New World Disorder

'An eloquent account of the drama and turbulence which buffeted the United Nations at the end of the Cold War. David Hannay was an adept and skilful diplomat: he uses his insider knowledge to describe the workings of the UN and the world of high diplomacy with style and grace. A wonderful resource for all those who want to understand how the United Nations works and why it remains the world's indispensable institution'

Kofi Annan, former United Nations Secretary General

'As our representative at the UN during a crucially difficult time David Hannay is remembered for his rigorous and clear sighted determination. He now uses these qualities to describe in detail the main discussions and decisions of which he was part, dealing with Iraq, Bosnia, Rwanda and a host of other issues. He clears away many of the over simplifications which have clouded thinking about the UN. His book should be an essential tool for the present generation of politicians and diplomats dealing with international affairs'

Douglas Hurd, former UK Foreign Secretary

'It is hard to think of anybody better equipped to write on the United Nations. David Hannay has seen the organisation from the inside and as a would-be reformer. He brings the subject to life not only by drawing on his own experience, but also through his sharp wit and cool analysis'

Professor Lawrence Freedman, King's College, London

'A frank and full memoir ... Lord Hannay has no illusions about the UN, but equally no doubt about its indispensability. He is explicit about its failings, but his blunt criticisms are always tempered by understanding and constructive proposals, and occasionally salted by a certain black humour'

Professor Michael Howard

New World Disorder

The UN after the Cold War:
an Insider's view

David Hannay

I.B. TAURIS

LONDON · NEW YORK

Published in 2008 by I.B.Tauris & Co Ltd
6 Salem Road, London W2 4BU
175 Fifth Avenue, New York NY 10010
www.ibtauris.com

In the United States of America and Canada distributed by
Palgrave Macmillan, a division of St. Martin's Press, 175 Fifth Avenue,
New York NY 10010

ISBN: (HB) 978 1 84511 719 1

A full CIP record for this book is available from the British Library
A full CIP record is available from the Library of Congress

Library of Congress Catalog Card Number: available

Designed and Typeset by 4word Ltd, Bristol, UK
Printed and bound by TJ International Ltd, Padstow, Cornwall, UK

Dedication

To all those who have worked over recent years to make the
United Nations more effective and more equitable

David Hannay was a British diplomat for 36 years. He was Britain's Permanent Representative to the European Union and then, between 1990 and 1995, to the UN. Following his retirement from diplomatic service, he was the British Special Representative for Cyprus and a member of the UN Secretary-General's High-Level Panel on Threats, Challenges and Change. He is the author of *Cyprus: The Search for a Solution.*

Contents

Chapter I

A personal introduction

By the beginning of 1990 I had been serving for more than four years as Britain's permanent representative and ambassador to the European Communities (EC). The first three years of my time had been a period of considerable progress in Britain's often fraught relationship with the rest of Europe. It was too good to last. By the end of 1988 Britain was once again sailing back into stormy seas. Margaret Thatcher had made clear in her Bruges speech of September of that year her visceral aversion to any further integration. The determination of most of our European partners to press ahead with the project for an economic and monetary union and a single currency set them and the British government on a collision course. And the handling of our policy towards the prospect of a re-unified Germany, in the period following the fall of the Berlin Wall, set us at odds not only with our main European partners, but also with the US administration.

Permanent representatives do not make policy, although they are often close to its making; and they then have to execute it. I was as elated and encouraged by the successes of the earlier years as I was worn down and depressed by the difficulties that then arose. Moreover, from the time of the falling out between the prime minister and her foreign secretary and chancellor of the exchequer over Britain's membership of the Exchange Rate Mechanism at the Madrid European Council in the summer of 1989, it had become clear that Margaret Thatcher no longer welcomed or paid much attention to such advice as I put forward. Negotiations were due to begin in mid-1990 on two extremely contentious projects in the Inter-Governmental Conferences on Economic and Monetary Union and on Political Union; and those negotiations were bound to last for a substantial time and to lock in whoever was involved at senior official level. It was time to go, reluctant though I was to leave the European scene in which I had been a supporting actor for most of the previous 25 years.

In those days appointments, and none more so than senior appointments, were wrapped in mystery. None of the relative transparency, with jobs advertised and applied for and organised collective consideration of a range of candidates, which now exists, was then in place. The sort of posts to which I might aspire were effectively in the gift of the foreign secretary and the prime minister – and there were three different foreign secretaries, Geoffrey Howe, John Major and Douglas Hurd, in office during the period in question. I had been asked during the first half of 1989 whether I would be content for my name to be considered for the job of permanent under-secretary and head of the diplomatic service which was due to become vacant on Patrick Wright's retirement in late 1990; and I had said that I would. Thereafter silence fell, apart from the odd rustling in the undergrowth. A bureaucratic game of musical chairs ensued which resulted in the top job going to someone else and my being appointed to the post they had been slated for: Permanent Representative to the UN in New York.

My lack of previous UN experience was some cause for concern, but my lengthy labour in the stony vineyard of multilateral diplomacy seemed likely to be of use; and the attractions of a large bilateral post, of which my brief period in Washington in the mid-1980s had been my only previous experience, were not compelling. When I did have time to think about the future during my last months in Brussels, and Brussels was the sort of job where one did not have much time to think of anything except how to get through the next week, I speculated that the next job would be a slightly less intensive and high-pressure one than Brussels had been. How wide of the mark that was to prove.

Nothing illustrates better the extent to which Saddam Hussein's invasion of Kuwait in August 1990 came like a bolt from the blue than the fairly leisurely arrangements made for the transition in New York between me and my predecessor there, Crispin Tickell. On leaving Brussels at the end of July, the Foreign Office agreed that I could take a month's leave and get to New York at the beginning of September; Tickell too was to use up the leave owing to him before taking up his appointment as Warden of Green College, Oxford, in the autumn; and

Tickell's (and my future) deputy, Tom Richardson, would hold the fort during August in New York. Following the Iraqi invasion of Kuwait on 2 August, the Foreign Office finally caught up with me at a small game reserve on the border between South Africa and Lesotho. Clearly there had to be a permanent representative in New York to handle what was evidently a major crisis. Which was it to be? The answer was fairly obvious. It was decided that Tickell should stay in New York through August and that I should stick to the plan to arrive and take over at the beginning of September.

So, when I did arrive in New York, it was to be plunged straight away into the deep end. And thus it continued, without any noticeable let up, until the day of my retirement, when I left New York, five years later. It is the story of those five, pretty tumultuous years which makes up a major part of this book. They were years during which the UN was thrust closer to the centre of the world stage than it had ever previously been, except for brief, episodic moments of prominence during a Cold War which had effectively paralysed its decision-making capacity. They were years too when the UN, and in particular its principal member states, of which Britain was one, sought to get to grips with the challenges of the post-Cold War world which were so different from those the international community had previously faced. During that time the UN faced the challenges of straightforward interstate aggression (Iraq), of international terrorism (Libya), of the proliferation of weapons of mass destruction (Iraq again, North Korea), of civil war and state failure (Afghanistan, Haiti, Rwanda, Somalia, Yugoslavia), of complex, multifaceted peacekeeping (Cambodia, El Salvador, Mozambique) and of environmental degradation (the Rio Summit). That list in itself shows why, if one was looking for a label to give to this new phase of history, 'new world disorder' would be a good deal closer to the mark than the one coined at the time, 'new world order', even if some of the characteristics of a new system of international order did begin to emerge amidst the chaos, the many failures, the successes and the half-successes. Perhaps no single statistic illustrates better the hectic pace of those years than the fact that the first Security Council resolution in whose negotiation I participated in September 1990 was numbered 666 (whose Cabalistic significance seemed to escape most of the participants – the numbering being sequential from the establishment of the UN 45 years earlier, in 1945). The last resolution before I left in July 1995 was numbered 1005. In those five years the Security

Council thus adopted half the number of resolutions it had in the previous 45.

Within months of my retirement in 1995, I was asked to take up a newly created appointment as British Special Representative for Cyprus, the object of which was to revive and strengthen the UN's long-running efforts to achieve a settlement of that dispute. For the next seven years I worked closely with successive UN Secretary-Generals (Boutros-Ghali and Annan), as well as successive UN Special Envoys for Cyprus in an area of UN activity – the use of good offices and mediation – of which I had previously had little experience. We came close to a settlement in 2003–4 in the successive iterations of what was called the Annan Plan. But in the end this plan, while endorsed in a referendum by two-thirds of the Turkish Cypriot voters, was rejected by three-quarters of the Greek Cypriots; and the problem remained unsolved.

And then, shortly after giving up my Cyprus appointment in 2003, the UN Secretary-General, Kofi Annan, invited me to be a member of a 16-strong, high-level international panel to which he gave the task of identifying the threats and challenges facing the UN in the twenty-first century, and the changes it needed to make if they were to be successfully handled. The panel took a year to produce its report, 'A more secure world: our shared responsibility', with more than 100 recommendations for action, which was tabled in December 2004, immediately endorsed by the Secretary-General and passed on to the member states. There then ensued nearly a year of advocacy and of negotiation leading up to the UN Summit of September 2005 in New York, when some of the recommendations were adopted and many left in limbo.

I am not a great enthusiast of diplomatic memoirs, particularly not those which concentrate on trivia and which undermine the necessary trust which has to exist between officials and political leaders. But diplomats, like politicians, business leaders, the military and many others do contribute to the shaping and making of historical events. And it is right therefore that they should make their contribution to the recording of them. I hesitated for some ten years since I left New York before putting pen to paper, often being asked whether I was going to leave some record of the time I spent there. Gradually an idea has taken shape of writing something which is not simply a diplomatic memoir in classic terms but which would also help the reader to understand how that most misunderstood of international organisations, the UN, actually works. It is certainly not a full history of the UN, not even a history of it during the period in question, but it is an attempt to describe how important decisions come to be taken, enlivened with a certain amount of personal anecdotage to relieve the often tedious and confusing jumble of acronyms and institutional turf-fighting with which so many accounts of the business of international organisations is burdened. The object is to make the UN more comprehensible to the ordinary reader, and also to enable judgements to be made about its strengths and weaknesses, avoiding so far as possible the mood swings between the hope that the UN can achieve almost anything and the fear that it can achieve almost nothing, which characterise the views of so many around the world.

I have naturally had to struggle with the problem of hindsight and the need to avoid shaping the story and the events to fit what we now know has subsequently happened. History is made by individuals and groups of people driving quite fast in foggy conditions, while it tends to be described and analysed by people with 20/20 vision or as close to that as they can achieve within the parameters of their own views and prejudices. I have tried to confront the problem by describing what happened at the UN in terms of what we knew at the time and with, as the principal written record, the UN documents which were actually endorsed then. I have then tried to analyse and to draw lessons from what was decided and done. No one but myself has any responsibility for these judgements.

Chapter II

The United Nations at the end of the Cold War

By the summer of 1990, when this story begins, most of the developments and decisions which came to be known as the ending of the Cold War had already occurred. The countries of Central and Eastern Europe had broken away from the tutelage of the Soviet Union and of their own Communist parties, with the final episode, the overthrow of President Ceausescu's regime in Romania, already six months behind; the Warsaw Pact was dead; and all this had taken place with the acquiescence of President Gorbachev, with virtually no violence or loss of life and certainly no confrontation between the superpowers and their respective allies. The two parts of Germany were about to become one again, following treaty arrangements negotiated between the former occupying powers. Soviet troops had withdrawn from Afghanistan under internationally agreed and supervised arrangements. In the south-west corner of Africa, Cuban troops had been withdrawn from Angola, and Namibia had been brought to independence with the withdrawal of South African troops and the successful completion of a complex UN peacekeeping operation. Free and fair elections had been held in Nicaragua and the defeat of the Soviet and Cuban-backed Sandinista government peacefully accepted.

Elsewhere around the world disputes which had either in effect been proxy wars between the superpowers or which had been sustained or aggravated by their support were beginning to be addressed and resolved. The final stages of settling the Iran–Iraq war were in hand. All the external powers involved in Cambodia's long agony were now co-operating to bring it to an end. Further progress in Central America, in

El Salvador in particular, looked possible. Attempts were being made to deal with some of the worst of Africa's trouble spots, in Angola, Mozambique and Western Sahara. In South Africa itself, in an unexpected knock-on effect of the end of the Cold War, the apartheid regime was beginning to give ground. Some particularly long-running disputes such as those over Palestine and Kashmir looked as intractable as ever, but there was hope that the winding down of Soviet/US rivalry would bring beneficial effects there too.

The trends were therefore clear and irreversible. What was a great deal less clear was how far they would go, and what would take the place of the frozen certainties of Cold War diplomacy. How was the world going to cope with future threats to international peace and security when they came along? And what form would they take? What would be the impact of the emergence of the USA as the sole superpower left standing? How would that affect its own actions; and those of others?

The UN had been as caught by surprise as its member states by the end of the Cold War. The ending of the threat of a possible armed confrontation between two nuclear superpowers, a threat which it had been recognised from the outset the UN would be completely powerless to prevent or to mitigate, in itself lifted a massive dead hand from its day-to-day existence. At the same time the willingness of the USA and the Soviet Union to cooperate in winding down disputes which they had previously fostered, and which they had almost invariably prevented the UN from taking any useful action to resolve, meant that much that had previously been assumed to be politically off-limits to the UN now ceased to be so. The successful peacekeeping operation in Namibia, which was concluded in the first half of 1990, had demonstrated a UN capacity to mount and conduct much more complex operations, with elaborate civilian and state-building dimensions in addition to the classic military disengagement provisions of earlier UN peacekeeping. And, although that operation had at one point teetered close to failure, it had been pulled through with the active cooperation and support of the main member states involved. All this meant that the UN had suddenly emerged from the wings of international diplomacy to a position much closer to centre stage than it had ever occupied before.

The end of the Cold War also had important implications for the UN's developmental, economic and social work. In place of the tension between the free market economic prescriptions of the West and those of the command economies of the Soviet Union and China, which had largely dominated and paralysed much UN activity in the economic and social fields for 45 years, there remained only one agenda: 'globalisation'. The blind alley of the so-called New International Economic Order was left behind. Frustrated by the Cold War jousting at the UN, most of the practical negotiations and progress on economic and developmental issues had drifted away from the UN into the institutions dominated by the Western powers, the General Agreement on Tariffs and Trade (GATT), the International Monetary Fund (IMF) and the World Bank. The question now was whether the UN's relevance and capacity to deal with at least some of these issues could be established; and whether the UN could provide the forum and identify the policies for handling new global challenges, of which those from environmental degradation and climate change were beginning to move sharply up the international agenda.

The institutions and resources with which the UN was equipped to face this fundamentally rearranged international scenario were those with which it had survived the long years of Cold War frustration. A number of its members, the USA and Britain prominent among them, were as determined to hold its budgetary limits to a zero real-growth yardstick as they had been before the Cold War ended. Most of the ministers, diplomats, and officials of the Secretariat, who collectively were responsible for running the UN and for shaping its decisions, had known no world other than that dominated by the Cold War. As many were bemused and alarmed by the removal of all the familiar landmarks as those who were invigorated and inspired by the opening up of new and wider opportunities for the organisation to fulfil the objectives set out in its Charter. Many from developing countries were doubtful whether their predicament would be given sufficient prominence in the new world that was emerging and at least some of them regretted the passing of a situation in which they could play off one side in the Cold War against the other. Some of these ambiguities and cross-currents are reasonably well captured in the following excerpt from an analysis I made shortly after my arrival in New York in 1990:

> The new arrival at the UN in 1990 cannot fail to be told that
> here is an organisation under-going a renaissance. Every
> speech, even on the most informal occasions, and there are
> very many speeches at the UN and virtually no occasion is too
> informal to make one, proclaims the fact. The recent successes

– the ending of the Iran/Iraq war, Namibia, Afghanistan, Nicaragua – are ticked off; the robust and effective response to Iraq's aggression against Kuwait is extolled; the future challenges – Cambodia, Western Sahara, El Salvador – are noted with an optimistic assumption that they too will be successfully handled; and the liberating effects of the end of the Cold War are given much credit for this happy state of affairs. That is the conventional wisdom. Is it justified? I think largely it is. But there is a tendency to underestimate the fragility of the renaissance; to turn a blind eye to the fact that the extent of the renaissance is magnified by comparison with the extremely low straits into which the organisation sank in the '70s and early '80s; to forget that this heady new wine is being poured into some pretty cracked old bottles.

It is time now to look at these 'old bottles' and to consider how suitable they were for the tasks ahead in the post-Cold War world.

Chapter III

The work of the United Nations and its structure

It is a challenge to anyone writing about an international organisation to make the material comprehensible and capable of assimilation by the ordinary reader, or indeed by any reader who has not worked in the organisation in question; to avoid drowning in the alphabet soup of acronyms which proliferate in all such organisations; and also to avoid allowing the complexities of bureaucratic process to camouflage and obscure any proper analysis of the substance of the issues at stake. In no case is this challenge more acute than when dealing with the sprawling and fissiparous structure of the UN, its different central institutions and its many semi-autonomous agencies. That is the justification for preceding a narrative account of the UN's activities in the period following the end of the Cold War by a kind of snapshot of the structure and working of some of the UN's principal component parts at the outset of the period in question.

The UN ended the Cold War in terms of legal and institutional structures much as it began it in 1945, when the Charter came into force and set out the powers and functioning of the various main bodies of which the UN was composed: the Security Council, the General Assembly, the Economic and Social Council (ECOSOC), the Trusteeship Council, the International Court of Justice, and the Secretariat, to name only the most prominent. One major change had been made when, in 1965, the Security Council had been expanded from 11 members to 15, without, however, changing the role of its five permanent members (China, France, the Soviet Union, the UK and the USA) or diluting their power of veto. The Economic and Social Council, too, was enlarged from

18 to 54 members. And the addition, in 1948, of the Universal Declaration on Human Rights remedied an omission from the original charter of an element which was to be of increasing significance as time passed.

The functioning of none of the UN's component parts had run at all smoothly during the Cold War period, and none had been able to fulfil the objectives and aspirations set out in the Charter. Vetoes by the permanent members, particularly by the Soviet Union and the USA, had crippled the decision-making capacity of the Security Council; the same Cold War jousting had often dominated the activities of the General Assembly and the Economic and Social Council. Nevertheless, in the interstices of Cold War politics, progress had been made – an aggression (by North Korea against South Korea) had been reversed, a UN capability to conduct peacekeeping operations following a cease-fire between the combatants had gradually emerged and been success-fully tested on a number of occasions (in the Middle East and in Cyprus for example), and the role of the Secretary-General's good offices in damping down or resolving disputes had steadily developed and regis-tered some successes. Two other important issues, not directly linked to the Cold War but amplified by it, had contributed to the general paral-ysis and to the asymmetric way in which the UN had developed. The first of these was the successive rounds of hostilities between Israel and its Arab neighbours over the future of Palestine and the refusal of Israel and its ally the USA to allow the UN to play any significant role in the attempts at handling or resolving the dispute. The second was the ten-sion between the African members of the UN (egged on by the Soviet Union and China) and the West over how to deal with the apartheid regime in South Africa and over whether to impose economic sanctions on that country. Both these issues remained live ones at the end of the Cold War, although the second showed some early signs of losing its force and relevance.

Throughout those first 45 years of its existence, successive genera-tions of secretary-generals, of foreign ministers and of diplomats had been only too well aware of the dysfunctional nature of the UN and its main organs. But attempts to reform or adapt it had virtually all foundered on the rocks of Cold War considerations or of those arising from the other two long-running sources of tension. So, when the Cold War so unexpectedly came to an end, no one could be at all sure how the removal of the distortions it had imposed would affect the UN's activities and how these would now develop in the absence of the classic East-West confrontation with which all concerned were so familiar. The organisation was sailing into uncharted waters.

The Security Council

The establishment of a Security Council, and the powers given to it under the Charter, which included the imposition of economic and diplomatic sanctions and the use of force, was the single most ambitious and most innovative feature of the UN organisation; and, not surprisingly, the Security Council has remained ever since the main focus of public attention to an extent which has often led to the impression that the Security Council and the UN are synonymous. Even more innovative was the provision that enabled Security Council decisions to be taken by a qualified majority vote (nine members out of 15 in the post-1965 enlarged Council), mitigated by a power of veto for each of the five permanent members. All this represented a balance struck between the lessons learned from the failure of the League of Nations in the 1930s and the realities of post-war power politics. With the single exception of the authorisation of the use of force to repel North Korea's aggression against South Korea in June 1950 (which only occurred thanks to the Soviet Union's temporary absence from the Security Council), throughout the Cold War period the left hand of the veto in most cases nullified the sweeping powers conferred on the Council under the right hand of the Charter.

The physical surroundings in which the Security Council deliberated and reached its decisions in no way reflected its prominent position in the organisation. In contrast to the striking white marble exterior and the sweeping hemicycle of the General Assembly, the Security Council was tucked away in a far corner of the upended cigar-box-shaped building which housed the Secretariat. The room in which the Council debated in public and actually adopted any formal decisions was spacious enough, although dominated by an appallingly ugly, brutalist mural to which, fortunately, the members of the Council, who sat at a horseshoe-shaped table, were able to turn their backs. At either end of the horseshoe were seats for the representatives of the country or countries which were the object of the Council's deliberations and for non-member ambassadors who wished to address the Council. Beyond them were steeply ramped rows of seats for delegations not participating in the Council's deliberations and for members of the public. Unless the Council decided otherwise, all proceedings in the main chamber were televised and recorded verbatim.

The main business of the Council, however, the whole process of the shaping of decisions and the negotiation of texts, took place elsewhere, across a narrow corridor in the so-called informal consultations room – 'behind closed doors' as the media liked to describe it. This small, cramped room had just enough space to accommodate the 15 members of the Council sitting at a replica of the council chamber's horseshoe-shaped table. Immediately behind each ambassador's seat at the table were two seats for members of their delegation, each one immediately behind the other (thus making communication exceptionally difficult). Non-member delegations and ambassadors did not have access to this smaller room, where the proceedings were neither televised nor officially recorded. The informal consultations room could hardly have been more claustrophobic, particularly when, during sensitive negotiations, the narrow spaces behind the chairs tended to fill up with people standing; but it did also engender an intimate, often collegiate, atmosphere, and it encouraged direct debate and frank, sometimes tense, exchanges. On one side of the informal consultations room was a dingy antechamber, full of large armchairs and with a television set almost permanently switched on as a way of reminding delegates of what was going on in the real world outside. On the other side of the consultations room were two tiny, slit-like offices, one for the Secretary-General and one for the president of the Council.

The presidency of the Security Council rotated amongst its members on a monthly basis, following the alphabetical order (in English) of the countries on the Council at the time. Every month began with a series of meetings between the incoming president of the Council and each of his colleagues to discuss his (or her) and their priorities for the month ahead. Through this and a number of other procedural ways, the presidents did have some influence on the ways in which business was transacted during their month in office. But the extent of this influence tended to be exaggerated by those outside the Council; any attempt to exceed the purely procedural duties of the office was likely to bring the perpetrator up against the many subtle ways in which other members of the Council could slow down and complicate the business in hand. The fact that ambassadors of the permanent members might, if they stayed in New York for a five-year tour of duty, chair the Council as often as four times, while ambassadors of the non-permanent members, with two-year, non-renewable terms, were unlikely to do so more than once was just one of the many sources of friction and complaint arising from the distinction between permanent and non-permanent members.

The Security Council contained two groups which acted as such, the permanent members and the non-aligned members, and one consisting of those who did not fall into either of the other two groups and who were sometimes called the non-non-aligned, who generally did not act as a group. For most of the Cold War the permanent members (or the P5 as they tended to be called) were not a group at all, but were at daggers drawn. However, from the late 1980s onwards, as the intensity of the Cold War began to abate, they started to meet, at first informally over tea at the residence of the British ambassador and later more regularly and in a more structured way. At the outset their discussions were subject-specific, dealing with ways of supporting the Secretary-General's efforts to bring the Iran–Iraq war to an end. But gradually they became wider in scope; and they were coordinated on a rotating three-monthly basis by one of the members.

During the second half of 1990, when Iraq's invasion of Kuwait was at the top of the agenda, the ambassadors of the P5 met on more than 50 occasions, and their political counsellors, who were a kind of subset of the ambassadors, as many times again. This emergence of the permanent members as a group capable of acting together and of ironing out differences between themselves privately and before wider discussion in the Council began was an extremely significant development, with positive consequences for the Council's decision-making capacity. For one thing it greatly attenuated, even if it did not totally remove, the chance of a veto. And then the likelihood was that, if a group with as disparate interests as the P5 could resolve the differences between them, they would be able to pick up sufficient support from other members of the Council to make up the numbers needed for a qualified majority. But P5 solidarity was always fragile, as I analysed it at the time, and it could never be taken for granted:

> The influence of the five currently considerably exceeds the
> sum of their collective action partly because those outside an
> exclusive club of this sort always tend to exaggerate its

significance and partly because its members go out of their way to avoid crossing swords in public. But this unity is fairly precarious and it requires continuous effort to sustain it. The Americans are clearly *primus inter pares* and are set to remain so as their relative strength vis-à-vis the others is on the increase, and given the Soviet Union's accelerating collapse as a super-power; but they will need to nurse the other four along and take fuller account of their susceptibilities than some in Washington would wish to do if they are to make the most use of this instrument which has served them (and us) so well over the Gulf crisis.

The non-aligned group in the Security Council also had considerable potential influence. It too, like the P5, caucused regularly and had a coordinator; and, in theory at least, it normally had enough votes on the Council to deprive a resolution of the necessary nine votes to make a majority if all its members either voted against or even abstained. But, like the P5, its unity was fragile. Outside New York and infrequent ministerial meetings of its members, the Non-Aligned Movement did not really exist as a policy-making entity. The non-aligned group on the Council was drawn from three different regions, Africa, Asia and Latin America, which often had quite different interests (throughout the 1990–1 Gulf crisis for example, its three African members voted solidly with the P5, while the Asian and Latin American ones did not). With the end of the Cold War it faced an existential question: what was it non-aligned with or from? For all these reasons the non-aligned group was more reactive than proactive; but it was often influential in shaping Council decisions and could never be ignored.

Security Council action takes a number of different forms, the clear distinctions between which are often poorly understood. At the lowest level the Council can, after discussing a matter in informal consultations, authorise its president to speak to the press on its behalf. Such press statements can be useful in sending a public signal of the Council's involvement in a particular issue and of the direction in which its deliberations are moving; and they tend to be better than saying nothing at all after a meeting and leaving the field open to speculation. But they have no real force and only limited impact; and they are always liable to be undermined by press briefing by individual ambassadors anxious to put across their own particular reading of a situation.

One step up the scale is a presidential statement. This is not, as it would seem, a statement by the President of the Security Council alone, but one agreed to textually, in advance of a full, public meeting of the Council, by all its members. Presidential statements cannot, however, form the basis for policy decisions with far-reaching practical consequences; the fact that they have to be adopted by unanimity means that negotiation of a text lends itself to progressive watering down and the incorporation of contradictory views; and they tend not to be taken very seriously by those on the receiving end of them.

Next up the line is a Council resolution. This instrument is a clear statement of collective policy-making, involving the whole Council, whether it is adopted by unanimity or by a majority. It can contain detailed material such as, for example, the mandate and modalities of a peacekeeping mission. It has political but not legal force on the wider membership (and is invariably described by the media as 'not legally binding', thus undermining its effectiveness). At the top of the Security Council's Richter Scale is a resolution based on Chapter VII of the Charter. To adopt this the Council must first formally determine that a threat exists to international peace and security (Article 39 of the Charter) and must include such a determination in the text of the resolution. This then opens up a whole toolbox, ranging from diplomatic or economic sanctions through to the authorisation of the use of force by a country or group of countries or the mandating of the use of force by the UN itself. Chapter VII resolutions had been few and far between during the Cold War years; they were to become frequent after it. Such resolutions impose a range of direct legal obligations on the whole UN membership, whether members of the Security Council or not.

The General Assembly

The General Assembly, which brought together the representatives of all the members of the organisation, emerged from the Cold War in the same way that the Security Council had, with the same powers and functions as it had gone into it. Like the Security Council, it had been impeded in carrying out those functions by Cold War rivalries and by the other major sources of tension, the question of Palestine and the handling of the apartheid regime in South Africa. Also like the Security Council, it had grown in numbers during that period, but the General

Assembly did so to a dramatic extent. When the Charter was signed there were 51 members; by the time the Cold War came to an end in 1990 there were 159 members; and the number was still rising, reaching 192 by the end of the period covered by the present book. So long as the Cold War lasted and all the UN's institutions were to a similar degree paralysed by it, the implications of this massive expansion in numbers for the transaction of business and decision-making had remained masked and in any case incapable of being seriously addressed. But that was coming to an end and, as I noted at the time:

> ... the impact of the renaissance [of the UN] on the various parts of the UN system has been singularly disparate . . . . The General Assembly has, both by contrast [with the Security Council] and in absolute terms, lost much ground . . . . This disparate impact is setting up many tensions which are only gradually beginning to surface.

The General Assembly was, moreover, handicapped by a good deal more than its massive increase in numbers and the failure so far to adapt its procedures to take account of this. In a number of different ways the Charter gave it less than it seemed to do in the way of influence and authority. The General Assembly appointed the Secretary-General and decided on the admission of new members. But in both cases it was required to act on the basis of a recommendation of the Security Council, there being no instance of the General Assembly having rejected such a recommendation or having forced one on an unwilling Security Council. And then the General Assembly's involvement in the whole critical field of threats to international peace and security was so hedged about with conditions and restrictions as to be virtually unusable. It could only in this field issue recommendations, not take decisions, and it was explicitly barred from doing even that in respect of any dispute or situation where the Security Council was exercising the functions assigned to it in the Charter (Article 12(I)). While attempts had been made to develop a decision-making capacity for the General Assembly when the Security Council was deadlocked (the 'uniting for peace' procedure), these had been, in the view of many observers, of dubious legality and were all the less likely to gather broad support once the Security Council was able itself to take decisions and if vetoes became the exception rather than the rule.

And, where the General Assembly did have allocated to it undoubted powers of decision, for example over human rights, over the development of international law, over disarmament and over budgetary matters and many issues relating to the administration of the organisation and its Secretariat, a system of committees with a notional membership of 150 or so was hardly an ideal or effective way to exercise them. There was indeed a fundamental dilemma built into the whole matter of the method of decision-making by the General Assembly. The Charter provided for decisions to be taken by a simple majority irrespective of the size or significance of the countries represented in the majority or the minority, except in cases of particular importance where the majority required was two-thirds, again without any account being taken of the size or significance of those voting either way. This system had been applied from time to time; but, since General Assembly decisions were, unlike decisions taken under Chapter VII of the Charter by the Security Council, not legally binding and since there was no provision for their enforcement, this was not a particularly effective way of proceeding other than in terms of gesture politics. And even in those terms, for example in the case of the 1975 resolution equating Zionism with racism, they could be quite counter-productive. So, over time, the balance had tilted towards resolutions being adopted by consensus, which had some advantages but also plenty of disadvantages, the main one being that such resolutions tended to emerge riddled with contradictory provisions and festooned with items of special interest to one or another delegation or group which made inclusion of them the price of their acceptance, while it was at the same time all too easy to knock out highly desirable provisions.

For all its weaknesses, however, the General Assembly remained completely indispensable for an organisation which had been set up and remained fundamentally intergovernmental. It provided a forum in which the whole range of international developments could be debated openly. Its ministerial session in September of every year gave a platform for the Secretary-General himself to set out his thinking on the way ahead and for foreign ministers and, increasingly, heads of government to participate and contribute their views – often, as for example in the case of President Gorbachev's speech in September 1988, in striking terms which marked a milestone in the winding down of the Cold War. If it could rid its agenda of the accretion of items which were reinscribed year after year at the insistence of individual countries or groups of countries for largely ritual debates and focus rather on a limited number of genuinely topical questions, it could help to influence the context in which day-to-day decisions were taken and also the direction in which the organisation as a whole moved. And it could, from time to time, endorse and register major shifts in policy, such as the need to address the problems of the environment.

The Economic and Social Council

ECOSOC suffered from the outset from having the weakest and the vaguest of the mandates for the institutions of the new organisation set out in the UN Charter. It could 'make or initiate studies and reports with respect to international economic, social, cultural, educational health and related matters' (Article 62 of the Charter); it could make recommendations to the General Assembly; it could call international conferences; it could obtain regular reports from the specialised agencies; but of authority and of the right to take decisions which would have a direct impact on the membership there was no trace. Nor were any resources put at its disposal. By the end of the Cold War, like the other institutions, its numbers had expanded, from 18 to 27 and then to 54, but no other changes to its powers and responsibilities had been made.

The Cold War had had a damaging impact on the work of ECOSOC too, with much jousting between the protagonists of the two competing economic systems, the free market economies of the West and the command economies of the East; and it had hampered any serious progress towards fulfilling the ECOSOC's remit on human rights and its oversight of the not very effective Commission on Human Rights (CHR). But ECOSOC suffered also from the fact that, from an early stage, the main Western powers decided to concentrate most of their international cooperative efforts in the fields covered by it on institutions which were not a full part of the UN system and which did not report to it – the IMF, the World Bank and GATT (later to become the World Trade Organisation, WTO) – where the countries with fully state-controlled economies were not represented. Meanwhile many of the UN's specialised agencies, each with its own system of governance and its own budget and financial resources, grew in influence in their respective sectors of activity. ECOSOC thus became something of a fifth wheel.

During the 1970s ECOSOC made full use of its ability to call conferences, and considerable progress was registered through meetings on the environment and development (1972), hunger and world food (1974), population growth (1974), the role of women (1975), employment and basic needs (1976), human settlements (1978) and science and technology (1979). From then on, however, ECOSOC's agenda was more and more dominated by a doomed attempt to create what was called a 'New International Economic Order' and by such dead-end diversions as work designed to regulate the activities of trans-national corporations. The 1980s thus became what one of the shrewdest observers, Enrique Iglesias, called 'a lost decade'; and ECOSOC's role and that of the UN as a whole on economic matters lapsed into what even some of its strongest supporters described as 'constructive dissent'.

The Secretary General and the Secretariat

The role of the UN Secretary-General and of its Secretariat is covered in a remarkably skimpy manner in the 1945 Charter. This in fact proved to be more of a strength than a handicap, as successive Secretary-Generals skilfully worked to enlarge their field for action. Those efforts did not entirely escape the malign impact of the Cold War, a major crisis developing in the 1950s over a Soviet attempt to impose a tripartite structure on the office ('the troika') which would have condemned it inevitably, as was intended, to complete stasis. But, once that onslaught had been repelled, the holder of the office gradually but steadily emerged as a key player on the international stage, both as what has been called a kind of secular pope, able to use the bully-pulpit of his office to direct attention to the burning problems of the hour, but also as an international mediator and as the head of an organisation with a capacity to conduct elaborate and effective peacekeeping operations. The personality of the holder of the office mattered quite a lot. Dag Hammarskjold (1953–61), still to this day probably the outstanding UN Secretary-General, made more progress than his two successors U Thant (1961–71) and Kurt Waldheim (1972–81). The last Secretary-General of the Cold War period, Javier Perez de Cuellar (1982–91), was an exceptionally competent diplomat, but very much one steeped in the unwritten rules of that period: always preferring to operate quietly behind the scenes; and always reluctant to put his head above the parapet when the major powers became engaged in an issue or crisis. The fact that the office of the Secretary-General emerged in such good shape from the Cold War, with the ending of the Iran–Iraq war, the brokering of the withdrawal of Soviet troops from Afghanistan, a successfully completed peacekeeping operation in Namibia and a series of achievements in bringing peace to the countries of Central America under its belt, owed much to his stewardship.

The UN Charter may have been skimpy in its definition of the function of the Secretary-General, but it did already indicate the two main axes along which he was expected to work. It stated flatly that 'he shall be the chief administrative officer of the organisation' (Article 97) and he 'may bring to the attention of the Security Council any matter which in his opinion may threaten the maintenance of international peace and security' (Article 99). At the same time it made very clear the subordination of the Secretary-General to the main institutions: 'he may perform such other functions as are entrusted to him by these organs' (Article 98). This has proved over the years a source of strength, for example in the case of the emergence of UN peacekeeping, nowhere mentioned in the Charter as a major function of the job, but also a source of weakness in the shape of the micro-management to which the Secretary-General is subjected, by the General Assembly in particular. The twin axes laid down in the Charter also foreshadowed a dichotomy in the job which it was not easy for one person to straddle successfully, either in terms of the use of his time or in terms of the skills required to carry out the two quite different tasks. These contradictions remained more or less dormant so long as the Cold War limitations on the development of the office were in force. This dormancy was not likely to last for long once the Cold War came to an end.

The UN Secretariat suffers greatly, like that of every international organisation, from the need to have represented in it at every level the whole gamut of its membership and, as a subset of that requirement, from a lack of full control by the Secretary-General over the appointment of its senior officials. The main result of this is an extraordinary unevenness in the quality of its officials, ranging from world-class operators, often working intolerable hours, to time-servers whose bureaucratic skills are modest. This unevenness is always strange and frustrating to those schooled in a meritocratic national administration, but is a characteristic which seems to be endemic in international organisations. The Cold War, which had been fought out vigorously and grimly in the corridors of the Secretariat, had also taken its toll; and left its mark in an unwillingness to take any initiative or to run any risks, leading to even the smallest matters being referred up to the 38th floor for decision (the top floor of the UN building where the Secretary-General and his closest advisors had their offices). I noted at the time that the Secretariat 'seems somehow bemused by the turn of events [the end of the Cold War], not quite sure whether it heralds a threat to its vested interests or an opportunity to be seized with both hands'.

The media

The revolutionary impact of the end of the Cold War on the UN was not the only such seismic shift occurring at that time. Almost simultaneously, but quite coincidentally, the world was undergoing a revolution in communications, the most recent of a series of such revolutions which had occurred since the late nineteenth century. The aspect of that revolution which most immediately and most directly affected the UN and the other component parts of what has been somewhat loosely termed the 'international community' was the arrival of the 24 hours a day, seven days a week, global news cycle, the most prominent manifestation of which was a hitherto little known US television news channel, Cable Network News (CNN). With the hyperbole which was one of the less attractive characteristics of the 24 hours a day news cycle, CNN came to be known as the 16th member of the Security Council.

The UN was not well equipped to cope with this particular revolution and nor were its principal member states. The UN, in the form of the Secretary-General and the Secretariat, had traditionally operated an extremely reactive, rather than pro-active, communications policy. They had taken the view that their crucial role as a trusted intermediary in often delicate negotiations could only be damaged by saying too much in public about what they were doing. They also took the probably wise view that they could not hope to win in any public exchanges over differences of policy between them and one or more of their principal member states. These considerations were entirely legitimate ones, but they did not leave either the Secretary-General or the

Secretariat well placed to manage, let alone to guide, the new media phenomenon in which stories flowed in from conflict areas in quite different time zones from New York and then flowed out again from New York back to those conflict areas. The principal member states for their part had barely thought about the problem at all; and they had not really considered the implications for their own classic methods of handling the press through regular briefings at fixed times of the day of a situation in which the main international focus of the biggest story of the day might turn out to be the discussions and decisions of the Security Council in New York, an organisation which had neither a communications policy nor a press spokesman. What was said to the media about a particular meeting of the Security Council tended to depend on the whim of the particular president of the Council that month and on the willingness or unwillingness of its individual members to be waylaid on their way out of the meeting at a hastily assembled group of microphones and cameras clustered in a cramped corridor just outside the Security Council's suite of offices.

The new phenomenon had plenty of positive features. The ubiquity of television and radio reporters and their increasing ability to transmit reports without having to pass through channels controlled by the host government meant that a steady, reasonably objective and remarkably rapid flow of information became available both to decision-makers in capitals and to those in New York. This often resulted in a strong light being shone into various nooks and crannies which governments would much rather have kept well away from the public gaze. But there were negative features too, as the sheer cumulative mass of reporting and the visual impact of often shocking pictures were beamed into the living rooms of hundreds of millions of viewers around the world. The effects could be of two contradictory kinds, one a 'push' effect and the other a 'pull' one, not unlike the operation of the tides. At first the media tended to build up a 'something must be done' mood; but later on they could just as well contribute to a powerful regressive pressure (as was, for example, the case with the images of the body of a US helicopter pilot being dragged through the streets of Mogadishu in October 1993). To label those features as positive or negative is not intended to be a value judgement, less still to suggest that they could or should be suppressed; but merely to underline the fact that these were new factors of which careful account had to be taken by both governments and international organisations if they were not to be swept off

their feet and if they were to be able to formulate appropriate and effective policy responses.

*   *   *   *

I am conscious of not having covered in this introductory chapter on
the working of the UN and its structures at the time of the end of the
Cold War a fair number of important parts of the UN family. I have
said nothing of the International Court of Justice; and nothing too of
the specialised agencies, each with its own structure of governance and
its own resources. But this is not intended to be a comprehensive
history of the UN system even during the period covered by this book;
and I have therefore concentrated on those parts of the system where
both the impact of the Cold War and the impact of its ending were
the greatest.

Chapter IV

1990: Reversing an aggression

The invasion of Kuwait by Iraq on 2 August 1990 was the first act of aggression committed after the end of the Cold War. As such the response of the international community to it was always going to be of wider significance than the purely regional dimension within which Iraq tried to situate it. It was the failure to understand these wider implications and the shifts which were taking place in international politics and the power relationships between, in particular, the five permanent members of the Security Council that led to Saddam Hussein's major miscalculation of the likely consequences of his actions.

The Iraqi invasion and its conquest of Kuwait, which was accomplished within a few hours, did indeed come like a bolt from the blue to the UN, although it did not come out of an entirely clear sky. Tension between Iraq and Kuwait over the payment of Iran–Iraq war debts, the price of oil and the ownership of a cross-border oilfield had been on the increase for several weeks. There had been attempts to mediate by other Arab countries, in particular by President Mubarak of Egypt, and by the Arab League (AL). The general view was that this was the best way to avoid a full-blown crisis; and it was the expression of this view by the then US Chargé d'Affaires in Baghdad to President Saddam Hussein that was subsequently, quite unjustifiably, represented as a kind of amber light for the military action he then took. In reality Saddam Hussein needed no amber light. He clearly calculated that he would get away with his aggression, as he had done when he attacked Iran in 1980, or would, at worst, suffer a slap on the wrist. At no stage in the run-up to hostilities had anyone involved seriously contemplated recourse to the UN. Indeed, as events subsequently unrolled, ambassadors in New York wryly recalled how the Iraqi and Kuwaiti ambassadors had patrolled the corridors of the UN building explaining how unjustified it would be for this matter to come to the UN and how their two governments were going to work things out, perhaps with the help of other members of the AL. This failure to make any use of the UN machinery for preventive purposes was part of an old pattern which would continue to recur in other circumstances, as we shall see. And the inadequacy of regional organisations as a substitute for the UN was also to recur.

The first response to Iraq's aggression

The Security Council's first response to Iraq's invasion came on the same day in the form of Security Council Resolution 660, which forth-rightly condemned Iraq's invasion and demanded that it withdraw its forces immediately and unconditionally. It went on to call on Iraq and Kuwait to begin intensive negotiations to resolve their differences, with the support of the AL. This latter reference to negotiations may have given some comfort to Saddam Hussein, but he would have been wiser to note two other aspects of the resolution. The first was that it was explicitly adopted under Chapter VII of the UN Charter involving a determination that Iraq's invasion constituted a breach of international peace and security, thus opening the way to the wide range of measures, including the use of force, provided for under Chapter VII. And the second was that the resolution was supported by 14 members of the Security Council, with only Yemen not participating in the vote. The resolution was thus supported by all five permanent (i.e. veto-wielding) members of the Council, including China and the Soviet Union, and even by Cuba, which was at the time a non-permanent member.

Four days later, faced with Iraqi unwillingness to comply with the previous resolution, the Security Council went much further and applied comprehensive mandatory economic sanctions against Iraq under Security Council Resolution 661. The resolution banned all imports from Iraq, thus including Iraq's main export of crude oil; and all exports to Iraq except for supplies intended strictly for medical purposes and 'in humanitarian circumstances, foodstuffs'. This latter provision reflected the fact that Iraq was a large net importer of foodstuffs and could not feed its population without such imports. The resolution also imposed financial sanctions on Iraq, prohibiting the provision of any funds or other financial and economic resources to Iraq or to occupied Kuwait by any commercial, industrial or public utility. Once again all five permanent members of the Security Council voted for the resolution, with only Cuba and Yemen on this occasion abstaining. The sanctions thus imposed were, because they were based on Chapter VII of the Charter, legally binding on all states; and the Council established a Sanctions Committee to monitor observance. These sanctions were far more wide-ranging than any the Council had ever imposed during the Cold War. They were explicitly stated as being directed at restoring the authority of the government of Kuwait and to secure compliance with the Council's earlier demand that Iraq withdraw immediately and unconditionally from Kuwait.

The Iraqi response remained defiant and included the declaration of a 'comprehensive and eternal merger' between Iraq and Kuwait which was met with a further Security Council Resolution, 662 of 9 August, which decided, again with mandatory legal force and this time acting unanimously, that the annexation of Kuwait had no legal validity and was null and void. Then on 25 August in Security Council Resolution 665, the Council crossed another threshold when it addressed the issue of enforcing sanctions and in particular the need to prevent Iraqi or other oil tankers evading the embargo. In a first reference to 'Member states cooperating with the government of Kuwait', which was to become UN-speak for the coalition of the willing, established to restore Kuwait's sovereignty and independence, the Council authorised such states as were deploying maritime forces to the area 'to use such measures as are commensurate to the specific circumstances as may be necessary under the authority of the Security Council to halt all inward and outward maritime shipping in order to inspect and verify their cargoes and destinations and to ensure strict implementation of the provisions laid down in Resolution 661'. This somewhat tortuous language was, after some sucking of teeth by Margaret Thatcher in London, accepted as authorising the use of force to prevent evasion of the embargo and was thus applied, bringing pretty well all Iraq's overseas shipments of oil to a halt. Again this resolution was supported by the five permanent members of the Security Council, with only Cuba and Yemen abstaining.

The final turn of the screw in this sequence of resolutions imposing and enforcing sanctions against Iraq came with Resolution 670 of

25 September, which was adopted on this occasion by the foreign ministers who were in New York for the annual opening of the General Assembly. Resolution 670 overrode a whole range of international agreements relating to civil aviation and decided that no state should permit aircraft to take off from their territory and go to Iraq or Kuwait or to come to their territory from Iraq. With the adoption of this resolution all flights in and out of Iraq ceased, with the exception of any specifically authorised by the UN in certain, very carefully circumscribed, circumstances, e.g. for the UN Military Observer Group monitoring the ceasefire on the Iran–Iraq border. Thereafter all movement in or out of Iraq had to take place by road, in almost every case by driving from Baghdad across the desert to the Jordanian frontier.

By this time, less than two months after Iraq's original invasion of Kuwait, the international community had reacted with a hitherto completely unprecedented degree of unity and determination and had crossed several important rubicons in terms of the use of coercive measures against a state in flagrant breach of its international obligations. But none of this had had any noticeable effect on the ruler of Iraq's determination not to yield to pressure, however much his people might be suffering from sanctions. The stage was thus set for a debate over whether there was any hope of sanctions compelling Iraq to disgorge Kuwait or whether other, more forceful measures would be required. And every step which Saddam Hussein took and every statement he made merely weakened the hand of those who pleaded for sanctions to be given more time to work and strengthened the case for moving towards the use of force.

A massacre in Jerusalem

The inability of the UN to do anything effective about the Arab–Israel dispute and the situation in the Occupied Territories in Palestine had been a running sore for many years. Successive Israeli governments had no confidence in the impartiality of the UN or in its capacity to provide security within the context of any agreements which might be reached; and successive US administrations had used their powers of dissuasion, and where necessary their veto, in the Security Council, to block any attempt to give the UN any role in the sporadic efforts to reach a settlement or to respond to unacceptable actions committed by

Israel in the Occupied Territories. Arab countries, following the lead of the Palestine Liberation Organisation (PLO), which had observer status at the UN, regularly initiated debates in both the Security Council and the General Assembly without any serious prospect of getting a mandate for action, but to air their grievances at the way the UN machinery was being hamstrung and to gain support for their cause in the court of world public opinion. In this, throughout the Cold War period, they received the enthusiastic support of the Soviet Union, manoeuvring for tactical advantage in their wider contest with the West. The latest round in this exercise in frustration had taken place as recently as May 1990, when the Security Council had held a special meeting in Geneva to enable the Chairman of the PLO, Yasir Arafat, to appear before it, but had been unable thereafter to reach any agreed conclusions. Iraq's invasion of Kuwait had temporarily driven this, along with many other issues, off the Security Council agenda, but not far and not for long.

It was one of the characteristics of life on the Security Council that, thanks to New York's geographical position in the Western hemisphere, many of the most dramatic and critical events had occurred elsewhere in the world while the members were still asleep. So it was on 8 October, when news came through that Israeli security forces had opened fire on a crowd of Palestinian demonstrators at the Muslim holy place in Jerusalem (the Al-Haram al-Sharif), killing a substantial number ('over twenty' was the nearest to a precise figure that could be reached after many weeks of unseemly wrangling over the body count) and wounding many more. The Israeli story was that the demonstrators had been throwing stones from the Muslim site up above down onto Jewish worshippers at their own holy site in the wall of what they call the Temple Mount. Whatever the truth of this allegation, the Palestinian version being that the demonstrators had been throwing stones at the Israeli security forces and that these had only accidentally fallen on the Jewish worshippers below, it was quite clear from the outset that the Israelis had used grossly disproportionate force against the demonstrators. To compound the difficulty of handling the matter, the place where the incidents took place was not regarded by the Israelis as part of the Occupied Territories at all, but rather as part of the inalienable territory of their own capital city, while for the whole of the rest of the international community, including the USA, it was indeed part of East Jerusalem, which had been occupied by the Israelis in 1967. As I listened to the BBC World Service that morning over breakfast I registered that, as the current president of the Security Council (alphabetical rotation having brought the UK to that hot spot a mere three weeks after I had arrived in New York), I was in for an extremely demanding few days.

The massacre in Jerusalem would have been difficult enough to handle at the best of times; but in the middle of the crisis over Iraq's seizure of Kuwait it was a great deal more so. Iraq's aggression had in fact split the Arab world, with most Arab countries roundly condemning it and working from the outset to get it reversed, but with a small number, which included Jordan and Arafat's PLO, as well as Yemen, currently the only Arab country on the Security Council, sympathising more or less openly with Saddam Hussein and always looking for opportunities to head off or to split the coalition gathering against him. Yemen, and above all the PLO as the aggrieved party, were in key positions in the debate that was about to get under way in the Security Council. These two, while quite justifiably determined to secure an unambiguous condemnation by the Security Council of what the Israeli security forces had done and some UN action to enquire into the circumstances of the massacre, had another, at first hidden, agenda; this was to bring forward a resolution which would provoke an American veto and thus strain, if not break, the coalition gathering against Saddam Hussein. The majority of the members of the Council were committed to preventing that outcome, the Americans themselves with the caveat that doing so should, to the extent possible, avoid putting their relations with Israel under too great a strain. The stage was set for a difficult negotiation. It was to take five days and three nights to achieve a unanimous resolution – Security Council Resolution 672.

Oddly enough the sending of a UN mission of enquiry to the region, although strongly opposed by the Israelis, was the least contentious of the elements of a resolution and was rapidly recognised as common ground by all members of the Council. Much greater difficulty arose over the condemnation of Israel and its terms. In the past US administrations in general, and the Bush administration in particular, had stymied or vetoed such explicit criticism. On this occasion the circumstances were so clear-cut and the offence so great that it was clear from the outset that only a veto would prevent outright condemnation. After some delay and considerable backtracking in Washington, the Americans decided that this point would have to be conceded, but they were determined that the condemnation should not be exclusively of the Israeli security forces but must include the Palestinian use of violence too. This met much resistance; and in the end they had to settle for the addition of the single word 'especially' in the sentence 'condemns especially the acts of violence committed by the Israeli security forces'. Even greater difficulties arose over the reference to 'all the territories occupied by Israel since 1967', where the Palestinians wanted an explicit mention of East Jerusalem. This the Americans, under massive pressure from the Israelis, refused to concede, which was bizarre given their own view that East Jerusalem and the Al-Haram al-Sharif were indeed part of the Occupied Territories. And there we remained agonisingly stuck for many long hours, stretching into days.

It was during that time that I first realised how little help the UN Secretariat officials who serviced the Security Council were when the president found himself in a tight corner. Used to the European scene in Brussels, where the Secretary-General of the Council would have been sitting beside me as I chaired the Committee of Permanent Representatives, feeding me with any number of tactical ideas and drafting fixes, I was at first taken aback by the flat refusal of UN officials to venture any advice at all. Nor did anything useful come out of London. In the end I resorted to an old Brussels device known as 'confessionals', when I saw each member of the Council separately in private and talked through the remaining difficult points. This, or perhaps heavy lobbying in capitals, eventually did the trick.

Throughout it all the most difficult delegation to handle was the Palestinian one, partly because of the problems they had in getting clear instructions from Arafat in Tunis, partly also because of divided counsels in their New York team and the hidden objective of splitting the coalition. In the end acquiescence, if not agreement, was reached on the basis of an approach which left any reference to East Jerusalem out of the text of the resolution, but which had me, as president of the Council, responding at the public, official meeting held to adopt Resolution 672 to a question from the Yemeni ambassador by stating that it was indeed the Council's view that East Jerusalem was a part of the territories occupied by Israel in 1967. The Americans accepted this, as did the other members of the Council, and we had unanimity. Immediately after the Council meeting at which I had confirmed the point about East Jerusalem, the Israeli Chargé d'Affaires (Benjamin Netanyahu, the previous ambassador, having left before I arrived), normally a mild-mannered person, came up to me white with rage and said that I had just ceded his home town. And the head of the Palestinian delegation in New York was abruptly fired for reasons which were never fully explained but which almost certainly included the failure to sustain a deadlock. It had been a narrow squeak.

Following this climax there were a number of aftershocks, but none with the same explosive potential. The Israelis, predictably but unwisely, refused to receive the Secretary-General's emissary, Jean Claude Aimé, who was sent to enquire into the circumstances of the massacre. The Council simply put the ball back into their court with another resolution (673), which deplored the Israeli refusal to receive the mission and asked them to reconsider. They never did; and Aimé's mission was thus stillborn.

Then, in December, when the Yemenis held the presidency of the Council, they revived the whole issue again and situated it in the wider framework of the need for a renewed effort to resolve the whole Arab–Israel dispute. This led to a great deal of tactical manoeuvring, with four successive procedural votes being taken to prevent the tabling of drafts which the Americans would have felt required to veto; and then finally to the adoption by unanimity of a further resolution (681) and of a presidential statement. This latter contained the following: 'they agree that an international conference, at an appropriate time, properly structured, should facilitate efforts to achieve a negotiated settlement and lasting peace in the Arab-Israel conflict. However they are of the view that there is not unanimity as to when would be the appropriate time for such a conference'. Even by the standards of international diplomacy this was an agonisingly tortuous text. And, at the time, most people regarded it as pretty inconsequential. But a year later, in the aftermath of the Gulf War, the US administration did swallow their long-standing aversion to an international conference and summoned the parties to the Madrid meeting, which, after many diversions and delays, led on indirectly to the Oslo process and President Clinton's assemblage on the White House lawn in September 1993. In any event, that concluded the efforts by Saddam Hussein and his supporters to construct a link between the issue of Kuwait and the Arab–Israel dispute and thus to muddy the waters which were beginning to close over his head.

Iraq: towards the use of force

Amongst the foreign ministers who flocked to New York in September 1993 for the annual ministerial debate at the UN General Assembly, the vast majority took a firm line on the need to reverse Iraq's seizure of Kuwait in terms which were consistent with, but made no mention of, the eventual use of force. There was, however, one significant exception, the Soviet foreign minister Edvard Sheverdnadze. In his speech to the General Assembly on 25 September, buried in an otherwise unexceptionable statement, was a phrase which clearly opened the door to eventual Soviet acquiescence in the use of force. If Saddam Hussein had had ears to hear or eyes to see he would have interpreted this, as many other observers did, as a signal that, in certain circumstances, the Soviet Union might actually support the use of force. The significance of this could hardly be exaggerated since the Soviet Union had for long been Iraq's principal international supporter and arms supplier and was the holder of large sums of Iraqi debt; and it was, given China's clear air of detachment from the crisis, far the most likely wielder of a Security Council veto against any resolution authorising the use of force. But, that distant rumble of thunder apart, the emphasis in the General Assembly debate was all on the need to make sanctions work. And the level of US and other troop deployments to Saudi Arabia at that stage meant that any prospect of hostilities, whether authorised by the UN or, as preferred by others like Margaret Thatcher, under cover of the provisions of Article 51 of the UN Charter recognising the inherent right of self-defence (for Kuwait and its allies), was still a good way away.

At the very end of September 1990 the British prime minister herself came to New York briefly for a summit meeting which assembled more than 50 heads of state and government to sign the UN Convention on the Rights of the Child, the first and one of the more useful of a series of such summits which were to be called in the 1990s. She saw President Bush, also in New York for the summit, and no doubt discussed the Kuwait crisis, but I was not involved in that meeting nor did she see any need to seek my views on the next stages at the UN. The time, if ever there really was one, when she was needed to prevent Bush from going 'wobbly' was long past, and the key decisions were going to be taken by the US president, at that moment heavily immersed in the mid-term Congressional election campaign.

A couple of days after that, from 1 to 3 October, Douglas Hurd was back in New York for a ministerial meeting of the Conference on Security and Cooperation in Europe (CSCE; shortly afterwards to become a fully-fledged international organisation). Tom Pickering, my US opposite number, and I were summoned across by our respective bosses, James Baker and Hurd, to the Javits Centre where the CSCE meeting was taking place. Having for some time wandered round the cavernous depths of the conference centre overlooking the Hudson River, on the opposite side of Manhattan to the UN, the four of us finally found a small, unlit room for our meeting. Not much time was wasted on the immediate next steps in the Kuwait crisis at the UN. It was agreed that we would give the Security Council a couple of weeks' pause, since signs of resolution fatigue were evident, but that then, before the end of the month and under UK presidency, we would press for another resolution aimed at tightening the screws further on Iraq, although it was recognised that there was not a lot of scope for further sanctions measures. Baker then asked Pickering and me what our estimate was of the chances of getting through the Security Council a resolution authorising the use of force against Iraq. Guided for the first time by some process of telepathy which always seemed to operate over the next two years when we worked together, we replied in identical terms. We did believe such a resolution could be achieved, particularly now the Soviet Union had signalled its possible support. But it could not be done in the classic way, with the bulk of the negotiations in New York, backed up with some supporting fire from our embassies in Security Council capitals. This was a hugely important and hugely political step. It would require personal contact at the political level with foreign ministers and heads of government in their capitals to ensure that our colleagues on the Security Council, several of whom were past masters at inventing their own instructions, received a firm steer. And it would have to be done in November when the USA held the chair in the Security Council. Baker did not say much, but it was very clear that he personally was leaning towards the Security Council route, principally for reasons of domestic policy, seeing this as the best way to secure Congressional support. Hurd, not surprisingly considering the prime minister's views, said little. Having run through the membership of the Security Council and the prospects for influencing each of them to vote for such a resolution, with only Cuba identified as irremediably hostile, the meeting concluded.

A strange sequel to this meeting followed. On our way out to Kennedy Airport I asked the Foreign Secretary whether he wanted me to report the meeting in the normal way by telegram, no Private Secretary having been present. 'Yes', said Hurd, 'Why not?' And I duly reported it deadpan, with no comments or advice. The next day I received a somewhat flustered call from the Foreign Office. On the instructions of No. 10, copies of the telegram were being withdrawn from distribution; no reference was to be made to it in any subsequent communication. Such was the mood in the last months of the Thatcher government.

From the middle of October onwards we were heavily engaged in New York in negotiation of a further sanctions resolution. This proved far from straightforward for two reasons. Firstly we were scraping the bottom of a fairly empty barrel so far as new measures were concerned. Nevertheless Security Council Resolution 674, as it was to become on adoption on 29 October, did contain some important new elements. Member states of the UN were invited to collate and to pass on to the Council substantiated information about Iraqi breaches of international law on the treatment of civilians and human rights abuses; this could have been a small opening towards an international tribunal had it been subsequently decided to set one up, which in the event it was not. Then Iraq was reminded of its liability under international law for any loss, damage or injury arising in regard to Kuwait or third states; and states were invited to collect relevant information regarding their claims for restitution or financial compensation. Thus the foundations were laid for the post-war Compensation Commission.

The second problem arose from the determination of a small group in the Council (Colombia, Cuba, Malaysia and Yemen), which inevitably came to be known as the 'Gang of Four', to switch the emphasis away from sanctions and towards some ill-defined mediatory role for the UN Secretary-General. The rest of the Council was equally determined, as was Perez de Cuellar himself, to avoid the Secretary-General being put in the impossible position of appearing to mediate between mandatory Security Council resolutions and an aggressor. At the end of much ill-tempered debate, a text emerged which merely stated that the Council 'reposes its trust in the Secretary-General to make available his good offices as he considers appropriate, to pursue them and to undertake diplomatic efforts in order to reach a peaceful solution to the crisis .... On the basis of resolutions 660, 662 and

664 ....' This could hardly be regarded as a mandate to mediate and was not so regarded either by the Secretary-General or by the Iraqis.

Early in November three developments occurred in rapid succession which transformed the situation both on the ground in the Gulf and in New York. The USA and other 'member states cooperating with the government of Kuwait' began to deploy much more substantial military forces to Saudi Arabia, thus making the prospect of expelling the Iraqi army from Kuwait by force a realistic possibility at some not too distant moment in the future; secondly James Baker began a marathon tour of Security Council capitals to persuade governments to vote for a use-of-force resolution; and thirdly Pickering and I received instructions to begin consulting the permanent members of the Security Council on the text of such a resolution. Baker's travels took him first to London, where I was amused to see press photographs of him at No. 10 with Margaret Thatcher, as the prime minister, smiling through, I suspect, slightly gritted teeth, announced that our two governments would be going to the Security Council seeking a use-of-force resolution.

The normal practice, for the British government at least, was to send its mission in New York instructions as to what it wanted to see in a resolution but to leave the actual drafting to New York, assisted, as we were, by a resident Foreign and Commonwealth Office (FCO) legal adviser. But not on this occasion. Instead we received a fully finished text, undoubtedly the work of the FCO's principal legal adviser, Frank Berman, with dire warnings not to tinker, or let others tinker, with it. The text had already been agreed with the Americans in Washington. It was short and to the point, but not without subtlety. It authorised member states cooperating with the government of Kuwait, unless Iraq fully implemented its obligations under previous resolutions (carefully enumerated), to 'use all necessary means to uphold and implement' those resolutions. The overall objective, and this was to become highly relevant to post-war developments, was stated as 'to restore international peace and security in the area', thus casting the net a good deal wider than the simple expulsion of Iraqi troops from Kuwait. The resolution also requested all states to provide appropriate support for the actions so authorised (a provision which seems to have eluded the notice of the Belgian government when they subsequently refused to allow the export of artillery ammunition to the UK during the course of the military operations).

Meetings of the P5 to consider the text began immediately. We met in a tiny, virtually unfurnished flat opposite the UN building, which the Chinese had taken specifically for the purpose of their three months as coordinator of P5 meetings; it came to be known as 'the Chinese take-away' (their own UN mission office was uptown, beyond the Metropolitan Opera and thus unacceptably inconvenient for meetings, which were by then taking place almost daily and sometimes more than once a day). Around the table was a lot of varied diplomatic experience: Tom Pickering (USA), a gregarious, tactically brilliant and hugely effective operator, previously ambassador in Nigeria, Jordan, Israel and El Salvador; Yulii Vorontsov (Soviet Union), a cynical, disciplined former deputy foreign minister, who had been sent to Kabul to preside over the withdrawal of Soviet troops from Afghanistan and had been a long-standing No. 2 at the Soviet Embassy in Washington, where he had had many dealings with Henry Kissinger during the heyday of détente; Li Dao Yu, an epitome of Chinese imperturbability and subtle inflections, with a nice sense of humour; Pierre Louis Blanc, a Gaullist through and through (he had been the General's last press secretary), unhappy with the direction of French policy but far too loyal to say so; and myself. As soon as discussion began, Vorontsov said that the Soviet Union expected to be able to vote for the resolution so long as it included one further element, a 'pause of goodwill' of a month or six weeks which would give Iraq a last chance to comply. Pickering and I duly reported this, pointing out that, from the New York point of view, the delayed triggering of the authorisation could be a real advantage, not just because it showed a reasonable and moderate approach but also because it kept firm control of the timetable during the period which looked likely to elapse between the adoption of the resolution (end of November) and the allied forces in Saudi Arabia being ready to commence military operations. The pause was accepted by Washington, London and Paris and the text redrafted accordingly, setting 15 January 1991 as the date of its expiry. The Chinese made clear throughout that they would abstain and not veto; and no pressure was put on them to do otherwise. When we went out to consultations with the other members of the Council, no further changes were proposed or made. Interestingly enough in the light of subsequent debates about UN enforcement action, no suggestion was made that military action should take place under UN auspices (or under a UN flag as had been the case in Korea many years before). It was simply assumed that, given the size of the Iraqi armed forces, only a coalition of the willing, led by the USA, would be up to the task.

While this process was under way, I went back to London for a very brief visit, whose original object had been to allow me to meet the whole range of ministers interested in developments at the UN and who had not been available in early September before my departure. This objective was totally frustrated by the fact that I arrived on the day after Margaret Thatcher had failed to get the necessary majority to defeat Michael Heseltine's challenge to her as leader of the Conservative Party and while she was engaged in consulting her cabinet colleagues one by one as to whether she should go on to a second round. The corridors around the ministerial suites in the House of Commons, where all this was taking place, were full of scurrying figures and whispering groups, the air of conspiracy so thick you could have cut it with a knife; but not one minister was available to discuss the UN. I was, however, able to see the Leader of the Opposition, Neil Kinnock, as a result of a previous consultation with Douglas Hurd, who had agreed this would be a good idea. I sat down with Kinnock and Charles Clarke (his Chief of Staff and subsequently Home Secretary) and briefed them thoroughly on all that was going on in New York. Kinnock was refreshingly frank and supportive and made it clear that he would support the government policy on the use of force; he dismissed the activities of a group of his own back-benchers led by Tony Benn, opposed to this course, with a cheerful expletive. In the days that followed, as the Conservative leadership election, following Thatcher's resignation, produced a new prime minister and a new government (although not a new Foreign Secretary), I reflected how fortunate Britain was to have such a robust political system and one capable of mustering bipartisan support for a genuinely important decision. It is always good for an ambassador to know that there are no wobbles behind him.

The resolution (678) on the use of force was duly adopted on 29 November by 12 votes in favour, with two voting against (Cuba and Yemen) and one abstention (China). A fair number of foreign ministers attended the session, including Baker, who was presiding, and Hurd. Despite the groundbreaking nature of the decision being taken, there was not much tension, Baker's lengthy diplomatic odyssey having nailed down publicly most of the votes needed. The only remaining doubt was over Yemen. My own view was that there was little or no chance of getting the Yemenis to vote in favour. Ali Abdullah Saleh, the president of Yemen, was close to Saddam Hussein and genuinely admired him; and the Yemenis had abstained on or voted against pretty well all the previous resolutions. But the Americans persisted up to the last moment. Faced with endless prevarication by the Yemeni ambassador, who purported not to be able to contact his foreign minister in Sana'a, I recall an exasperated Pickering picking up his mobile telephone (rather bulky in those days and still in their infancy), punching in about 20 numbers and passing the machine to Abdullah Al-Ashtal saying 'He's on the line'. It was to no avail. And an irritated Baker observed audibly after the vote: 'Well that's one less bilateral aid programme'. Shortly after the adoption of the resolution, President Bush took everyone completely by surprise by announcing that he had asked Baker to seek a meeting with the Iraqi foreign minister Tariq Aziz. This move turned out to be a tactical master-stroke since it ensured that, for the month or so that it took to set up and to hold the meeting, no-one else ventured onto the turf; and no one in New York tried to reopen issues which had been settled by Resolution 678.

*　*　*　*

So 1990, the first half of which had been a relatively quiet period for the post-Cold War UN, with the winding down of the successful peacekeeping operation in Namibia, and the reduction of hostilities in Central America after the defeat of Nicaragua's Sandinista government at the polls, ended with an unforeseen aggression having been met with an unexpectedly robust response and with a number of quite unprecedented decisions having been taken. But all still remained to play for. My own view at the time set out the balance:

> It is not easy to offer any very meaningful predictions for 1991 since the crystal ball is entirely dominated by the saturnine features of the ruler of Iraq. It is no exaggeration to say that the whole future development of the United Nations in the area of international peace and security depends to a great extent on the outcome of the Gulf crisis. If Saddam Hussein is successfully expelled from Kuwait, whether peacefully or by force, not only will the UN have a large amount of follow-up work to do on regional security and other matters, but it will receive a tremendous shot in the arm. Indeed a successful

outcome may lead to an altogether excessive euphoria about the capacity of the UN to resolve regional issues in the post-Cold War era. Be that as it may, we will certainly in those circumstances find a major increase in the business flowing towards the UN and major increased demands on its resources.

If, on the contrary, the Gulf crisis and the UN's so far remarkably robust handling of it turn out to be a failure, whether because of dissension in the alliance, successful manoeuvring by Saddam Hussein or a loss of will by the United States, to name only three of the ways in which matters might go wrong, then I fear that the UN renaissance may indeed turn out to be a false dawn. In such a perspective it would be hard to see the UN successfully playing the sort of pro-active role it has over the Gulf in other disputes which are likely to be of a less clear-cut nature and less susceptible to effective economic and military action. After all there can be few countries more vulnerable to economic sanctions than Iraq and few against which the marshalling of a multinational military force is geographically and politically so feasible.

So a very great deal rides on this issue. If all goes reasonably well, I think we will then need to give serious thought as to how we wish to see the UN operating, particularly in the field of peacekeeping and peacemaking in the post-Cold War era. With the United States unwilling, and in the long term unable, to carry the whole burden itself, with the Soviet Union ceasing to have a world-wide intervention capacity and throwing its weight behind a UN approach and with middle-ranking powers, including the UK, France, Germany and Japan either unwilling or unable to sustain independent activity in the future, there is a great deal to be said for thinking imaginatively about an expansion of the UN's capabilities and activities in the field of collective security.

Chapter V

1991: War and peace; and state failure

The first half of 1991 was entirely dominated by the crisis with Iraq over its seizure of Kuwait, by the last feeble twitches of diplomatic activity to avert a war, by the war itself and by its complex aftermath. But, during the second half of the year, the first round in what were to become the wars of the Yugoslav succession was forcing its way up the UN's agenda. And the mounting of the so far largest ever UN peacekeeping operation, in Cambodia, was beginning to move from the planning to the operational phase. So the whole issue of overstretch, both of political energy and of resources, began to loom over the organisation, just when the success of the UN's reversal of Iraq's aggression brought a whole mass of additional issues on to the Security Council's plate.

The first two weeks of 1991 were a period of waiting: waiting to see whether the last contacts with Saddam Hussein's regime would lead to any shift in the Iraqi position towards compliance with the UN's resolutions; waiting also to see when the authority conferred on the coalition under Resolution 678, which became effective on 16 January with the expiry of the 'pause of goodwill', would lead to actual hostilities.

As occurred at the beginning of January every year, the membership of the Security Council changed, with five of the elected members leaving at the end of their two-year term (Canada, Colombia, Ethiopia, Finland and Malaysia) and five others (Austria, Belgium, Ecuador, India and Zimbabwe) arriving. This changing of the guard had, during the Cold War, been the object of much feverish speculation and much positional manoeuvring, as calculations were made both by the newcomers and those remaining on the Council of just where each government stood on the East-West spectrum. But that sort of calculation had now become pretty academic and, with the early months of the year being completely monopolised by Iraq, on which the key decisions had already been taken, there was no noticeable shift in the balance of attitudes. Cuba and Yemen remained outside any likely majority; India and Zimbabwe were somewhat unknown quantities but firmly opposed to Saddam Hussein's aggression; and Ecuador appeared rather less volatile than Colombia had been, and with an ambassador, Jose Ayala Lasso (subsequently to become the first UN High Commissioner for Human Rights), who became over time that most valuable of people to have on the Council, a representative of a small country with few particular axes to grind and with an aptitude for reconciling conflicting views and building bridges between groups in disagreement with each other.

War in the Gulf

The last two diplomatic efforts to avert hostilities between Iraq and the US-led, UN-authorised coalition arrayed against it were rapidly played out. First Baker met Tariq Aziz, the Iraqi deputy prime minister, in Geneva on 9 January. The meeting was a standoff, with not the slightest sign of give on either side. Baker insisted on Iraq's full compliance with the UN's, by then 12, mandatory resolutions; Tariq Aziz breathed defiance. Thereafter an extremely reluctant UN Secretary-General was finally propelled briefly into the centre of the stage, mainly by those numerous countries who still hoped, against all indications, for a diplomatic miracle. Perez de Cuellar's visit to Baghdad on 13 January proved as unfruitful as Baker's to Geneva. He was treated with scant respect by Saddam Hussein, who seemed impervious to warnings that military action was now very close. Ahead of the visit the French, in one of those wobbles which probably reflected as much as anything domestic difficulties in Paris over participating in a US-led military operation, tried to persuade the other members of the P5 that the Security Council should give Perez de Cuellar a vague mandate to work for compromise. This approach, which would have put the Secretary-General in the impossible position of negotiating between an aggressor and a set of clear, legally-binding UN resolutions, found no takers; and the French did not persist to the point of raising their ideas in the Council itself.

On the afternoon of 16 January, the members of the Security Council were meeting in the claustrophobic confines of their informal consultations room, conducting a desultory discussion of the latest situation on the West Bank and Gaza, when a latecomer, hastening through the empty ante-chamber, noticed that the television set there, switched as usual permanently to CNN, seemed to be emitting a series of lightning flashes against a black background. Somewhat naively he suggested to the Council members that there seemed to be something wrong with the television set; in fact the Coalition's air attacks on Iraqi targets, including those in Baghdad, had just begun. The consultations room emptied rapidly; and the ambassadors assumed a role to which they were to become accustomed in the weeks ahead, that of spectators of events over which they had no control.

The six-week period of hostilities – roughly five weeks consisting exclusively of the aerial bombardment by coalition forces of targets in Iraq and Kuwait, and less than one week of land operations, which resulted in the expulsion of all Iraqi forces from Kuwait – was largely uneventful at the UN's headquarters in New York. The only attempt to interfere with the military operations came from a group of member states outside the Council, led by the Arab countries of the Maghreb (Algeria, Libya, Mauritania, Morocco and Tunisia), who called for an urgent Security Council debate, their hope being that such a debate would reveal a public groundswell of opinion in favour of a call for a ceasefire. This call for an urgent debate triggered off much manoeuvring in the corridors and also in the Council but no action. Outside the Council the ambassadors of the main Arab countries who were members of the Coalition (Egypt, Syria and Saudi Arabia) lobbied actively to discourage any efforts to interfere with the process of expelling Iraqi forces from Kuwait. Within the Council, manoeuvring focussed around whether or not any debate should be held in public (as those calling for it wished) or in private, as was possible under the rules of procedure if the Council so decided. A procedural vote on 13 February decided that the meeting should be held in private, with nine votes in favour, two against (Cuba and Yemen) and four abstentions. This vote demonstrated clearly that there would be insufficient support in the Council for any attempt to adopt a resolution calling for a ceasefire; and that, together with the failure to stage a public debate, meant that the debate itself became something of a damp squib, merely providing a platform on which a large number of non-members registered their views on the crisis.

Neither the US decision to call a halt to military operations (on 28 February) nor the subsequent negotiations between US and Iraqi military representatives on the terms of a cessation of hostilities (at Safwan on 3 March) came anywhere near the Security Council. At US instigation the Council did, however, adopt a resolution (686) on 2 March which effectively rubber-stamped what had been happening on the ground up to then and gave the USA carte blanche for the cessation of hostilities negotiations which had yet to take place. This resolution noted that Iraq had by now, on 27 February, accepted all the mandatory Security Council Resolutions adopted following its invasion of Kuwait; it focussed on a number of short-term aspects such as the release of prisoners and third-country nationals, the cessation of missile attacks, and the return of property. It was entirely silent on the wider issues which would need to be addressed in the post-war period. Despite the rather peremptory way in which the text was tabled and negotiated, neither Pickering nor I being able to answer even quite simple questions about what was happening on the ground, no real problems arose in the Council. The relief there that the USA and its coalition allies had called an early halt to military operations and had clearly decided not to continue their offensive into Iraq itself was palpable and overcame any irritation about the manner of handling this phase. But both Pickering and I expressed misgivings to each other and to our governments should this become the pattern for the future. We need not have worried.

The mother of all resolutions

Within days of the adoption of the cease-fire resolution, Pickering telephoned and, having advised me to take a deep breath, revealed that it had been decided in Washington and agreed between Washington, London and Paris that the whole post-war process in the Gulf was going to be handed over to the UN and negotiated within the Security Council. This far-reaching, and completely unexpected, decision had important, and, in the short term at least, entirely positive consequences for the UN's standing and credibility as a key player in securing international peace and stability. It also meant that an enormous workload descended on Security Council delegations, in particular on those of the P5, as streams of instructions began to issue from

Washington and London covering the whole gamut of issues that needed settling, the Iraq–Kuwait border, the future sanctions regime, compensation for damage done by Iraq, weapons of mass destruction, missing persons and the return of Kuwaiti property, and many other complex questions. On this occasion, unlike the resolution authorising the use of force (678), we were merely given the main elements of what was required, not fully worked-up texts, which it was left to us in New York to draft.

The negotiation of this massive resolution, which came to be known as the 'mother of all resolutions' when it was adopted as Security Council Resolution 687 on 3 April, went quite remarkably smoothly considering its scope. Nor was its name (a snide reference to Saddam Hussein's supposed naming of the recent hostilities as 'the mother of all victories') pure hyperbole, since it gave birth to a peacekeeping operation and three fully-fledged international bodies (one for the demarcation of the frontier between Iraq and Kuwait, one for calculating the losses and compensating victims of Iraq's aggression and one for bringing about the destruction, removal or rendering harmless of all Iraq's weapons of mass destruction and its ballistic missiles with a range of more than 150 kilometres). All texts began by passing through the mesh of the P5, which was in almost continuous session for a whole month at either ambassadorial or counsellor level. Thereafter they went to the Council as a whole. And the final outcome was adopted by 12 votes (including China), with only one vote against (Cuba) and two abstentions (Ecuador – for totally extraneous reasons – and Yemen).

The main elements of this unprecedented resolution were as follows:

(i) **The Iraq–Kuwait border**
Dispute over the precise delineation of this border, both the land border and its maritime prolongation, had arisen frequently, both before and since Kuwait's independence had been recognised, most recently in the run-up to Iraq's invasion of Kuwait in August 1990. The border had never been properly demarcated, although an agreement negotiated between Iraq and Kuwait in 1963, after a previous crisis had almost led to hostilities, did exist; and there were also British maps, dating from the period when Britain had been responsible for Kuwait's external relations, which contained such oddities as references to the number of date palms along the

road south of Safwan which determined where the border lay. Given what had happened the year before, even if it was legitimate to doubt whether the border was the real casus belli between the two countries, this situation could not be allowed to continue. But rectifying it was far from straightforward. For the UN Security Council itself to have imposed a border would have been a hugely innovative step into an area where it had always previously been considered that it was for the two or more parties in a border dispute themselves to negotiate a settlement (or to agree to submit the matter to the International Court of Justice), a step with all sorts of potentially troubling implications for other border disputes, for example that between India and China. It was certainly a step too far for the Chinese and for a number of other countries. The solution found was to ask the UN Secretary-General to make arrangements to demarcate the boundary using as a basis the existing 1963 agreement and drawing on the British maps. Even this ingenious compromise was too much for the Ecuadoreans to swallow (they had a long-running border dispute with Peru which some years later led to brief hostilities) and forced them into an embarrassed abstention on the resolution as a whole.

Simply demarcating the border was, however, clearly not a sufficient measure to ward off a recurrence of the dispute in the future, given in particular the disparity in the size and military capacity of the two countries. So consideration was also given to the need to guarantee its future inviolability. This too was not entirely straightforward, if only because such an explicit Security Council guarantee had never been given before. The principal question was whether that guarantee should contain a degree of automaticity should the border be transgressed. Again this was a step too far for China and some others. So the guarantee was given; but future action, including explicitly the key phrase about the use of 'all necessary means', the codeword for the use of force, would depend on a further Security Council decision, i.e. it could be blocked by the veto of a permanent member.

In addition it was decided that a UN peacekeeping observer mission should be established on the Iraq–Kuwait border to deter violations of the border and to conduct surveillance of an asymmetrical demilitarised zone which would extend ten kilometres into Iraq and five kilometres into Kuwait. This mission was never regarded as more than a tripwire against Iraqi incursions. Some consideration was given by the USA to extending its remit to cover also the Iraq–Saudi border (since Iraq had violated that border too in the course of the recent military operations), but this idea was dropped in view of the great length of the border involved. This peacekeeping mission had one novel characteristic: hitherto UN peacekeeping missions had always required the agreement of the parties to the dispute and six-monthly renewals could be blocked in the Security Council. In this case when the mission was formally set up (Security Council Resolution 689 of 9 April), it was made clear that Iraq did not have any veto over its continuance and that it would require a decision of the Security Council to terminate it, a reversal of the normal procedure, thus ensuring that this could only happen with the agreement of Kuwait's coalition allies.

(ii) Weapons of mass destruction

The fact that Iraq had programmes for the development of weapons of mass destruction (WMD) and for the construction of missiles which could deliver them was no secret. It had made extensive use of chemical weapons in the Iran–Iraq war and also in the military operations against its own Kurdish population (thus breaching its obligations under the 1925 Protocol for the Prohibition of the Use in War of Asphyxiating, Poisonous or Other Gases). Its nuclear programme had been a cause of concern for many years and had led to the bombing of the Osirak research reactor by the Israelis in June 1981; it was widely supposed that Iraq was developing nuclear weapons (in contravention of its obligations under the Nuclear Non-Proliferation Treaty (NPT)). Less was known about its efforts to develop biological weapons (in contravention of the Biological and Toxic Weapons Convention of 1972), but there was much speculation and suspicion. Its missiles had been used, admittedly not to very good effect and only armed with conventional warheads, to bombard Tel Aviv, Riyadh and other targets during the recent hostilities.

Both before and during these hostilities, much anxious consideration had been given in Washington and London as to what was to be done about these WMD programmes in the event of Saddam Hussein accepting the existing UN resolutions, which made no explicit mention of them, and withdrawing from Kuwait. The idea that he might be allowed to continue to develop these weapons programmes clandestinely was not appealing, particularly as it was so clear that they played an important role in his blackmailing diplomacy towards his neighbours. With the decision by the coalition allies following the ceasefire not to go further into Iraq, this quandary now had to be resolved.

The solution consisted of requiring Iraq to accept unconditionally the destruction, removal or rendering harmless under international supervision of all its WMD programmes and of its ballistic missiles with a range of more than 150 kilometres; of establishing a special commission (known as the UN Special Commission (UNSCOM)) to carry out this work in respect of biological, chemical and missile capabilities; and of tasking the International Atomic Energy Agency (IAEA) to do the same with Iraq's nuclear installations. All this was duly incorporated in the resolution, although not without some technical difficulties over the drafting and, unusually, some friction between London and Washington. The friction arose over whether, as some at least in Washington wanted, the nuclear task should also be given to the Special Commission and not to the IAEA.

That the IAEA had been fooled by Saddam Hussein and its inspectors hoodwinked over the extent and nature of his nuclear programme was not in doubt; and there were plenty of politically motivated arms control experts in a Republican administration who had no time at all for IAEA safeguards and would happily have seen them sidelined and discredited. The view in London (and fortunately there were some in Washington who took that view too) was that it would be extremely unwise to deprive the IAEA of its proper responsibilities on nuclear matters and that this provided a golden opportunity to strengthen the IAEA's capacity to conduct more intrusive inspections in future. In the end the parallel-track approach, with UNSCOM and the IAEA working in tandem, which was in any case almost certainly the only approach which would have been acceptable to the other members of the Security Council, was adopted.

The outline solution to the WMD problem in Resolution 687 was rapidly followed up by a further resolution (699 of 17 June), which actually set up UNSCOM on the basis of a plan which had been submitted by the Secretary-General in May and which gave

UNSCOM and the IAEA a full and detailed mandate for carrying out their remits. At the same time it was decided that Iraq would ultimately bear the full costs of carrying out these tasks. The inspectors from both organisations duly went to work and soon uncovered evidence of massive stockpiles of chemical weapons and the ruins, destroyed by allied bombing, of nuclear installations designed to produce fissile material for nuclear weapons. All this was documented in a series of reports to the Security Council. Of biological programmes and weapons there was at first little trace and the Iraqis continued for several years to deny their existence. The extent of the nuclear programme in particular far exceeded pre-war intelligence estimates and this intelligence failure offers one of the explanations for the failure in the other direction which took place in the run-up to the invasion of Iraq in 2003.

The work of the inspectors did not, however, run at all smoothly and a soon-to-be-familiar pattern of Iraqi concealment, obfuscation and obstruction of their work began, as Saddam Hussein played cat and mouse with them, a process which was to continue for the whole period up to the withdrawal of the inspectors in 1998 prior to military action being taken by the Coalition allies. The first major instance of this pattern occurred within a few weeks and gave rise to Security Council Resolution 707 of 15 August, which condemned Iraq's violations of its obligations under Resolution 687 and required it to remedy them. Resolution 707 is of some interest because it set out more clearly and explicitly than did any other resolution the link between Iraq's cooperation with UNSCOM and the IAEA, the absence of which 'constitutes a material breach of the relevant provisions of that resolution [687] which established a cease-fire and provided the conditions essential to the restoration of peace and security in the region [the wording of Resolution 678, which authorised the use of force in the first place]' and the continuing authority to use force which was to be so hotly contested by those who opposed the invasion of Iraq in 2003.

(iii) Compensation for war damage

The actual period of hostilities may have been short and the number of casualties relatively small, but the damage caused by Iraq's invasion of Kuwait was great. Many thousands of migrant workers and their families, mainly coming from other Arab countries and from the Indian subcontinent, had lost their livelihoods and had had to be evacuated; much indiscriminate damage had occurred in Kuwait City at the time of the invasion and later; missile attacks on Saudi Arabia and Israel had fallen on cities; and, in the last days of the military campaign, the retreating Iraqi troops had quite deliberately set out to inflict the maximum damage they could on Kuwait's oil installations, starting massive conflagrations which took many weeks to extinguish and causing severe environmental damage throughout the Gulf region.

The idea of holding Iraq to account for the costs of its aggression had already been raised before the war started (in paragraphs 8 and 9 of Resolution 674 of 29 October 1990, when Iraq was reminded of its liability for any damage that was inflicted and member states were invited to collect information relevant to their claims 'with a view to such arrangements as may be established in accordance with international law'). Previous international experience over war reparations, particularly after the First World War, had not been satisfactory. The terms had tended to be dictated by the victors, rather arbitrary and massive figures which confused direct damage caused by the war with punitive elements imposed for having started it were established at the outset, in a process which lacked transparency and accountability; and the effects on the economy of the country being required to pay compensation were poorly understood and, in the view of many later commentators, beyond their capacity to bear. All this was present in the minds of those working on the resolution; the precedents provided evidence more of pitfalls to avoid than of ways to proceed.

Resolution 687 did not therefore attempt to establish an overall figure for how much Iraq should pay by way of compensation. It defined what was to be compensated: 'direct loss, damage – including environmental damage and the depletion of natural resources – or injury to foreign governments, nationals and corporations' on a basis which contained no punitive element; it established a fund to pay such compensation and an international commission to administer the fund; and it directed the Secretary-General to make recommendations as to the percentage of the exports of Iraq's petroleum products which should be used to furnish the fund with the resources needed to pay compensation (petroleum and petroleum products being virtually Iraq's only exports) 'taking into account the requirements of the people of Iraq'. A further resolution was then adopted some two months later (Resolution 692 of 20 May) approving the Secretary-General's proposals for the Commission's Governing Council and method of operation, locating it in Geneva. The Governing Council and the Commission were given complete independence and freedom of action over determining acceptable claims and the levels of compensation. And then, in one further resolution (Resolution No 705 of 15 August), the Council, acting on the Secretary-General's recommendation, set 30 per cent of Iraq's oil export revenue as the percentage ceiling for Iraq's payments.

This last decision did not emerge without a certain amount of behind-the-scenes jostling, since some in Washington wanted a higher figure. But in the end counsels of moderation prevailed, as did the feverish lobbying of France and the Soviet Union, both of whom could see the chances of their ever being able to recover Iraq's massive debts to them arising from the pre-war supply of military equipment receding into a very distant future. For a considerable time the fund had virtually no resources, since Iraq was prevented by the sanctions regime from exporting legally, and few compensation payments could be made. But the work of sifting, analysing and adjudicating on the claims was able to proceed; and the ground was well prepared for the later period when the oil-for-food scheme came into operation (in 1996) and began to provide a substantial flow of resources into the fund, thus enabling compensation payments to be made.

(iv) The sanctions regime

The economic sanctions regime imposed on Iraq in August/ September 1990, following its invasion and seizure of Kuwait, had been put together in some haste and in a series of steps not all of which were mutually consistent or easy to apply (an account of the sequence of measures taken is set out in the preceding chapter of this book). The objectives had been as much political as economic, to shock Iraq into recognising that it had made a mistake in invading Kuwait and to persuade it to withdraw from that country without the need for the use of force. In this objective it had failed, although economic sanctions had certainly weakened Iraq in the run-up to hostilities. In the aftermath of the war a full-scale review of the sanctions regime was clearly necessary; and this was brought home with considerable force by a report on the impact of the war and sanctions on the civilian population of Iraq, which was circulated to the Security Council by the Secretary-General following a visit to Iraq by Under-Secretary-General Martti Ahtisaari.

The first thing that needed to be done was to decide the objective of any continuance of the sanctions regime, given that the original objectives, the restoration of Kuwait's independence and the establishment of peace and security in the region, had in one case been achieved and in the other was simply too vague to be operable. Given that Saddam Hussein remained in charge in Iraq and that the threat he represented to his neighbours had not been removed, there was no suggestion by any member of the Security Council that the continuation of economic sanctions was not necessary. It was decided therefore to link the lifting of sanctions very precisely to the completion of the actions set out earlier in the resolution for the destruction, removal or rendering harmless of all Iraq's programmes for weapons of mass destruction and of ballistic missiles with a range of more than 150 kilometres – 'upon Council agreement that Iraq has completed all actions contemplated …. The prohibitions shall have no further force or effect'. The object was to provide a clear and measurable yardstick for the Council's use when it came to lift sanctions and also to give the regime in Iraq a major incentive to cooperate fully with the weapons inspectors. Unfortunately it did neither of these as effectively as had been hoped. The fact that the final word on the lifting of sanctions rested with the Council meant that a resolution to that effect could always be blocked by the veto of a Permanent Member; and both Saddam Hussein, by playing a never-ending game of cat-and-mouse with the inspectors, and successive US presidents and British prime ministers, by making public statements implying that they would not agree to the lifting of sanctions so long as Saddam Hussein remained in power, sapped its credibility and clarity.

The new resolution also set out with greater precision than before the way the sanctions regime was intended to apply to different categories of Iraq's imports: medicine and health supplies were outside the regime and merely had to be notified; foodstuffs

were to be dealt with under an accelerated 'no objection' procedure in the Sanctions Committee; materials for essential civilian
needs and humanitarian purposes were to be dealt with similarly;
all arms supplies and military technology and services were
banned completely until the Council decided otherwise (the
detailed systems to implement this ban were subsequently
approved by the Council in Resolution 700 of 17 June); and all
supplies relating to programmes for weapons of mass destruction
were banned and excluded from the provisions for the periodic
review of the sanctions regime. It was provided that the main sanctions regime would be reviewed by the Council every 60 days and
the arms embargo every 120 days.

These review provisions were systematically misunderstood and
misinterpreted by almost all concerned, the media in particular,
which persisted in confusing the word 'renew' with 'review' and
thus in announcing every two months that the Council had agreed
to renew sanctions against Iraq. It did nothing of the sort. The
reviews were just that, unless and until a resolution was proposed
and adopted to 'reduce or lift the prohibitions'; and no such proposal was in fact made until after the overthrow of Saddam
Hussein in 2003, even though a number of delegations (France,
Russia and China in particular) argued for the easing of sanctions
during those periodical reviews. For a long time there would not
have been a majority in the Council for such a resolution; and,
much later, the near-certainty of a US and UK veto, taken together
with Saddam Hussein's less-than-compliant behaviour, discouraged any attempt to go down that road.

There remained, however, one major obstacle to operating the
new, more sophisticated sanctions regime in a manner which
would relieve the impact on ordinary Iraqi civilians. The financial
sanctions imposed and the ban on Iraqi exports of oil meant that
there were inadequate resources available to finance even those
imports which were permitted. No one doubted that there were in
fact substantial financial resources in the hands of senior members
of the Iraqi regime, nor that some resources were generated by
smuggling or by the acquiescence of the international community
in the continuance of Iraqi oil exports to Jordan. But Saddam
Hussein had other purposes to which to put such resources and in
any case the sums involved would have been inadequate to the

needs. So in August 1991 the Council adopted two resolutions (706 and 712) which provided for the internationally controlled sale of agreed quantities of Iraqi oil, the cash generated by which would be put in an escrow account and used for the purchase of humanitarian supplies, medicines and foodstuffs.

This was the first version of what subsequently became known as the 'oil-for-food' scheme. In the event it was stillborn. Lengthy negotiations between the UN Secretariat and Iraqi officials to work up the agreed operating details of such a scheme, which could have been put for approval to the Sanctions Committee, ran into the sands, the Iraqi side insisting on provisions which would have left the scheme even more open to fraud than the similar scheme, approved much later (in 1995), turned out to be. The main problem at this stage was not, however, technical but political. Saddam Hussein was clearly reluctant to agree to any scheme which might lessen the pressure on the Security Council to lift sanctions. He saw the well-publicised sufferings of his own people as the best lever for raising that pressure, and measures taken to alleviate their sufferings as likely to prolong the duration of sanctions. There were certainly tensions within the Iraqi regime over whether to permit such a scheme to go ahead, with Tariq Aziz, the long-serving foreign minister and then deputy prime minister and a frequent visitor to New York, the leading protagonist in its favour. But Saddam Hussein, not for the first nor the last time, chose to gamble and underestimated the determination of the international community.

Saving Kurds and losing Shi'a

History is full of mishaps, often subsequently portrayed as conspiracies or plots, which have major unwanted consequences. One such mishap was the timing of the Kurdish and Shi'a uprisings in Iraq in March 1991. It is hard to believe that, if those risings had taken place a week or two earlier, the USA would have negotiated a cease-fire agreement with the Iraqi military which left the bulk of Saddam Hussein's elite Revolutionary Guard troops available to be deployed against the rebels and which permitted them to use their attack helicopters. As we have seen earlier in this chapter, the UN was in no way involved directly in those decisions. But it had to try to cope with the consequences when the Iraqi repression of the risings led to a massive exodus of Iraqi Kurds across the border into Turkey and a rather lesser but still substantial flow of Kurdish and Shi'a refugees into Iran. That this was a man-made humanitarian disaster was not in doubt. But what could be done about it? And by whom?

The precedents for a collective, UN response, intervening in what were unmistakably events occurring within a sovereign, independent member state, were non-existent. Major man-made humanitarian crises had occurred during the Cold War years and interventions had taken place – for example, when India intervened in what was then East Pakistan, or when Tanzania intervened in Uganda to overthrow Idi Amin, or when the Vietnamese invaded Cambodia to overthrow the Khmer Rouge regime of Pol Pot – but in no case had the intervening country sought UN authorisation for its actions nor did they give great prominence to the humanitarian arguments for intervention, even though in all three cases those were quite compelling. In every case the intervenors and their main backers had had solid, realpolitik arguments for downplaying the humanitarian dimension and for denying flatly that a precedent might be being created which could be of wider application.

The day before the Council was due to adopt the 'mother of all resolutions', an extremely nervous and worried French Chargé d'Affaires (Jean-Marc de la Sablière, Blanc having retired and his successor Jean Bernard Mérimée having not yet arrived) telephoned Pickering and me to say that he had received instructions to try to insert at the last moment into Resolution 687 some provisions requiring the Iraqis to stop hostilities against the Kurds and Shi'a. The prospect was a daunting one not simply in terms of delaying what was an urgently needed resolution but, far more fundamentally, because trying to insert into a mandatory, Chapter VII-based resolution provisions which amounted to a humanitarian intervention in the internal affairs of Iraq was likely to prove unacceptable not only to the Soviet Union and China but quite possibly to other members of the Council too. After some frantic telephoning between Washington, Paris and London, it was agreed that the French would not press the case for an amendment to Resolution 687 but that we would all three start work urgently, immediately after Resolution 687 was adopted, on a Chapter VI, i.e. non-mandatory, resolution on the Kurds and the Shi'a. We were as good as our word, but it was uphill work. We were trying to take the Council over a Rubicon that had not hitherto been crossed. In the end we mustered a mere ten votes (nine being needed to adopt a resolution), with Cuba, Yemen and Zimbabwe voting against and China and India abstaining. The key vote was that of the Soviet Union, which had serious qualms; but the tide of US/Soviet cooperation was running strongly and carried us over.

The resolution (688), adopted on 5 April, only three days after the previous one, was in all conscience pretty feeble, at least on the face of it. It condemned the repression of the Iraqi civilian population which threatened international peace and security in the region (a key phrase hinting at possible future use of Chapter VII); it demanded that Iraq end this repression and undertake an open dialogue to ensure the human and political rights of all Iraqi citizens; it insisted that Iraq give access to international humanitarian organisations; it requested the Secretary-General to pursue his humanitarian efforts in Iraq and to use all the resources at his disposal to address urgently the critical needs of the refugees and displaced Iraqi population. But it, by definition, contained no enforcement provisions (which would have required the use of Chapter VII); and the pattern of voting on the resolution made it clear that, if we had reverted to the Council with a request for increased authority we would have been very unlikely to have got it. So, in terms of what could be done on the ground in Iraq, we were going to need to improvise, making what use we could of the somewhat flimsy cover provided by Resolution 688.

By now the pressure for robust intervention, in particular to protect the Kurds who were fleeing in huge numbers and in appalling climatic conditions across the mountainous borderlands between Iraq and Turkey, was very strong in Europe and was overcoming earlier hesitations in Washington. A combination of the Coalition's imposition of no-fly zones in northern and southern Iraq, of operations by coalition forces based in Turkey to protect refugees close to the border and the deployment of the UN's humanitarian agencies in the camps on both sides of the border, taken together with Iraq's sullen acquiescence and decision not to mount any military challenge, resulted in the gradual stabilisation of the situation and over time the reversal of the refugee flow. But what worked for the Kurds, thanks to the contiguity of a NATO and coalition ally in Turkey, did not work for the Shi'a, whose suffering was hardly alleviated at all by the various measures and many of whom remained in refugee camps in Iran. The UN Secretariat and agencies had the trickiest task of all, involving securing Iraqi consent or at least acquiescence in all they did but operating without any serious military protection in a region which could at any moment become a war zone. Overall they performed creditably and the Secretary-General, Javier Perez de Cuellar, overcame his initial doubts and gave strong support.

Yugoslavia: the failure of a state

During the first nine months of 1991, as Yugoslavia slid towards disintegration and then, following declarations of secession by Slovenia and Croatia in June, tipped over into an increasingly vicious civil war, the UN remained a detached bystander, heavily preoccupied, as we have seen, by the war in Iraq and its aftermath. Yugoslavia was, of course, itself a UN member state in good standing, a troop contributor to peacekeeping operations, quite recently an elected member of the Security Council and one of the three founder members of the Non-Aligned Movement. Its federal government, while gradually losing all authority and fading into irrelevance, strongly resisted any attempt to bring their plight formally before the UN. For them such a move would have implied recognising that this was an international issue, not one involving the domestic affairs of a member state and thus outside the terms of reference of the UN Charter (the key reference in the Charter – Article 2(7) – stating 'Nothing contained in the present Charter shall authorise the UN to intervene in matters which are essentially within the domestic jurisdiction of any state or shall require the Members to submit such matters to settlement under the present Charter').

There was much sympathy for this point of view at the UN, particularly among the members of the Non-Aligned Movement who had been distinctly uneasy about the humanitarian intervention in northern Iraq earlier in the year; and so the active and popular Yugoslav permanent representative, Darko Silovic (a Croatian, but no friend of secession), was able to fend off any suggestion that the UN should play a role in the rapidly deteriorating situation. Nor did any of the other main players at the UN show much enthusiasm for UN involvement. The members of the European Community (EC), Britain and France among them, were heavily involved in their own diplomatic efforts to broker a peaceful outcome to the Yugoslav crisis; and, while few of them shared the hubristic claim of the Luxembourg foreign minister that this was 'Europe's hour', they were not as yet prepared to recognise that their own efforts were proving inadequate. The US administration was reluctant to be drawn into another messy foreign entanglement. The Soviet Union was entirely absorbed in its own internal upheavals. And the Chinese disliked the whole concept of intervention. Moreover the phenomenon of state failure, of which Yugoslavia was daily becoming a clearer example, was at that stage not well understood, nor were its knock-on implications in terms of wider threats to international peace and security.

By September, however, all these reasons, or excuses, for inaction had become unsustainable. In the east of Croatia fighting in and around the town of Vukovar had reached an intensity which recalled scenes from the Second World War, with heavy artillery bombardments and persistent reports of atrocities against civilians. The Yugoslav federal government's resistance to the issue being brought to the UN had weakened. The Europeans realised that their diplomatic efforts needed wider international support. The outcome was a Ministerial-level meeting of the Security Council (the ministers were already in New York for the annual general debate in the General Assembly) and the adoption of Security Council Resolution 713 of 25 September, the first of a very long series devoted to the Yugoslav crisis.

The resolution itself was an uncomfortable straddle between the various tensions which had prevented the issue being taken up earlier; somewhat surprisingly it was adopted by unanimity. The preamble welcomed the fact that the Yugoslav government itself favoured the convening of the Security Council, and the resolution commended the efforts of the Europeans, including the summoning of a conference on Yugoslavia, and expressed its full support for them. But at the same time as making it clear that it wanted the European peacemaking role to continue, it invited the UN's Secretary-General to offer his assistance and to report back to the Council. From this small acorn was to grow the UN peacekeeping mission in Croatia and a joint peacemaking role for the UN Secretary-General's personal envoy, Cyrus Vance, formerly US Secretary of State during the Carter administration. The one immediately operational element in the resolution was the imposition of an arms embargo 'on all deliveries of weapons and military equipment to Yugoslavia until the Council decides otherwise'. Given how extremely contentious the arms embargo subsequently became, it is worth noting that its inclusion in this first resolution (and the subsequent tightening up of its implementation in Security Council Resolution 724 of 15 December) provoked no disagreement in the Council. The concern to avoid other countries in the region or even outside it being drawn into the conflict or becoming involved as arms suppliers to one or other of the parties weighed heavily in the balance at this stage.

In the months that followed the adoption of this first resolution, Vance's efforts on the ground gradually bore fruit in the form of cease-fire arrangements between the Croatians and the Yugoslav army and the preliminary preparations for the deployment of UN peacekeepers to the three parts of Croatia where most of the fighting had taken place (Eastern and Western Slavonia and the Krajina). But those preparations were continually being interrupted by cease-fire violations, and in December the Security Council in Resolution 724 stated flatly that 'the conditions for establishing a peacekeeping operation in Yugoslavia still do not exist'. Meanwhile the Europeans' parallel efforts, led by their principal envoy Lord Carrington, formerly British Foreign Secretary and Secretary-General of NATO, to negotiate a peaceful transition to a post-war Yugoslavia, by now clearly involving the break-up of the previous entity into its component federated parts, were being subjected to rising tension within the EC itself between two alternative ways of proceeding. One view, whose most prominent protagonist was the German foreign minister Hans Dietrich Genscher, favoured the early recognition as independent sovereign states of Slovenia and Croatia and their admission to the UN.

The other view, held by the British and French governments and by Carrington himself, was that recognition should only be granted as part of an overall package covering all the former component parts of Yugoslavia, and containing commitments by all to the borders between them and to the equitable treatment of the ethnic minorities which would be established by this settlement. The UN Secretary-General and Vance were firmly of this second view; and they were increasingly concerned about the implications of early recognition, which it was unlikely to be possible to limit to Slovenia and Croatia alone, for Bosnia and Herzegovina, where up till then an uneasy calm had prevailed. The Americans were also of this view, although their continuing semi-detached attitude towards Yugoslavia had been damagingly signalled earlier in the autumn when Baker had said 'the US has no dog in this fight'. The tensions came to a head early in November when Perez de Cuellar, with some encouragement from the French, British and US governments, wrote to Genscher pleading with him not to rush his fences on recognition. The German government brushed this intervention aside (and Genscher went so far as to complain to Douglas Hurd about my role in its genesis); and in December they won the backing of the whole EC for recognition which followed in early 1992. The negative consequences were to be felt soon enough, as Bosnia too slipped into open war and Macedonia teetered on the brink of it.

Cambodia: putting the pieces together again

Cambodia's torment had continued for 30 years. Dragged into the Vietnam War against its will by a combination of Vietnamese infiltration through its territory and US retaliation in an attempt to interdict it, the country emerged from that period in the hands of the genocidal Khmer Rouge led by Pol Pot. This regime had caused the deaths of up to one-third of the population and reduced the country to ruin. In its turn it was overthrown following a Vietnamese-backed military invasion which brought to power Hun Sen, a former Khmer Rouge commander. Over this period huge numbers of Cambodian refugees fled to neighbouring Thailand, where they were housed in camps along the Thai–Cambodian border. A civil war continued, with both the Khmer Rouge and the Hun Sen regime relying on outside support, mainly Chinese in the case of the Khmer Rouge, and Soviet and Vietnamese in the case of Hun Sen. The international community, led by the USA, refused to recognise Hun Sen as the government of Cambodia and continued to recognise the Khmer Rouge as such. Throughout this tragic and sorry sequence of events the UN had played only the most marginal of roles. Cold War politics ensured that any attempt to bring the Security Council into play would be met by a veto of one or another or several of the permanent members. There was a demeaning annual scrap over the seating of the Cambodian delegation to the General Assembly, the seat remaining in the hands of the Khmer Rouge. And the international community picked up the tab for the cost of the refugee camps, where the UN High Commission for Refugees did sterling work. It could be said that Cambodia was one of the main, and least intended, victims of the Cold War.

As the Cold War began to lose its force at the end of the 1980s efforts to remedy the situation in Cambodia got under way. The French government was active diplomatically, as were Japan, Australia and the countries of the Association of Southeast Asian Nations (ASEAN). The Western powers became increasingly embarrassed by their backing for the Khmer Rouge; and the Soviet Union was reducing its support for a whole range of Third World regimes. Crucially representatives of the P5 began to discuss the Cambodian issue and found that they could identify common ground and the need to make an entirely fresh start. A ministerial conference on Cambodia in Paris in 1989 provided a continuing framework for making more progress. So far the discussions had all taken place away from the UN, with senior officials of the P5 from capitals making the running. But, even at this preliminary stage, care was taken to include as an observer to the talks the UN Secretary-General's special representative Rafeeuddin Ahmed, who ensured a UN input into the shaping of a Cambodian settlement. A Security Council Resolution (668 of 20 September 1990) gave its blessing in very general terms to the framework for a comprehensive political settlement.

Now, in the second half of 1991, all that changed, as the international action shifted definitively to New York and what was to be to date the UN's largest ever peacekeeping mission began to emerge from the mists. A carefully choreographed sequence of events started with the installation in June of Prince Sihanouk as Chairman of the Supreme National Council of Cambodia, which contained representation of all the warring factions, and that body's decision to call a voluntary ceasefire, to renounce foreign military assistance and to invite the UN to send a survey team to Cambodia. Then in July a meeting of the Co-Chairmen of the Paris conference on Cambodia, together with representatives of the P5 and Indonesia, took place in Beijing and called for the withdrawal of foreign military forces, the ceasefire and the cessation of outside military assistance to be effectively verified and supervised by the UN. On 16 October Security Council Resolution 717 was adopted by unanimity; it established a UN Advance Mission in Cambodia, to be deployed as soon as the signing in Paris of agreements for a comprehensive settlement had taken place. Signature of the agreements duly took place on 21–23 October. And on 31 October Security Council Resolution 718 was adopted, again by unanimity, giving full support to the agreements signed and requesting that the Secretary-General should submit at the earliest possible date his implementation plan, together with costs, for the establishment of a UN Transitional Authority in Cambodia (UNTAC). Before the end of the year, appointments of a commander and deputy commander for the military components of UNTAC were made; and offers of military personnel from 22 member states – including from all five permanent members of the Security Council, itself a major innovation, Cold War practice having been to avoid P5 troop contributions – were made and accepted. It was clear that the next two years would see a major focus on efforts to bring the Cambodian peacekeeping mission to a successful conclusion.

Slipping towards peacekeeping overload (Western Sahara, El Salvador, Angola)

During the course of 1991, three more peace operations, in addition to those in the former Yugoslavia and in Cambodia, which have already been mentioned, began to take shape. Each in its way was positively influenced by the end of the Cold War; but each inevitably placed more burdens in terms of troop deployments, of finance, of civilian dimensions and of demands on mediating skills and time on an already hard-pressed UN machine. Each one of the three was very much a new-style peace operation; that is to say, something much more complex and multifaceted than the classic peacekeeping operations of earlier years, which had principally consisted of overseeing and monitoring an already existing ceasefire agreement between two previously warring parties, usually states. In the case of Western Sahara, that function of monitoring a ceasefire did exist, but in addition the operation included the sensitive task of registering voters for a referendum which would determine the fate of the territory and then of organising that referendum. In El Salvador the task involved not only the military aspects of bringing a civil war to an end, but also human rights monitoring, civilian police functions, land reform and the supervision of free and fair elections. In Angola there was a rather similar mix to that in El Salvador.

The international dispute over the formerly Spanish-administered territory of Western Sahara had lasted ever since Spain withdrew from the territory in 1975–6 at the end of the Franco era. The subsequent partition of the territory between Morocco and Mauritania (the latter of which later withdrew from its portion) was contested by many of the indigenous Sahrawi inhabitants, who enjoyed the backing and material support of Algeria, the other country contiguous to the territory; a low-intensity guerrilla war began; large refugee camps housing Sahrawi refugees grew up close to the Algerian border with the territory at Tindouf; and the Moroccans constructed a major sand barrier (the Berm) to protect the main inhabited and economically valuable parts of the territory. The dispute also had a Cold War tinge in that the Sahrawi and Algeria enjoyed the support of the Soviet Union, while Morocco was close to the West, in particular to France and the USA. But this Cold War dimension was by no means the only external factor. The then regional organisation, the Organisation of African Unity (OAU), leaned strongly towards the Sahrawi side of the argument, resulting eventually in Morocco's withdrawal from that organisation.

UN efforts through use of the Secretary-General's good offices gradually established the shape of a peace plan, with progress accelerating as the ending of the Cold War removed that element from the equation. But Algeria's and the OAU's support of the Sahrawi was not greatly affected by that development and there was therefore still not that solid regional support for the peace process which was to prove so crucial in the resolution of other conflicts. The most straightforward part of the process involved the deployment of a peacekeeping force to oversee a ceasefire, and that was in due course (from 1992 onwards) successfully accomplished. But the task of registering voters for a referendum to decide whether the territory should become independent, as the main Sahrawi political organisation, the Polisario Front, wanted, or part of Morocco, was built on shifting sands. From the outset both sides were clearly determined to use the registration process to bring about the only one of the two contradictory outcomes that they were prepared to accept, the Sahrawi by limiting the franchise as closely as possible to a pre-existing Spanish census and the Moroccans by extending it to include a wider range of the nomadic tribes of the region. There was some suspicion, also from the outset, that UN mediators had given incompatible indications to each side as to the way the registration process would be conducted, and thus as to its likely outcome. Be that as it may, the registration process was quickly bogged down. So the peace operation which was launched with Resolution 658 on 27 June 1990 and Resolutions 690 of 29 April and 725 of 31 December 1991 remained stuck in mid-stream, neither a complete failure nor a success.

El Salvador's civil war, which was at the heart of a series of inter-locking conflicts involving also Nicaragua, Honduras and Costa Rica and, from the outside, the USA, which supported successive Salvadorean governments, and the Soviet Union and Cuba, which sup-ported the communist-led insurgents in El Salvador, had continued throughout the 1980s despite a number of regional efforts to bring it to an end. The ending of the Cold War brought first the holding of free and fair elections in Nicaragua which resulted in defeat of the Sandinista government in that country and the withdrawal of Nicaraguan support for the Salvadorean rebels. This was followed by a willingness of all concerned, including the Bush administration in the USA, to encourage the UN Secretary-General and his skilful personal envoy to the region, Alvaro de Soto, to intensify their work to broker a peace settlement in El Salvador. Their efforts were backed by very close cooperation between a group of mainly neighbouring countries who were called 'the friends of the Secretary-General' and included Colombia, Mexico, Spain and Venezuela. The Security Council, some-what riskily in the eyes of some, authorised in Security Council Resolution 693 of 20 May the deployment of a team of human rights monitors in advance of an overall peace settlement. Then, in the very last days of Perez de Cuellar's mandate as Secretary-General, on 31 December 1991, that overall settlement was achieved and the deploy-ment of a full peacekeeping mission was approved in Security Council Resolution 729 of 14 January 1992. Although this peacekeeping opera-tion was not without a certain number of alarms and excursions in the following two years, it was a major success which brought an end to the conflicts in Central America, with the sole exception of some continu-ing purely internal problems in Guatemala.

The UN had first become involved in Angola in 1989–90 in connec-tion with the verification of the withdrawal of Cuban troops from that country which had been an essential part of the deal that enabled Namibia to be brought to independence and which was completed in May 1990. This deal had not addressed the continuing civil war in Angola between the government and the UNITA rebels led by Jonas Savimbi. But a post-Cold War grouping of countries consisting of the Soviet Union, the USA and Portugal negotiated in May 1991 a settle-ment with the Angola warring parties, known as the Bicesse Accords. In this case, in sharp contrast with the Cambodian negotiations in which senior UN political and military advisors had been fully involved in the negotiations at each stage, the UN was only brought in at the last moment and simply presented with a fait accompli; and this despite the fact that the whole task of implementing the agreement involving monitoring ceasefire agreements across a very large country, demobilising and disarming substantial numbers of armed men and incorporating them in a new national army, and overseeing the holding of elections, was simply dumped in the UN's lap. The Security Council authorised a new, second mission to Angola in Security Council Resolution 696 of 30 May, thus launching what was to turn out to be a seriously under-resourced operation with an inadequate mandate.

These three additional operations, like those in Yugoslavia and Cambodia, clearly demonstrated how difficult it is for the UN to resist overstretch or to decline to take on a mandate even when there might be doubts as to the viability of the basis on which it was being asked to operate. In each individual case the arguments in favour of UN involvement in peacekeeping were compelling: in every one, lives, often many lives, were being lost prior to the decision to deploy; in none were there alternative volunteers to take on the task. The UN is sometimes in a position to say 'Yes, but … ', and it should probably have been more willing to do so as the first rush of post-Cold War peacekeeping engulfed it, but it does not enjoy the luxury of saying 'No'.

Choosing a new Secretary-General

Every five years the UN community in New York gives itself over to the delights of electioneering, as the time comes round to choose a new Secretary-General or to reappoint the incumbent. 1991 was one of those years. The electorate is a rather special one, with one vote per member state in the General Assembly. But the real electorate is smaller than that – the 15 members of the Security Council – since the Charter provides that the General Assembly makes the appointment *on the recommendation of the Security Council*; and in the Security Council, of course, each of the five permanent members has a veto. Although in theory the General Assembly could reject a name recommended by the Security Council, it could not substitute one of its own; and this has never happened, not least because the Security Council has members from all the different geographical regions and thus in itself represents some kind of a balance.

The last real election (Perez de Cuellar having been reappointed unopposed in 1986) had taken place ten years earlier, in 1981, at the height of the Cold War. It had been a Grand Guignol occasion, with the Chinese vetoing Kurt Waldheim (standing for a third term) several times on the grounds that it was Africa's turn; the Americans vetoing Salim Salim, the African candidate, several times; and Perez de Cuellar emerging at the end of all this from the traditional smoke-filled room as a compromise candidate with whom everyone could live. In 1991, not surprisingly therefore, the Africans were determined to have their turn and this time they did not repeat the mistake of only fielding one candidate. The two leading African candidates were Boutros Boutros-Ghali, the deputy prime minister of Egypt, and Bernard Chidzero, the finance minister of Zimbabwe. In addition there were some other African names more or less in the frame; but Olusegun Obasanjo was handicapped by the fact that a military regime was in power in his home country of Nigeria and Olara Otunnu, a former Ugandan foreign minister, was even more handicapped by the fact that President Museveni would not put his name forward at any price. While some members of the Security Council, the USA in particular, remained averse to regional pre-emption, and thus to accepting that it had to be an African, it rapidly became clear that no non-African had the slightest chance of getting a majority of votes even if they were not going to be vetoed by the Chinese, who were as insistent as they had been in 1991 that it should be an African. One or two distinguished European names, Gro Harlem Brundtland, the Norwegian prime minister, and Hans van den Broek, the Dutch foreign minister, were briefly considered but got virtually no support on the grounds of regional preference.

So it soon came down to a two-horse race, with the African votes split along classic Anglophone (Chidzero) and Francophone (Boutros-Ghali) lines. Britain gave strong, and the USA rather lukewarm, support to Chidzero. The French ran a hyperactive and effective campaign for Boutros-Ghali. Of the two candidates, Boutros-Ghali was ubiquitous, Chidzero less so. Neither said a word publicly about how they would handle the job and neither had much direct UN experience; they concentrated on telling each interlocutor in private what they thought he or she wanted to hear. Meanwhile the Security Council went through an agonising process of what were called straw polls. At first there was a long list and it was permissible to support more than one name.

Votes were at this stage not differentiated between permanent and non-permanent members to avoid any premature consideration of potential vetoes. The object was to winnow out the field, which it did quite successfully, those with minimal support being dropped from succeeding rounds.

The whole process got off to a somewhat shaky start due to there being one properly completed voting list short in the first rounds of Council votes. It turned out that the Council president's directions (in English) to 'tick' names was not only incomprehensible to the ambassador of Zaire but also to the French interpreter, there being apparently no word for 'tick' in French. The main uncertainty related to a possible use of the veto by one of the permanent members. Once it was clear that it was going to be an African, there was no risk of a Chinese or Russian veto; we never contemplated one; the Americans sucked their teeth for a long time over Boutros-Ghali but concluded that, given the key role President Mubarak had played in the Gulf War and was playing in the US efforts to restart the Middle East peace process, there could be no question of a veto by them; only the French murmured from time to time that the inadequacy of Chidzero's knowledge of the French language might be a serious matter. But they were not put to the test, since their lobbying bore fruit; there was a decisive shift in the council towards Boutros-Ghali, and it was then rapidly agreed to recommend his name unanimously (Security Council Resolution 720 of 21 November). In truth the better candidate had won; and Boutros-Ghali's wide political and diplomatic experience had told over Chidzero's almost exclusively economic expertise.

In parallel with the election a large group of UN ambassadors and senior officials from the UN Secretariat had been meeting regularly to consider reforms to the secretariat which might be recommended to the incoming Secretary-General. The most important of these was the idea of appointing a Deputy Secretary-General, who would be able to take some of the management and administrative burden off the Secretary-General. It was already beginning to become clear, as the dust from the end of the Cold War settled and as the increased demands on the organisation built up, that not only was the job of Secretary-General becoming seriously overloaded, but also we were looking for a person who possessed two completely different sets of qualifications: one set those of a super-diplomat and political operator who could head off conflicts, help to resolve impasses and broker deals; and the other set those of an effective manager and administrator who could run a large bureaucracy and a burgeoning number of complex overseas peace operations. Of course we might find both sets of qualities in one person, but it would probably make more sense to look for two, with complementary skills.

That was the thrust of the main proposal which we deputed Peter Wilensky, the Australian ambassador, to put to the incoming Secretary-General on our behalf when he came to New York just before Christmas. Boutros-Ghali turned it down flat. He interpreted it, quite wrongly, as an attempt to constrain his own freedom of action. It was to take quite a few more years and the replacement of Boutros-Ghali by a Secretary-General in Kofi Annan who knew the problems inside out from his lifetime career with the UN, to secure the appointment of a Deputy Secretary-General; and even then there was not at first any really precise and well thought-through division of responsibilities between them.

The end of an empire

The UN world in New York is to some extent insulated from the realities of life and politics in each of its nearly 200 member states. Business goes on in its institutions irrespective of upheavals around the world. Decisions with far-reaching implications continue to be taken. Throughout the first half of 1991 everyone was conscious of the gradual weakening of the central institutions of the Soviet Union and the emergence of Russia, with its elected leader Boris Yeltsin, as an alternative power centre. But this did not impact directly on the UN, where the policy direction set from 1989 onwards by President Gorbachev and his foreign minister, Edvard Sheverdnadze, of broad cooperation with the main Western powers in handling international crises masked the extent of the waning authority and influence of the Soviet Union. Then came the August coup against Gorbachev. That also was too short-lived to have any direct impact at the UN. The Soviet Chargé d'Affaires (Vorontsov was on holiday near Moscow), a strong liberal, told me afterwards that, immediately after the coup, he received instructions to inform the UN Secretary-General of the new regime that had taken over. He had put his instructions at the bottom of his in-tray and done nothing. The immediate crisis was soon over.

But, from that point onwards, it was clear that some sort of breakup of the Soviet Union was under way. A major symbolic line was crossed on 12 September when the three Baltic states (Estonia, Latvia and Lithuania), whose existence had been wiped from the map in 1939 by Stalin when they were incorporated into the Soviet Union, were admitted as members of the UN with full Soviet acquiescence (in another milestone marking the end of the Cold War, the two Koreas had already been so admitted on 8 August). Other component parts of the Soviet Union were to follow in 1992, the only exceptions being the Ukraine and Belarus, which were already, bizarrely, full members of the UN as a result of a deal done at the time of the UN's establishment in 1945.

The demise of the Soviet Union had some potentially tricky legal and procedural implications at the UN given in particular its status as a permanent member of the Security Council. A number of countries, Japan and Germany in particular, were keen to open a debate on permanent membership and to advance the case for their being added to that select category. The existing permanent members, and in particular the Russians themselves, had no interest at all in allowing such an uncontrolled and open-ended debate to get under way. So some careful thought had been given in capitals and in New York to the modalities of proceeding at the UN by the time late in December when the formal decisions on winding up the Soviet Union and its succession by the Russian Federation were taken. A formal notification of this succession was duly made to the Secretary-General; and the next day Vorontsov appeared in the Security Council sitting behind a name-plate marked 'Russian Federation' (and thus placed slightly higher up the alphabetical order than he had been the day before!). A good deal of surprise and some irritation was expressed at the speed and smoothness of this transformation; but it was never faulted either procedurally or legally.

*   *   *   *

'1991 was a tumultuous year at the UN', thus my contemporary and not particularly original view. Clearly the high point was the reversal of Iraq's aggression against Kuwait, which was complete by the time of the ending of hostilities at the beginning of March. The implications for the UN of this event were far reaching. At the time I suggested 'the UN in its original and basic role of the guarantor of collective security against aggression has come firmly back into the centre of the stage'.

In light of the UN's subsequent travails this may seem a little overstated. But it was surely singularly important that, right at the beginning of the post-Cold War period, such a salutary example was set of the determination, will and capacity of the international community to resist acts of aggression. No other act of aggression in the twentieth century – and there had, after all, been plenty of them – was reversed so rapidly and at such low cost in human life as this one. And, although no clear causal links can be drawn, it is nevertheless the case that there have been few acts of aggression by one state against another, and none as clear-cut as this one, in the 17 years or more that have followed.

Another crucial moment was the passing of a resolution on the internal repression in Iraq of the Kurds and Shi'a which followed shortly after the end of the war. On this my contemporary judgement was more cautious:

> the Shi'a and Kurdish uprisings fell fair and square in that area
> of internal affairs which had hitherto been regarded as strictly
> off-limits for the UN. It was little short of the miraculous that
> we managed to get through SCR 688 which provided support
> for our subsequent attempts, more successful for the Kurds
> than for the Shi'a, to shield them from Saddam's vengeance.
> That we were able to do as much as we did with UN support
> and under UN cover was more a tribute to Saddam's pariah
> status than a harbinger of any fundamental shift in
> international opinion.

With the benefit of hindsight and in light of the unanimous endorsement by the 2005 UN Summit meeting of the international community's collective responsibility to protect those whom their own governments are unwilling or unable to protect, that judgement seems unduly pessimistic; but it does illustrate how far there still was to go.

In many ways, therefore, 1991 was a genuine vintage year for the UN. As it looked at the time:

> if anything the trend that had brought the UN back to the
> centre of the world stage is strengthening, as success brings
> wider support and increased, perhaps excessive, expectations.
> The cooperation between the Five Permanent Members of the

Security Council has come intact through a year of hectic
activity, its strength perhaps best demonstrated by its
members' determination not to let even the dissolution of the
Soviet Empire interfere with its further development.

This positive trend at the UN cannot be properly understood, however, without reference to two major areas of policy where developments far away from the UN itself had had an extremely beneficial
impact. In the months following the Gulf War, the US administration
showed clear signs of a determination to revive the Arab–Israel peace
process, which had been in a dormant, or, as many would have said,
moribund, state as a result of the Israeli government's negativism since
Yitzak Shamir had become prime minister. Those efforts culminated in
the Madrid international conference in November 1991, which, while
it was short on concrete results, contained some prospect of breaking
the deadlock. This opened the door to the reversal at the UN of the
hugely provocative 'Zionism is racism' General Assembly resolution
and also to a marked toning down of the annual crop of Palestine resolutions. The second area was South Africa where, following the release
from prison of Nelson Mandela in February 1990, a negotiating process
between the National Party government of President De Klerk and the
African National Congress was pointing the way ever more clearly to
the dismantling of the apartheid system. These developments were
beginning to drain some of the poison from issues which had quite
understandably disenchanted two major UN constituencies (the Arab
and African countries) over the preceding decades.

But evidently not all in the garden was lovely; and warning signals
were already evident. As I saw it at the time:

perhaps the biggest threat in 1992 is overload. There are
already plenty of signs of the UN machine creaking and
groaning under the demands put on it …. A lot will depend
on whether the new Secretary-General grasps the nettle of
Secretariat reform firmly or whether he recoils after he
receives the first, inevitable sting. If the leading members
states, ourselves included, want the UN to carry a bigger load,
then we will have to help it to do so. Partly that will mean
more money. Peace-keeping is expensive; but it is as well to
remember that failing to keep the peace is more so. It will also

I believe mean an imaginative approach to the role our armed forces can play in UN questions now that the taboo on involvement by the Permanent Five has been lifted.

More specifically the strains over handling the opening stages of the crisis following the collapse of Yugoslavia and the inadequacy of the resources allocated to the peacekeeping mission in Angola were sowing the seeds of future setbacks.

Chapter VI

1992: The crest of the wave

1992 turned out to be the peak of the UN's first post-Cold War period of successes, the moment when it was possible to hope, if not yet to be sure, that the organisation was set on a new path, destined to become an effective component of the system of collective security, as it had originally been designed to be in 1945. An unprecedented gathering of world leaders around the Security Council table at the end of January set the tone; and the new Secretary-General's subsequent paper 'An agenda for peace' showed the way. Nor were concrete successes lacking. Iraq no longer dominated the agenda so completely, as it had done the year before. Peacekeeping successes, or successes to come, were registered in Cambodia, El Salvador and Mozambique. In June the Earth Summit, as it was called, in Rio de Janeiro saw the signature of two conventions, on climate change and biodiversity, the first serious steps towards addressing problems which were to bulk much larger in the years ahead. Right at the end of the year a massive US-led humanitarian intervention took place in Somalia to bring food and medical supplies to a population, victims to anarchy and the depredations of warlords; and the operation was approved by a unanimous vote in the Security Council. But the dragons teeth sown in previous years were sprouting too. The UN became bogged down in Bosnia and was swept aside by a renewal of the civil war in Angola. States were failing and the UN was in many cases proving unable to prevent that happening and poorly equipped to deal with the consequences when they had failed.

The year came in with a new Secretary-General and with Britain in the chair of the Security Council. The five new, elected members coming onto the Security Council were Cape Verde, Hungary, Japan, Morocco and Venezuela. Of these Japan was to play a surprisingly muted role, determined to offer no hostages to fortune and to make no enemies in its search for a permanent seat; Morocco was at the extreme moderate end of the Arab spectrum; and Cape Verde became another of those invaluable elected members always on the look-out to broker compromises and to reconcile differences. The departure of Cuba at the end of 1991 removed one potential obstacle to the holding of a high-level Security Council meeting.

The outgoing Secretary-General, Javier Perez de Cuellar, worked up to the last moment of his period of office, being rewarded on the final day of 1991 by the key agreement between the Government of El Salvador and the rebel forces, which enabled a full-scale UN peace-keeping mission to be deployed and, in due course, one of the organi-sation's most successful peace operations to be completed.

The new Secretary-General, Boutros Boutros-Ghali, was duly sworn in at one of those ceremonies which did so much to emphasise the caste system at the UN. The ceremony took place in the grandeur of the General Assembly Hall, with every ambassador in his country's place in the sweeping auditorium; every one, that is, except for the ambassadors of the five permanent members of the Security Council, who were up on the platform, standing alongside the new Secretary-General. The symbolism could not have been clearer. In my view it could not also have been more unwise, but, like many other things at the UN, it was not something that could easily be changed.

Boutros-Ghali, who spoke perfect French and excellent English, was a man of charm and erudition. He had an encyclopaedic knowledge of international, and in particular of African, affairs garnered during his long years as deputy foreign minister to Presidents Sadat and Mubarak, when his membership of the Coptic minority in Egypt had alone pre-vented him from rising higher. He was forceful and decisive, perhaps sometimes too much so for his own good in the new and sensitive role he was assuming. He personally knew and had worked with many of the heads of government and foreign ministers who made up his world-wide constituency. He was also a man of courage, who had played an important role in fashioning and implementing Sadat's highly con-tentious policy of rapprochement and peace with Israel and in the Camp David peace talks, under the aegis of President Carter, which had led up to it. He did, it is true, have some of the weaknesses of his strengths. His management style could best be described as Pharaonic. (Shortly after taking office he was asked by a journalist how he planned to cope with the Byzantine nature of the UN bureaucracy and its resistance to change, and he replied: 'As I did with the Egyptian bureaucracy, with a mixture of stealth and brutality'.) He tended to underestimate the limitations on the authority he wielded. He could be impatient with the intricacies of UN diplomacy and with the need to get all the many institutional wheels to mesh together. He was a great believer in building up backchannels behind the backs of the UN ambassadors to their masters in capitals, a practice which won him more enemies than it gained him advantage and which, in the case of his third US ambassador, Madeleine Albright, was to prove fatal to his prospects for a second term of office. One thing was clear from the outset: life with Boutros-Ghali was going to be interesting and eventful.

A first Security Council summit

I had first floated with London the idea of a January 1992 Security Council Summit, with Britain in the chair, back in the summer of 1991, once the elections to the Council had produced an alphabetical outcome which made that a real possibility. I pointed out that the new Secretary-General would be arriving at a particularly important time for the UN, with the tide of changes brought about by the ending of the Cold War at full flood and with new tasks being piled onto its plate with little thought having as yet been given as to how these were to be handled, and where the resources in men and money were to come from to do so. It would surely be good to indicate to the world that the leaders of the 15 members of the Security Council intended to give the incoming Secretary-General their full backing. I suggested two prior conditions that would need to have been met before we could afford to launch the idea of a summit, which I believed was likely to be welcome to most members of the Council; first the British government itself would need to have decided that there would not be a general election in the autumn of 1991; and second the project would have to have the support of the president of the United States.

The reaction in London to the flying of this kite was muffled and unclear. Indeed this was an interesting idea, but it was too soon to take any decisions about it. Silence then ensued for many months, well beyond the moment at which it became clear that there was not going to be an autumn general election in Britain and well beyond the time it would ideally have been wise to start planning a summit and consulting other members of the Council about its form and content. I assumed the idea had withered on the bough; and shortly before Christmas I left with my family for a short skiing holiday in Vermont, designed to prepare for the rigours of January's chairing of the Security Council. There I was with some difficulty run to earth by the Foreign Secretary with the news that he and the Prime Minister would indeed like a Security Council summit to take place the next month. It was clear that what had tipped the balance in favour of a summit were the pre-Christmas events in Moscow, the disappearance of the Soviet Union and its replacement by the Russian Federation, and the accession to power of President Boris Yeltsin. The summit would provide an early opportunity to meet the new leader and to bolster his authority. Did I think it was now too late to organise a summit under our presidency? I said it certainly was very late to be doing so, but not, I thought, impossibly so. US support was essential if we were to succeed; and I would need to broach the prospect of a summit with each of my Security Council colleagues when I saw them one by one, as was the invariable practice, right at the beginning of January to discuss that month's Security Council business. From that point on the idea would be in the public domain. These conditions were accepted.

US support certainly could not be taken for granted. While the prospect of an early opportunity for a Bush/Yeltsin meeting was likely to prove attractive and there were no absolutely conversation-stopping members of the Council (Cuba having rotated off the Council at the end of 1991), the presence of a Chinese leader at the meeting was, in the context of the Tiananmen Square killings and the subsequent freeze in high-level contacts with leaders of the regime, highly problematic (and the Chinese in the event made it as problematic as they could by choosing to be represented by Li Peng, the prime minister and the leader most closely associated with the killings). But Bush, who was contacted by No. 10 during an official visit to Australia, accepted John Major's proposal; and his UN ambassador Tom Pickering was able to fend off all the subsequent efforts by John Bolton, the Assistant Secretary for International Organisations at the State Department, to torpedo the meeting.

I duly began the preparations for the summit at the beginning of January, having set the last possible date for holding it under British presidency, 31 January, to provide sufficient time. The new Secretary-General and the members of the Council responded very positively to the idea of holding the summit, so the first hurdle was crossed with ease. Thereafter things got a good deal trickier. Both the form and the content of any summit outcome bristled with difficulties if it was to be anything more than a glorified photo-opportunity. In theory we could have aimed for a Security Council resolution to be adopted by the leaders, thus leaving open the possibility of adoption by a majority vote if any member or members of the Council proved sticky on a particular point. But the idea of actually voting down a head of government at such a meeting had only to be considered to be discarded. So we went from the outset for a presidential statement which, since it required unanimity, was a risky strategy, opening the possibility of a text emptied of real content. In the event the preparation of the document went better than I had expected. Ideas flowed in both from members of the Council and from some outside it; of the latter the two most notable being a strong push by the German government, not best pleased to find itself excluded from the proposed summit, that renewed support be given to strengthening the international disciplines against the proliferation of weapons of mass destruction, and an approach by the Chilean permanent representative, Juan Somavia (later to become Director-General of the International Labour Organisation), on behalf of the developing countries, asking, somewhat surprisingly, that development issues should not be forgotten; a surprise given the usual eloquent complaints from non-members of the Security Council that the Council was prone to extending its outreach into areas which, under the Charter, were none of its business.

There was much pressure to address the issue of international terrorism. And all members of the Council were clear that something needed to be done to strengthen the authority and the capacity of the UN to handle the mass of peacekeeping tasks which were landing on its plate. The challenge was to find something that could be done in this respect in the short period of time available for preparing the summit which went beyond warm but necessarily empty words. Drawing on my Brussels experience, I suggested that we invite the new Secretary-General to table, by 1 July, his analysis and recommendations for strengthening and making more effective the capacity of the UN for preventive diplomacy, for peacemaking and for peacekeeping. This idea was backed by all. Less straightforward was the need to ensure some reference to human rights, where the Chinese were, not surprisingly, extremely sensitive.

In the end the outcome was encouragingly positive and substantive and included the following:

(i)   A commitment to 'the collective security system of the Charter to deal with threats to peace and to reverse acts of aggression. All disputes between states should be peacefully resolved in accordance with the provisions of the Charter'.

(ii)   An expression of deep concern over acts of international terrorism, with emphasis on 'the need for the international community to deal effectively with all such acts'.

(iii)   The agreed remit to the Secretary-General to submit his analysis and recommendations on preventive diplomacy, peacemaking and peacekeeping by 1 July.

(iv)   A forceful and unambiguous statement that 'the proliferation of all weapons of mass destruction constitutes a threat to international peace and security' – thus opening the way to the subsequent adoption of mandatory measures under Chapter VII of the Charter to deal with this issue; and a commitment to work for the conclusion by the end of 1992 of a universal convention, including a verification regime, to prohibit chemical weapons.

(v)   A clear recognition of the indivisibility of security and development. 'The members of the Council agree that the world now has its best chance of achieving international peace and security since the founding of the United Nations. They undertake to work in close cooperation with other United Nations Member States in their own efforts to achieve this, as well as to address urgently all the other problems, in particular those of economic and social development, requiring the collective response of the international community. They recognise that peace and prosperity are indivisible and that lasting peace and stability require effective international cooperation for the eradication of poverty and the promotion of a better life for all in a larger freedom'.

The negotiation of the document and the run-up to the meeting was not without its moments of anxiety. The Indian government, a non-signatory of the NPT with a developing nuclear weapons capability, had considerable difficulties with the section on non-proliferation, compounded by the fact that the Indian prime minister was, at the critical moment, in transit to New York (in fact in the VIP suite at London Airport). Having by then settled the text with all other delegations, I said I did not intend to call any further meeting of the Council ahead of the summit itself (a popular move, as ambassadors were beginning to flow out to Kennedy Airport to meet their leaders); if any member wanted such a meeting, they would have to ask for one; if not, the document as it now stood would be on the table for adoption at the summit. This worked; and no attempt was made to reopen the text.

A rather more esoteric, but classically diplomatic problem, of a sort more appropriate to the Congress of Vienna than to a one-day meeting in Manhattan, arose over the order of speakers at the summit. The problem began with a call from No 10. President Mitterrand had telephoned John Major to say that, unless he was the first speaker, he would not attend the summit but would send his prime minister; Major had conceded the point. Even a diplomatic lifetime spent far from the delights of the rules of protocol left me in no doubt that trouble was now in store. The normal UN practice of an alphabetical order had been junked. What was to go in its place? For days we juggled with different formulas but none of them worked, the Chinese in particular being super-sensitive to any order of speakers that appeared to downgrade Li Peng. Finally I called a meeting of all 15 ambassadors in my flat (to have called a meeting in the UN building would have revealed the existence of a serious problem, which would have been grist to the mill of the international press). At the meeting I was rescued by Pickering, who said that the White House had told him that President Bush was really not concerned at what point he spoke. With that miraculous development all the pieces fell into place.

The summit meeting itself was something of an anti-climax, as all these UN gatherings tend to be, given that the outcome is invariably and necessarily agreed in advance. The occasion was lent some style by the attendance of King Hassan of Morocco in national dress and accompanied by two tea-pourers carrying huge brass flagons of mint tea. The first appearance on the international stage of President Boris Yeltsin, both his physical appearance and his eloquent and direct speaking style, did not disappoint. And again, as usual, as much if not more attention was paid to the numerous bilateral meetings held by the participants as to the couple of hours they spent sitting round the Security Council's horseshoe-shaped table.

Looking back at the 1992 Security Council summit 15 years after the event, two salient points emerge. The first is that the Summit did in fact identify rather clearly the main threats and challenges that faced the international community in the post-Cold War world. It set out a relatively coherent intellectual framework within which the UN needed to move forward into an era which was clearly quite different from that which had preceded it. The identification of indirect, as well as direct, threats to peace and security in the form of economic and social deprivation and environmental degradation established effectively one single, broad agenda which needed to be addressed, not two quite separate agendas, one dealing with security issues and the other with development. The need for a collective response to the threat from international terrorism was noted long before Osama Bin Laden had put in an appearance on anyone's radar screen; the importance of the disciplines guarding against the proliferation of weapons of mass destruction, the need to strengthen those disciplines, and the direct threat to international peace and security if there was a break-out from them, was set out unambiguously, well before the nuclear ambitions of North Korea and Iran came over the horizon; the case for strengthening the UN's capability for conflict prevention, peacemaking and peacekeeping was recognised, as the demand for those commodities expanded exponentially. If there was one major element missing from the equation, it was the failure to recognise, and to prescribe remedies for, the phenomenon of state failure. By the time of the Summit, that phenomenon was already all too prevalent in many regions of the world – in Cambodia, in Afghanistan, in Somalia, in Haiti and, of course, in the former Yugoslavia. But there was a reluctance to address it as a generic problem, principally because to do so involved stepping firmly across the line of non-interference in the international affairs of a UN member state. And there was an ignorance at the time of the wider damaging consequences that could flow from state failure in the form of providing safe havens for terrorists, creating conditions for genocide and ethnic cleansing, and pulling whole regions of the world into instability and conflict.

The second salient point unfortunately undermined almost all the credit due to the first. This was that the follow-up and implementation of the Summit policy statement was inadequate and defective in the extreme. Boutros-Ghali and his officials duly tabled their report 'An agenda for peace' at the end of June 1992. It was a well-argued and well-presented analysis of what needed to be done to strengthen the UN in its role as international problem-solver and peacekeeper. Its main weakness was that, in the euphoria of the moment, it overstated the case for, and the capacity of, the UN itself to undertake peace enforcement operations. Events in Somalia and Bosnia were soon enough to demonstrate that the UN was ill-equipped and unsuited to directing such operations. But this did not invalidate the other prescriptions in 'Agenda for Peace'. Unfortunately the member states, both in the Security Council and in the General Assembly (which was responsible for the budgetary and administrative aspects of peacekeeping), were too distracted by the rush of events to give any systematic consideration to the main recommendations in the document and opted instead for an approach best described as muddling through. The follow-up to 'An agenda for peace' ran into the sands in both institutions and no serious operational conclusions were agreed. A major opportunity had been lost.

Libya: a collective response to terrorism

The destruction of two civilian airliners, as a result of terrorist action, one American (PA103), over Lockerbie in Scotland, and one French (UTA772), over Chad, had taken place some years before the events described in this book. Since then painstaking work by investigators and prosecutors had pieced together evidence which pointed towards Libyan involvement, and by the end of 1991 the British and American legal authorities were ready to launch indictments against two named Libyans, both members of the Libyan Intelligence Service. The French investigations were also well advanced by this stage and pointed in the same direction. In November 1991, Pickering and I were asked by our two governments what action could realistically be taken in the Security Council in the likely event of Colonel Qaddafi, the Libyan ruler, refusing to surrender the two men for trial in the USA or Scotland. The situation was completely unprecedented. The Security Council had never before been involved in countering terrorism other than in the most general and unspecific terms. Libya was by no means the only government suspected of involvement in sponsoring terrorist acts.

When Pickering and I sat down to discuss how to respond to our instructions, I found that, for once, he was less sanguine than I was about the prospects of success. But we soon sketched out a carefully calibrated, step-by-step approach which we recommended as the only possible approach to mobilising effective Security Council support – and that far from certain of success. The first phase would involve our two governments formally sharing the facts with the other members of the Council by tabling the indictments at the UN. The second phase would consist of a first Security Council resolution; this resolution would be short and general and would do no more than urge the Libyan authorities to respond positively to the indictments; it would not be mandatory, i.e. it would not be based on Chapter VII of the Charter; and it would not refer in any way to the possible consequences of a Libyan refusal to cooperate, let alone to sanctions. The third phase, and the really problematic one, would be to seek targeted sanctions against Libya in the event of a refusal to cooperate; this second resolution would necessarily be based on Chapter VII of the Charter. We also recommended that the US and French cases be pursued in a single process, thus ensuring the support of France, a permanent member of the Security Council, and also of a wider range of countries and a wider regional spread than would have been the case if we had dealt only with the US flight (both flights were international ones with two different mixes of nationalities amongst the victims, thus ensuring support from the governments concerned for the action we were planning to propose). These recommendations were accepted in their entirety. The indictments were circulated as Security Council documents in December 1991.

The first resolution proved deceptively easy to pass despite its unprecedented nature and despite all concerned being fully aware that the Libyans were unlikely to respond to it positively, and that therefore the question of non-compliance was likely to arise only too soon. Resolution 731 of 21 January 1992 was passed unanimously. It condemned the destruction of the flights; deplored the fact that Libya had so far not responded to the requests to hand over those indicted; and urged the Libyans 'to provide a full and effective response to those requests'. The unanimous passage of the resolution was undoubtedly helped by the fact that it took place a mere ten days before the heads of state and government of the Security Council member states were due to come to New York for the summit meeting earlier described. Clearly no one much fancied sitting across the table from the presidents of the USA and France and the prime minister of the UK if they had refused their support in such a high-profile and domestically sensitive instance.

The second resolution was quite another matter and provoked a battle royal, with the outcome unclear until the last moment. The Council was presided over by Venezuela, whose flamboyant and effective ambassador, Diego Arria, made a major contribution to the resolution's passage. (I had presided over the Council in January.) The text tabled by the French, British and US governments based itself firmly on Chapter VII of the Charter, having determined that Libya's response to the indictments failed 'to demonstrate by concrete actions its renunciation of terrorism thus constituting a threat to international peace and security'. It imposed a comprehensive arms embargo on Libya; and it imposed sanctions on all civil air flights in and out of Libya and on all trade in aircraft or aircraft components with Libya; it also required the closing of all Libyan Arab Airlines offices and the downgrading of Libyan diplomatic missions, including those to international organisations.

The scope of the resolution was made wider than the simple handing over of the indictees and decided that 'the Libyan government must commit itself definitively to cease all forms of terrorist action and all assistance to terrorist groups and that it must promptly, by concrete actions, demonstrate its renunciation of terrorism'; it thus brought within its ambit the support which Qaddafi had given to the Irish Republican Army over the years, and also activities such as those in Germany which had led to the US bombing of Tripoli in 1986 and Libyan interventions across a whole swathe of African countries. As with the sanctions against Iraq, the measures were to be regularly reviewed (every 120 days); but, as with Iraq, there could be no lifting of sanctions without a further Security Council resolution, that is to say without France, Britain and the USA agreeing to it. Unlike the Iraqi case, these sanctions were far from comprehensive, only affecting one sector of the economy. They thus represented a first attempt to design targeted sanctions of a kind that would have more impact on the ruling elite than on the mass of the population. They were also intended to impact on the sector which had been the object of the terrorist attacks. And they were effective, all civil air flights in and out of Libya ceasing immediately and remaining suspended for several years. Security Council Resolution 748 of 31 March 1992 passed with ten votes in favour (the minimum to pass a resolution being nine), and five abstentions (Cape Verde, China, India, Morocco and Zimbabwe). It had been a close-run thing. The day after the resolution was adopted, the Venezuelan embassy in Tripoli was attacked by an angry mob and destroyed by fire (with, fortunately, no casualties).

The Earth Summit in Rio de Janeiro: the peoples' flags were palest green

Ever since the Stockholm UN conference on the environment and development in 1972, attempts had been made to move the international community on from vague verbal expressions of concern about climate change and the man-made causes of it to actual commitments to do something about it. As the scientific evidence accumulated, the pressure grew. But, quite apart from the inherent difficulty of getting agreement from 150 or so countries, each with different interests and geographical situations, to any concrete measures which would inevitably have far-reaching effects on the future management of their economies, the path towards what had come to be called a 'programme for sustainable development' was far from easy. There were still those who contested the scientific evidence or who argued that any action was either too late already or too costly, or a combination of both; those views were well represented in the USA, although they had not yet reached the pitch of opposition which was later to emerge to any binding commitments to reduce carbon emissions. The OPEC countries resisted any attempt to reduce the use of fossil fuels as likely to undermine the oil price. Many developing countries still regarded climate change as something of a developed world fad, nothing much to do with them and only too likely to divert scarce resources away from development programmes and to inhibit their future economic growth.

Despite all these reservations, however, a complex and laborious preparatory process ground forward, pushed on in particular by Maurice Strong, a Canadian business-man who had been appointed to be Secretary-General of the proposed international conference. A summit conference was scheduled for June 1992 in Rio de Janeiro; and the process of getting heads of government signed up to attend, John Major prominent and early amongst them, got under way. Most importantly of all, by the time the conference met, two binding international conventions, one dealing with climate change and the other with biodiversity, had been fully negotiated and were ready to be opened for signature at the conference itself. This need to pre-cook UN conferences by getting agreement on the substance in advance was to prove both a strength and a weakness, at Rio itself and then again and again at the series of further summit and ministerial meetings which were called through the 1990s (dealing with human rights, population, women's issues and social questions), and leading up to the Millennium Summit in 2000 and the summit to review progress towards the Millennium Development Goals (MDGs) in 2005. It was a strength in that the imminence of a high-level meeting and the need to reach agreement on the detail in advance of it often put effective pressure on negotiators to compromise and to broker agreements. But it was a weakness in that the outcome of the conference tended to be discounted in advance and the press then had a field day criticising the emptiness of the conference proceedings themselves. Nevertheless, the experience of going into such conferences without prior agreement certainly demonstrated where the balance of advantage lay. At Rio, for example, on issues over which no conclusions were reached in advance, such as the preservation of forests or the checking of desertification, no real progress was made during the conference itself and little was achieved in its aftermath.

The attendance of the prime minister and the Secretary of State for the Environment (Michael Howard), some evidence of interdepartmental friction in London in the run-up to the conference, and the rather shaky state of European coordination under an eccentric Portuguese presidency representative all made up a case for me to attend the Rio conference. The chance to get away from non-stop Security Council business in New York and the opportunity to see one of my sons, who was working with street children in Sao Paolo, made it even more attractive. The interdepartmental tension in fact originated not in London but in Washington, where the text of the biodiversity convention, which had been agreed by the Americans, as by the rest of us, at official level, was coming under sustained political onslaught in Congress. It was being argued that the convention would cripple US industrial and commercial interests in the biotechnology field. Ironically enough, the climate change convention, whose subsequently negotiated Kyoto Protocol was to cause such a storm in Congress, was not targeted in the same way. The upshot was that President Bush decided to override the advice of his environmental adviser to sign both conventions and opted to sign the one on climate change but not that on biodiversity. My telephone exchanges with London indicated that Michael Howard was inclined to follow the same route. I argued against this, pointing out that the main criticism of the biodiversity convention was that it was too weak to achieve its purpose of preventing further losses of biodiversity, not that it was too strong and might seriously damage our or anyone else's commercial interests; if we did decide not to sign, we risked being alone with the Americans, which would do nothing for the government's green credentials. This dialogue, which began between New York and London, continued on the somewhat fragmented basis of telephone calls between Rio (where I was by then) and the prime minister's party on an official visit to Colombia on their way to Brazil. It was decided we would sign both conventions in Rio. Nothing that has happened since suggests that we were wrong to do so.

The conference may have been an anti-climax; but it was certainly not a rest-cure. Every day I had to leave the delights of the Copacabana Palace Hotel, where our delegation was staying, at 6.30 a.m. to drive more than an hour to the conference site well to the south of Rio (supposedly chosen by the Brazilian government to be as far away as possible from the mass of non-governmental organisation delegates who were thoughtfully provided with a venue on the opposite side of the city). Each day was filled with a succession of coordination and negotiating meetings. It was extremely hot; the air conditioning at the conference centre, which was more like the setting for an agricultural trade fair than a conference on the environment, was deafeningly noisy; and the social side of the conference all took place in the evening in Rio, several traffic jams, and a good deal more than an hour's drive away by that time. Looking back on it, it is astonishing that anything got done at all. But, however weak the texts of the conventions, the conference did mark a turning point. From then onwards international legal frameworks for addressing the challenges of climate change and biodiversity did exist; what remained was to give them some teeth.

Yugoslavia: into the Bosnian morass

The early weeks of 1992 were the calm before the storm in Yugoslavia. The Security Council was mainly taken up with the authorisation and deployment of a substantial peacekeeping force to those parts of Croatia where there had been heavy fighting the year before between the forces of the now internationally recognised government of Croatia and the Serb-dominated Yugoslav National Army (Eastern and Western Slavonia and the Krajina). Following a ceasefire agreement reached between the parties in November 1991 in Geneva, the Secretary-General's personal envoy, Cyrus Vance, was able to sign an Implementing Accord on 2 January 1992. This opened the way to authorisation and deployment. Security Council Resolution 727 of 8 January endorsed the sending of an advance party of military liaison officers to monitor maintenance of the ceasefire; and at the same time it (unanimously) confirmed the arms embargo and made it clear that it continued to apply to all parts of the former Yugoslavia, irrespective of any change in their international status. Security Council Resolutions 740 of 7 February, 743 of 21 February and 749 of 7 April formally established the peacekeeping operation and urged as rapid deployment as possible to avoid any deterioration of the situation on the ground.

This was the first, but by no means the last, moment when the British government needed to decide whether, and if so on what scale, to become militarily involved in Yugoslav peacekeeping operations. It did not prove easy to reach a decision. A general election was imminent; the ceasefire which formed the basis for the operation was fragile; and the chances of a deeper and wider UN involvement in the former Yugoslavia were already too obvious to be dismissed. The UN Secretariat's Department of Peacekeeping Operations, which was as usual struggling to put together the elements of a large and complex operation, became increasingly frustrated by our delays over making up our mind. Eventually we offered a medical unit only. It was hardly a major contribution; and compared poorly with a number of other, often smaller European countries. We were not the only ones with hesitations; the new UN Secretary-General was extremely reluctant to see the organisation being drawn into a major and possibly open-ended commitment in Europe just when heavy demands were also coming forward from operations in Asia (Cambodia) and Africa (Angola and Western Sahara). But at this stage he kept his doubts largely to himself and accepted that his predecessor had effectively committed the UN to following through on Vance's peace-broking activities. He was in any case under heavy pressure from the European countries to do that.

But even during this period of relative calm, concern was steadily mounting at the prospect of new hostilities breaking out in Bosnia and Herzegovina. This Yugoslav republic, whose largest ethnic group was Muslim but which had substantial Serb and Croat minorities, was now, following the European Union's (EU; formerly the EC) decision to recognise the independence of states which decided to break away from Yugoslavia, moving steadily towards secession. The chances of the Bosnian Serbs accepting secession peacefully were not good; and rumours were already circulating that the Croatian (Franjo Tudjman) and Serb (Slobodan Milosevic) leaders had agreed to carve up the new state, leaving the Bosnian Muslims only a small rump of territory. The intermingling of the three ethnic groups meant that any outbreak of fighting between them was likely to lead to heavy casualties and much suffering for the civilian population. A March referendum in Bosnia on independence was boycotted by the Bosnian Serbs; it led to an overwhelming vote in favour; and shortly afterwards fighting began, in particular in the centre of the country around the capital, Sarajevo, which was soon in a state of semi-siege, with the Bosnian Serbs (effectively units of the Yugoslav National Army) bombarding the city with heavy artillery from the hills around it, and in the south around the city of Mostar, where Bosnian Muslims and Croats fought a particularly vicious battle for control.

At first the main effort to stop the fighting in Bosnia was borne by the Europeans; but their chief negotiator Lord Carrington had seen his hand greatly weakened by the EU's decision to remove the best incentive he had, to trade recognition of the new republics against a peaceful transition and fair treatment of minorities; and they only disposed of an unarmed civilian monitoring mission whose members could do little in the circumstances soon prevailing throughout Bosnia. The Security Council issued a presidential Statement on 10 April calling for a stop to the fighting and asking Boutros-Ghali to send Vance to the region to reinforce Carrington's efforts. Then on 24 April the Council issued a tougher statement demanding that all interference from outside Bosnia cease immediately; it also approved the sending of 100 military observers from the UN force by then deploying in Croatia to monitor the successive ceasefires in Bosnia, which were no sooner brokered than they were broken. On 29 April it welcomed Boutros-Ghali's decision to send his Under-Secretary-General for Peacekeeping Operations to look into the feasibility of a UN peacekeeping operation in Bosnia; but Marrack Goulding's report was that the conditions for such an operation did not currently exist and the Council, in Resolution 752 of 15 May, reluctantly accepted this, while asking the Secretary-General to review the feasibility of finding some way of protecting international humanitarian relief programmes. The resolution considerably sharpened its tone towards outside interference both by the Yugoslav National Army and by elements of the Croatian army, calling for their immediate withdrawal; there was also a first reference to the need to cease 'forcible expulsions of persons from the areas where they live and any attempts to change the ethnic composition of the population', subsequently to be known as 'ethnic cleansing'.

At this point a somewhat surreal series of ceremonies took place in New York as first Croatia and Slovenia (on 18 May) and then Bosnia and Herzegovina (on 19 May) were recommended by the Security Council and accepted by the General Assembly as new members of the UN. The grant of UN membership did nothing to halt the fighting on the ground, indeed it may well have intensified it; but it did completely change the rules of the game in New York and internationally. From now on any involvement by either Serbia or Croatia in military operations in Bosnia became an act of aggression and a breach of the UN Charter. Throughout the Bosnian crisis much ink was spilled by journalists and academic commentators as to whether it, and other conflicts in the former Yugoslavia, were in essence civil wars and not international conflicts. The point was not entirely theoretical since the argument ran that, if the conflicts were civil wars, then the international community should have nothing to do with them, limiting itself to humanitarian relief. In reality these conflicts were a complex mixture of civil war and international aggression. But, be that as it may, from May 1992 onwards they fell legally unmistakably on the latter side of the fence.

And, while the ruler of Serbia, Slobodan Milosevic, in particular, chose to ignore the change and to continue to support the Bosnian Serbs in their onslaught on the new republic, the consequences were not long in coming. On 30 May the Security Council, acting under the mandatory provisions of Chapter VII of the UN Charter, adopted Resolution 757 which condemned the Federal Republic of Yugoslavia (FRY) for its failure to desist from meddling in Bosnia, demanded also the withdrawal from the country of elements of the Croatian army, and imposed a comprehensive set of economic sanctions on the FRY, covering all trade except medical supplies and food, and also all financial transactions and civil aviation links, as well as calling for the reduction of diplomatic links. This package was based more on the Iraqi model than on the Libyan one. Although policing it proved a nightmare, with Yugoslavia's neighbours in some cases unable and in others unwilling to enforce the sanctions strictly, it did over time have a drastic effect on the Yugoslav economy, leading to massive shortages, economic collapse and rampant inflation. But, as in the case of Iraq, while it weakened the aggressor it did not bring about an early change of policy; and, as in Iraq, the burden of sanctions fell mainly on ordinary citizens and not on the authoritarian regime which was solely responsible for the political decisions against which the action was taken.

Four months later the isolation of the FRY was complete when its membership of the UN's General Assembly was suspended on the recommendation of the Security Council (Resolution 777 of 19 September), a step only once previously taken at the UN in the case of South Africa. The sanctions resolution and the resolution on the suspension of the FRY from the General Assembly occasioned the first break in Security Council unanimity over Yugoslavia, China and Zimbabwe abstaining on the sanctions resolution and China, India and Zimbabwe on the suspension. But on neither occasion was the action seriously contested, China in particular merely wishing to wash its hands of any such intrusive action but not to prevent it; and the unity of Russia (traditionally, and still to some extent, Serb-leaning), the European members of the Council and the USA (still semi-detached and refusing any involvement on the ground) was maintained.

Meanwhile Sarajevo remained effectively under siege, pounded by Bosnian Serb artillery from the surrounding hills, while the EU's peace facilitator, Lord Carrington, tried to bring about a ceasefire. Some very limited progress was made towards establishing an airlift into Sarajevo, with the UN being charged with its operation and the management of the airport (Resolutions 761 of 29 June and 764 of 13 July). Then, very early on 17 July, I was telephoned from London by Lord Carrington (Britain was at that time – from 1 July – the country holding the EU Presidency) saying that he had finally managed to get the acceptance of all parties to a ceasefire around Sarajevo. The most urgent task was to follow this up by deploying UN observers to monitor the implementation of the ceasefire, in particular by the Bosnian Serb artillery.

Carrington said he had already spoken to Boutros-Ghali, who had agreed to support such a move. Could I get some rapid action out of the Security Council? I said I would do my best; and, having spent most of the morning in consultation with the Under-Secretary-General for Peacekeeping Operations (Marrack Goulding) and the Security Council delegations principally concerned, it proved possible to get a unanimously backed presidential statement from the Security Council that afternoon supporting the ceasefire and deciding in principle that the UN should make arrangements for the supervision of all heavy weapons around Sarajevo. The Secretary-General was asked to report back to the Council on the modalities of this new deployment within one week. This was indeed lightning speed by UN standards. It soon, however, became clear that all was not well within the Secretariat. Boutros-Ghali, who had been entirely taken up throughout 17 July by the ongoing negotiations in New York between the leaders of the Greek Cypriot and Turkish Cypriot communities for a settlement of the Cyprus problem, which he was chairing, denied that he had ever committed himself to Carrington over any deployment of UN personnel and expressed extreme reluctance to see the UN drawn further into the Bosnian quagmire.

When the Security Council duly met on 24 July to hear the Secretary-General's report back, it was to be treated to a lengthy and intemperate tirade from Boutros-Ghali berating us for the precipitate way we had acted. This in particular put me, as the principal architect of the 17 July presidential statement, on the spot. Since, however, by then the ceasefire around Sarajevo had broken down comprehensively and the Bosnian Serb artillery were once again firing into the city, it clearly made sense to cut our losses over this diplomatic tiff. I suggested to the Council that 'Least said, soonest mended' should be our motto; and a statement was adopted papering over the cracks and concurring with the Secretary-General's view that the circumstances did not yet exist for the UN to supervise the heavy weapons around Sarajevo.

One conclusion to be drawn from this unhappy episode was that the existing, somewhat pantomime-horse, arrangements for dividing responsibilities between the EU (responsible for overall peacemaking in the former Yugoslavia, but with no military capabilities) and the UN (responsible for a peacekeeping operation in Croatia, the airlift into Sarajevo and steadily increasing humanitarian relief operations in Bosnia, but with no general peacemaking functions) could no longer be sustained. And this became very evident during a subsequent, rather tense round of discussions in New York between Carrington, Boutros-Ghali and Vance. Moreover the situation on the ground in Bosnia continued to deteriorate, with predictions of massive loss of life and suffering among the civilian population when the winter came. Against this background the British prime minister, in his capacity as EU president, and the UN Secretary-General decided jointly to call an international conference in London at the end of August 1992.

Even before that conference took place a number of European countries, with Britain and France in the lead, offered to deploy troops to Bosnia for the purpose of providing some protection for the UN's unarmed, civilian humanitarian workers who were doing their best to ensure that supplies of food and medicine got through to various communities beleaguered in the ethnic mayhem which by now had submerged virtually the whole of the country. This deployment, which was given cover by Security Council Resolution 770 of 13 August, was not at first a fully-fledged UN operation, the costs being met by the troop contributors; but a few months later this rather awkward half-way house arrangement was sorted out and the humanitarian protection mission became a full and normal part of the UN forces in the Former Yugoslavia (UNPROFOR). The deployment of a UN force into a war zone, albeit with a mandate limited to humanitarian protection, was an unprecedented one and it proved to be far from a complete success. On the plus side many thousands of Bosnians' lives were undoubtedly saved by the strengthened UN humanitarian operations, particularly in the first winter of 1992–3. But the troops, like the civilian humanitarian workers, could only, in the last resort, operate with the consent of the warring parties and those parties exacted their price in terms of supplies for themselves and various political manipulations. Those parties also drew their own conclusions about the firmness of purpose of the international community, or lack of it, to put an end to the fighting. Not for the first nor the last time in Bosnia the understandable determination of the outside powers not to be drawn into the hostilities as direct participants was taken by the Yugoslav parties as a licence to continue much as before.

At about this time too, the first substantiated reports began to surface in the press of prison camps in the Bosnian Serb-controlled areas, where Bosnian Muslims in particular were being subjected to torture, rape and malnutrition. Appalling photographs emerged and a trickle of outrage became a flood. These images strongly influenced opinion in Western Europe and most of all in the USA, where echoes of the Second World War holocaust were quick to be picked up and where criticism of the Bush administration's arms-length policy towards the former Yugoslavia became a steadily more prominent feature of the president's already faltering re-election campaign. In a first move by the Security Council, Resolution 771 of 13 August reminded all parties of their international obligations with respect to the treatment of prisoners under the 1949 Geneva Convention, called on them to desist from all breaches of international humanitarian law, including those involved in ethnic cleansing, and called on states, international organisations and the Secretary-General to collate any substantiated information and for the latter to submit a report including recommendations for additional measures to be taken. This led on to the establishment by Security Council Resolution 780 of 6 October of a Commission of Experts to examine and analyse the information which had been submitted. And that, in due course, was to lead the next year to the setting up of a War Crimes Tribunal for the former Yugoslavia, the first such instance since the tribunals at the end of the Second World War had been established by the victors in that war and the first ever, though not the last, occasion that the UN Security Council, acting under Chapter VII of the Charter, had taken such a step.

It was against this sombre background that the London conference met and achieved some modest, if unfortunately all too transient, progress. All the parties in the former Yugoslavia agreed to work for an overall peace settlement in an international conference on the former Yugoslavia which was to begin its work in Geneva immediately. At least the discordance between the EU and the UN activities was resolved, with David Owen, Lord Carrington's successor as the EU special representative, and Cyrus Vance, Boutros-Ghali's representative, acting as a single team and as joint co-chairmen of the Steering Committee of the Conference. They did indeed work well together and their efforts were to bear fruit the following year. All this diplomatic activity was welcomed and endorsed by the Security Council. But the Council was soon enough brought back to the reality of continued fighting in Bosnia and in Security Council Resolution 781 of 9 October established a No-Fly Zone in the airspace of Bosnia, which, since the Bosnians had no air force, was entirely directed at the Bosnian Serbs and their allies in Belgrade. This measure remained, however, for some time more or less a dead letter since no provisions were made to enforce the resolution and, unlike in Iraq, no one was prepared to take on that task.

As if the problems arising from the break-up of Yugoslavia were not already complex enough, another, quite separate issue now arose at the south-eastern extremity of the country, in Macedonia. This constituent republic of the former Yugoslavia had, like Slovenia, Croatia and Bosnia and Herzegovina, and unlike Montenegro at that stage, opted for secession and independence. It too had ethnic tensions between its predominantly Slav population and a substantial Albanian minority; it felt threatened by its much larger neighbour to the north, Serbia, whose pretensions to create a Greater Serbia affected Macedonia, which had virtually no armed forces of its own; and it had immediately fallen into a dispute with its southern neighbour, Greece, as a result of long-standing claims by irredentist elements in Macedonia to parts of northern Greece which the Greeks believed were reflected in the choice of the name and the flag of the newly independent state. This latter complication, compounded by a unilateral Greek decision to impose a trade embargo on Macedonia's main trade routes to the outside world (those through the FRY being cut off as a result of the sanctions against that country), resulted in yet another split in European unity, since all the members of the EU except Greece considered it an absolute priority to shore up Macedonia's fragile independence and to do everything possible to avoid the risk of Macedonia descending into the sort of chaos prevailing in Bosnia.

One result of the Greek–Macedonian dispute was that it had not been possible to agree on Macedonia's admission to the UN in May 1992, when the other three seceding countries had been accepted. In the autumn of 1992 President Gligorov of Macedonia approached the UN Secretary-General and asked for the preventive deployment of a small force of UN peacekeepers to his country to help stabilise the situation and in particular to monitor the border with Serbia. Boutros-Ghali consulted me privately, as he did no doubt other members of the Security Council, as to how he should respond. I said I would recommend to London that he should give a positive response and this was subsequently agreed. Other member states on the Council evidently did likewise, and Security Council Resolution 795 of 11 December unanimously authorised the preventive deployment which Boutros-Ghali had recommended. Quite apart from the intrinsic merits of this decision, which proved in the event to be the one unmitigated success of the UN's otherwise troubled involvement in the former Yugoslavia, this was another important step in the evolution of UN peacekeeping. In his document 'An agenda for peace', distributed in the summer of 1992, Boutros-Ghali had drawn attention to the potential advantages of preventive deployments as a means of conflict prevention. By definition they were a way round the problem of getting the consent of both parties to a territorial dispute because the deployment only took place on the territory of one of the parties. Unfortunately Macedonia remains to this day the sole example of this imaginative use of the UN's capabilities.

Cambodia: steady uphill work

The early months of 1992 saw decisions by the Security Council to set up UNTAC and to deploy its military elements. Security Council Resolution 728 of 8 January authorised the Secretary-General to provide assistance to the Cambodian authorities for mine clearance, an essential operation if the large numbers of refugees still in camps on the Thai–Cambodian border were to be able to return in any kind of safety. On 15 January the appointment of the Japanese Under-Secretary-General for Disarmament, Yasushi Akashi, as Special Representative for Cambodia was endorsed. Despite the last-minute nature of the appointment (the senior Secretariat official who had participated in the negotiation of the peace plan, Rafeeudin Ahmed, having refused the post) and notwithstanding his subsequent less than stellar performance as Special Representative for the former Yugoslavia, Akashi did a very workmanlike job in Cambodia, for which he deserved more credit than he was given. Then an initial appropriation of $200 million was endorsed on 24 January to enable UNTAC to get up and running. On 28 February, Security Council Resolution 745 formally established UNTAC, urged the rapid deployment of its military component, set the date of May 1993 as the latest for holding free and fair elections for a new Cambodian government and urged the Cambodia parties to agree to the full demobilisation of their armed forces.

So far, so good. But it was not to last. It soon became clear that the Khmer Rouge were reneging comprehensively on their obligations under the peace agreements. They refused to accept that UNTAC's writ ran in the parts of Cambodia they controlled, they prevented any of

UNTAC's military personnel from entering those areas, they refused to demobilise any of their armed forces and they continued to finance their operations by smuggling valuable tropical hardwood and gems out through Thailand. Throughout 1992 the P5 in New York had to contend with this situation and it did not prove easy. Li Dao Yu, the normally easy-going Chinese ambassador, was kept on a very tight rein by Beijing. China might have been ready to take a largely passive back seat when it came to dealing with Iraq or the former Yugoslavia, but Cambodia was a country within its own sphere of influence and the Khmer Rouge had been its protégés whom they had financed and armed. The Americans, regretting their earlier support for the Khmer Rouge, were all for denouncing them on each and every occasion and favoured the imposition of sanctions. The French tended to say that anything Prince Sihanouk wanted must be done, but, given the prince's often erratic and impulsive temperament, his twists and turns, and his close links to Beijing, this was not a straightforward prescription for policy. The Russians remained as committed to supporting Hun Sen as ever and thus normally joined the Americans in criticising the Khmer Rouge. Only the British, with virtually no interests in Cambodia, had no particular axe to grind; so I often found myself helping to broker acceptable compromise texts for the successive resolutions which the Security Council adopted in an attempt to strengthen Akashi's hand. A lot of time was spent deciding whether, and if so how explicitly and in what terms and with what consequences, to denounce the Khmer Rouge.

But it gradually became evident that the key issue was not the strength of the Security Council's verbal criticisms of the Khmer Rouge, nor even the imposition of sanctions on them, which all knew would prove virtually unenforceable, but whether or not to stick to the May 1993 timetable for elections and be prepared to hold them only in the parts of the country (the major part of it, fortunately) which were not controlled by the Khmer Rouge; and whether to accept the inevitable consequence of the Khmer Rouge's refusal to demobilise their troops by insisting on only partial demobilisation by Hun Sen and by the militarily much less significant royalists. Over time it became clear that the Chinese were determined to see the peace plan through to its implementation and were not prepared to allow the Khmer Rouge to torpedo it. So the job of brokering compromises among the P5 became steadily easier.

The process began with Security Council Resolution 766 of 21 July, which 'strongly deplored the continuing refusal by one of the parties to permit the necessary deployment of all components of [UNTAC] to the areas under its control'. Then Security Council Resolution 783 of 13 October:

> Deplores the fact that the Party of Democratic Kampuchea [the Khmer Rouge], ignoring the requests and demands contained in Resolution 766, has not yet complied with its obligations. Demands that the party [the Khmer Rouge] fulfil immediately its obligations under the Paris agreements .... And that it implement fully containment and demobilisation.

This same resolution confirmed the election date of May 1993. And then finally in Security Council Resolution 792 of 30 November: 'Condemns the failure by the Party of Democratic Kampuchea to comply with its obligations'. Of far greater practical and political significance the same resolution determined that UNTAC should proceed with preparations for free and fair elections to be held in April/May 1993 'in all areas of Cambodia to which it has full and free access as at 31 January 1993'. The resolution also imposed sanctions on the supply of petroleum products to any area of Cambodia controlled by a party not complying with the military provisions of the peace agreement; and it supported a moratorium on the export of logs from Cambodia. The die was now cast; and the Chinese had made it clear that the Khmer Rouge could no longer look to them for support. Every one of these resolutions was adopted by unanimity in the Security Council. It was the high-water mark of P5 collaboration.

South Africa: a hiccup in the dismantling of apartheid

As has been noted earlier the decision by the South African government to release Nelson Mandela and other African National Congress (ANC) prisoners, and the subsequent engagement of a negotiating process for the constitution and political arrangements of a post-apartheid South Africa, had had a remarkable lightening effect on the atmosphere at the UN. But the Security Council, which had long before imposed a mandatory arms embargo on South Africa and which had lengthily and fruitlessly over the years debated the imposition of wider economic sanctions, was not involved in the process at all. All concerned, including the ANC leaders themselves, had decided that it was better to keep these complex and sensitive negotiations away from the UN and to seek to resolve them through a domestic political dialogue within South Africa. This self-denying ordinance held until a rising tide of violence in South Africa, with growing tensions between the Zulus and their charismatic leader Chief Mangosuthu Buthelezi and the ANC and its supporters, culminated in a massacre in the Boipatong township on 17 June 1992. At this point the ANC and the many African governments which supported it decided to bring the matter before the Security Council. This understandable reaction contained some real risks, particularly as it became clear that the ANC and its supporters had no clear strategy as to what they wanted the UN to do, and that there were indeed tensions between those who wanted a large and continuing role for the UN (a number of African governments including Zimbabwe, which was a member of the Security Council and thus in a leading position amongst them) and those who merely wanted to use the Security Council to remind the South African government of the extreme isolation and precariousness of its international position, thus strengthening the faltering negotiating process within South Africa (the view of the ANC and its able and moderate representative at the New York proceedings, Thabo Mbeki, subsequently to succeed Mandela as president of post-apartheid South Africa).

My instructions from London were to favour a modest UN input to a resumed South African domestic negotiating process but to resist excessive denunciation of, or a move for increased sanctions against, the South African government. Those were, in the circumstances, sensible enough instructions; but they were not easy to carry out. For one thing the British government's track record on this subject, resisting sanctions even in the darkest hours of apartheid, was deeply suspect to all African governments. The US government, normally to be relied upon to take a similar line, on this occasion adopted a profile so low as to be virtually invisible, being preoccupied with the potential read-across to a hotly contested presidential re-election campaign. Other potential allies such as the French were not going to put at risk their relationship with the francophone African countries who were as usual vocal critics of South Africa and anxious to burnish their credentials. Fortunately the Secretary-General was himself determined not to allow the UN to

assume too prominent a role and to avoid any step which would interfere with the early resumption of the negotiations between the ANC
and the South African government. So, although the negotiation of
Security Council Resolution 765 of 16 July was distinctly tricky and we
were often virtually isolated, the outcome was pretty well as we (and, as
it turned out, both the ANC and the South African government)
wanted. The massacre at Boipatong and the other acts of violence were
roundly condemned without, however, blaming the South African government exclusively. The Secretary-General was invited to appoint a
special representative for South Africa but with a notably vague mandate pointing towards assistance to get the South African negotiating
process going again. Boutros-Ghali appointed Cyrus Vance, who was
already much involved in the former Yugoslavia. On the basis of his
subsequent report it was decided in Security Council Resolution 772 of
17 August to deploy some civilian observers to assist in the implementation of the National Peace Accord, which had by then been reached
between the different parties in South Africa. The debate in the Security
Council in July was notable for bravura performances by Chief
Buthelezi and by the South African foreign minister Pik Botha, himself
an old New York hand as South African ambassador; but the whole
weight of the debate demonstrated overwhelming pressure on the
South African government to bring its negotiations with the ANC to a
successful conclusion and to dismantle the whole apartheid regime.
The issue of South Africa did not return in any serious way to the
Security Council until 1994, after Mandela's election as the first president of a multi-racial, democratic South Africa, when the Council had
the welcome task of lifting all remaining sanctions against the country
(Security Council Resolution 919 of 25 May 1994).

Cyprus: an island divided still

The issue of Cyprus was, along with Kashmir and the Arab–Israel dispute, one of the longest-standing items on the Security Council's
agenda. But, unlike those other two, the UN had always stood at the
centre of international efforts to resolve the problem. Successive
Secretaries-General and successive UN special representatives had broken their teeth on the adamantine stubbornness of the parties in
Cyprus and on the unwillingness or inability of their two motherlands,

Greece and Turkey, to put effective pressure on them to reach compromises on the main issues at stake: territory, security, governance and property. The UN's efforts had been redoubled following the events of 1974 when a Greek-encouraged Greek Cypriot coup détat had precipitated two successive Turkish military operations which left the Turkish Cypriots (approximately 18 per cent of the population) in control of 37 per cent of the island and which also resulted in large-scale transfers of population – Greek Cypriots from the north of the island being ejected to the south, Turkish Cypriots from the south being sent north, movements which we would now call ethnic cleansing although the phrase was not in use at that time. In all that time only two very meagre documents had been agreed (in 1977 and 1979), setting the objective of the settlement negotiations as a bi-zonal, bi-communal federation (the original Cyprus independence constitution having been for a unitary state with elaborate safeguards for the Turkish Cypriot minority) but putting no flesh on those bare bones.

Most years the Security Council only thought about Cyprus twice, and then briefly, when the six-monthly renewal of the small UN force which patrolled the Green Line ceasefire zone between the two sides came up for decision. For a few days there would be a flurry of activity as representatives of the two Cypriot communities and of Greece and Turkey lobbied frantically for the inclusion or exclusion of this or that hallowed phrase in the renewal resolution; and the Council noted grumpily that no progress was being made towards a settlement. But 1992 was different. The new Secretary-General, perhaps encouraged by his predecessor who had earlier served as Special Representative for Cyprus and who had put much painstaking effort into assembling the pieces of a settlement jigsaw, decided to get the two leaders, George Vassiliou, the president of Cyprus and leader of the Greek Cypriot Community, and Rauf Denktash, the president of the unrecognised Turkish Republic of North Cyprus and leader of the Turkish Cypriot community, to New York and see whether, under his aegis, an agreement could be found. The Security Council strongly encouraged this initiative and set out the broad lines on which it was to be conducted in Security Council Resolution 750 of 10 April. Britain, which, as the former colonial power and having two Sovereign Base Areas on the island, had always played a prominent supporting role in the search for a negotiated solution, continued to do so. The British High Commissioner in Nicosia, David Dain, came to New York and was in daily touch with the different key delegations and with the Secretariat who were conducting the negotiations. And from time to time I got drawn in too.

Negotiating sessions were held from 18–23 June and then again from 15 July onwards. Boutros-Ghali threw himself into the negotiations with determination and commitment, which was indeed the reason why he was unsighted when a quick decision was needed on 17 July over the possible deployment of heavy weapons monitors to Sarajevo (referred to earlier in this chapter). Gradually he narrowed some of the gaps but he was unable to get full agreement, and time was beginning to run short as Vassiliou faced a re-election campaign in the winter and had made it clear that he would not be able to continue negotiating beyond the next session, scheduled for October. Boutros-Ghali consulted me at this stage as to whether he should go formally public with the 50-page negotiating document known as the 'Set of Ideas', which he had given to the parties, by sending it to the Security Council. I said I thought he should; and I also encouraged him to send forward with it the crucial redrawn map of the island, which he had also given to the parties, and which would have resulted in a substantial adjustment to the benefit of the Greek Cypriots (leaving the island split very roughly 72 per cent Greek Cypriot, 28 per cent Turkish Cypriot). I recognised that there were some risks in this approach but the advantages seemed to outweigh them. It should be possible to get a firm endorsement of the Security Council for the Secretary-General's approach and that would surely help him in the next, and possibly final, round in October. And, if the negotiations remained stuck then, at least the ground so far gained would remain as a benchmark for future efforts. Boutros-Ghali took this advice and sent forward to the Security Council both the Set of Ideas and the map; and the Security Council obliged by endorsing both unanimously in Security Council Resolution 774 of 26 August as the basis for reaching an overall framework agreement.

Unfortunately, even with this support, the October session ended without agreement other than to resume negotiations in March 1993. By then Vassiliou had been defeated by a wafer-thin majority in his re-election campaign by Glafcos Clerides, who had campaigned against the Set of Ideas. That particular set of proposals had therefore to be regarded as dead, although many of the component parts of it were to arise, like a phoenix from the ashes, some ten years later. In truth the hope of agreement in 1992 was always something of a long shot given

Denktash's unremitting negativism. Vassiliou was certainly negotiating in good faith and would have settled, though not at any price. But Denktash was as usual, and as he was to continue to do for many years thereafter until Turkey and his own people found a way to circumvent him in 2004, playing for a goalless draw. He used to say that he could have accepted 90 per cent of the Set of Ideas, and, once Clerides had come out firmly in opposition, spoke quite warmly about them, but he never told anyone which was the 90 per cent he could accept and what points were in the 10 per cent he could not. One other lesson emerged from the 1992 negotiations and that was that it was almost certainly unwise and doomed to failure, given the Cypriot proclivity for haggling over even minor points and the complete lack of trust between the two sides, to try to agree a framework, even one as detailed as the Set of Ideas, which required substantial further negotiation before it could be implemented. It was likely to make more sense in the future to get everything onto the table before seeking a decision; and that was in fact the approach followed in the next serious effort made to resolve the problem under the next secretary-general, Kofi Annan. Boutros-Ghali himself was rather bitter about the whole experience, feeling perhaps that his officials had overstated the chances of success; and he nursed a strong dislike of Denktash, which he often expressed quite indiscreetly and which made him an unlikely protagonist for a renewed negotiation.

Mozambique and Angola: one near-perfect peacekeeping operation, one failure

The peace settlement to the civil war which had been raging in Mozambique for many years between the government forces and Renamo, the South African-backed guerrilla movement, fell into the UN's lap virtually without it having lifted a finger. The negotiations were conducted, without any direct UN involvement, by the Italian religious foundation of San Egidio. But the settlement called for yet another major UN peacekeeping commitment and there was certainly no evading it. In truth the settlement came about not just because of the ingenuity and persistence of the Non-Governmental Organisation (NGO) intermediaries, but much more because of the mutual exhaustion of the warring parties and their recognition of the fact that a solution could not be found on the battlefield, and most of all because developments in South Africa undercut and reversed the whole policy of that country protecting itself by destabilising its neighbours. The pacification of Mozambique was thus of a piece with the parallel operation in the other former Portuguese colony in Southern Africa, Angola, but it was to prove a great deal more successful.

The Security Council moved promptly after the signature of the Mozambique peace agreement in Rome on 4 October and in Security Council Resolution 782 of 13 October authorised the appointment of a special representative and the despatch of 25 military observers. Then Security Council Resolution 797 of 16 December decided on the establishment of a full peacekeeping operation and looked forward to the holding of free and fair parliamentary and presidential elections in 1993. Despite some difficult moments during the operation, and in particular at the time of the elections, no major setbacks occurred and the whole process was successfully completed in the manner foreseen in the peace agreement. Perhaps because it went so relatively smoothly it attracted remarkably little attention from, and virtually no analysis by, the world's media.

Angola was quite another story. Although the early stages of the deployment of the pitifully small (much smaller than in Mozambique) military observer mission went ahead without too many problems, and parliamentary and presidential elections were held on schedule and in relatively satisfactory conditions at the end of September, the moment the results were declared, with the incumbent president Dos Santos defeating Jonas Savimbi of UNITA, all hell broke loose. Savimbi refused to accept the result, crying foul; and fighting began in Luanda, the capital, and elsewhere in the country; a number of UNITA's senior officers were killed summarily in the capital; and gradually a full-scale civil war got under way again. The military observer mission was quite inadequate to quell this drift back to war, and no one paid much attention to the frequent exhortations of the Security Council nor to the visit to Luanda by a mission of its members, a much less frequent occurrence then than it has subsequently become.

The enthusiastic and determined (British) UN special representative Margaret Anstee believed, and still believes, that if she had received a modest but prompt reinforcement of a battalion or two she could have saved the mission. Not many others shared that view, and the Secretary-General made no such request to the Council. Indeed, in a move which became typical of his management style, Boutros-Ghali forbade Anstee to brief the Security Council on a visit to New York, saying that only he could do that; and this edict was soon extended to other visiting special representatives. This high-handed behaviour, which took no account of the Security Council's responsibilities in authorising and mandating peacekeeping operations, was bitterly resented, not least by the smaller delegations on the Council, who lacked the means of the P5 governments to keep themselves adequately informed. Whatever the rights and wrongs of this particular episode, by the end of the year the Angola mission was on life support, being extended (in Security Council Resolutions 785 of 30 October and 793 of 30 November) for periods of only two months at a time. It gradually became clear that the whole painful process of putting the original Bicesse Accords together was going to have to be done all over again. Meanwhile the UN's humanitarian agencies continued to do what they could to alleviate the suffering of the Angolan people which was to continue for many a long day.

The question naturally arises as to why there should have been such a contrast between the outcomes of the operations in Mozambique and Angola. Partly it was a matter of the personalities concerned. Savimbi was a charismatic and viciously cruel warlord, absolutely unwilling (until his death in action in 2002) to accept defeat at the ballot box, while Dhlakama of Renamo was neither charismatic nor a warlord and, despite coming very close to rejecting the outcome of the Mozambican elections, allowed himself to be persuaded by massive, concerted international pressure to accept it; Chissano, the president of Mozambique, was certainly also a more straightforward and trustworthy figure than Angola's Dos Santos. Then the special representative in Mozambique, Aldo Ajello (a former Italian politician), proved exceptionally adept at mustering a broad spectrum of international support when the going got rough. He also had considerably more resources to draw on than Anstee ever had in Angola; but, in reality, he too would not have had sufficient resources to prevent or overcome a full-scale break-out from the peace agreement.

The most fundamental difference, however, lay in the difference in the resources available to the indigenous parties in the two countries. Mozambique is one of the poorest countries in the world, with few natural resources, and it had been ruined by years of civil war. Once external support was withdrawn – by the South Africans from Renamo and by the Soviet Union/Russia from the government side – the scope for resuming the conflict was very limited. Angola on the other hand is potentially one of the richest developing countries. It too had been ruined by years of civil war. But the combatants both had access to very substantial natural resources, the government side from Angola's growing offshore oil industry and UNITA from the diamond deposits of the interior; and with those resources they could buy arms, whatever embargoes the UN might try to impose (and no embargo was ever put on the government side, although one was imposed on UNITA).

Somalia: state failure in spades

Somalia was already a failed state (although that phrase was not in common usage at the time) well before the UN Security Council became involved in its affairs. With the overthrow and departure into exile of the former dictator, President Siad Barré, in 1991, the country began a slide into anarchy, and the institutions of the state gradually collapsed and virtually disappeared. A number of warlords, the two most prominent of whom vied for control of the capital Mogadishu and reduced much of it to rubble, exercised limited authority in different parts of the country. The former British colony of Somaliland, which had become part of Somalia in 1960, was now set on the path towards secession. But no one in the international community paid very much attention, although some of the UN's humanitarian agencies and a number of NGOs did noble work in trying and dangerous circumstances to relieve the suffering of the population. The hard fact was that, with the winding down of the Cold War and with the departure into exile of the pro-Soviet ruler of Ethiopia, President Mengistu, Somalia had lost all its geo-strategic significance which up to then had resulted in its being courted by both sides and also receiving considerable amounts of aid from both. It had in reality become an international orphan.

This discreditable state of affairs was finally brought to an end at the very beginning of 1992 when, on the somewhat dubious basis of a letter to the Security Council from the one remaining diplomat in the Somali delegation to the UN requesting that the UN become involved, the matter was taken up. Enthusiasm for stepping into an ongoing civil war was distinctly limited and the action taken by the Security Council in Resolution 733 of 23 January was remarkably limp. Admittedly Chapter VII of the Charter was invoked and a mandatory arms embargo was placed on the country; but no one was under any illusion that it would be respected or enforced. Beyond that the resolution was long on appeals to other organisations (the AL, the OAU, the Organisation of the Islamic Conference) to do something about the situation and short on anything else. It was not a resolution in which, as president of the Council that month, I took any pride. When the courageous Somali diplomat, who had set the ball rolling, came to see me before the Security Council formal meeting, she asked to sit at the table and to speak. I said she should certainly sit at the table behind the place-card 'Somalia' but I advised her not to speak in case anyone were to challenge her authority to do so and to avoid anything she said complicating the task of the UN's humanitarian agencies on the ground. She followed this advice; and the Council was thus able to sustain the fiction that it was operating with the consent of Somalia itself.

Then on 3 March the warring factions in Mogadishu signed a ceasefire agreement and asked for a small number of UN monitors to help stabilise the situation. The Security Council's response (Security Council Resolution 746 of 17 March) was to authorise the sending of a technical team under the UN's humanitarian coordinator and to urge that all parties cooperate over the delivery of humanitarian supplies. In due course (Security Council Resolution 751 of 24 April), the despatch of 50 UN observers to monitor the Mogadishu ceasefire was approved and that same resolution made a first reference to agreement in principle to the subsequent deployment of a 'UN security force'. At the same meeting the Council endorsed the Secretary-General's choice of Mohammed Sahnoun as his special representative, an experienced and wily, if somewhat strong-willed, former Algerian diplomat, with whom Boutros-Ghali was subsequently to fall out comprehensively and dismiss following disagreement over the question of the degree of coercion to be used in carrying out the mandate. Security Council Resolution 767 of 27 July authorised a mandate for a small security force and a 500-strong Pakistani unit was thereafter deployed. All these successive moves had two things in common: the first was that they were inadequate to the task in hand; and the second was that every step forward depended on the consent and cooperation of a number of heavily-armed Somali clans who tended to sell their cooperation at a high price in terms of control over and manipulation of the incoming humanitarian supplies. Meanwhile Somalia was crippled by an unprecedentedly severe drought, and malnutrition and starvation increased daily and began to attract growing attention from the world's media. In response to the deteriorating humanitarian situation, the evidence that the warlords were preventing the delivery of food to those who needed it and a security situation which made a mockery out of the March ceasefire, the Security Council authorised a substantial reinforcement of the UN force (Security Council Resolution 775 of 28 August) to a figure of 4,000, but these new contingents were slow in arriving and meanwhile the suffering of the Somali people was there for all to see, with the international community increasingly criticised for inaction. Even some NGOs began to appeal for more forceful external intervention.

This was the situation when, a few days after President Bush had lost his fight for re-election and completely out of the blue, the Secretary-General received a letter volunteering a large US expeditionary force to stabilise the security situation in Somalia and to facilitate the delivery of food and humanitarian supplies. This was an offer which could not be refused and, a few days later, in Security Council Resolution 794 of 3 December it was accepted. This resolution was probably the most astonishing single document to be agreed in the immediate post-Cold War period at the UN. For one thing it swept aside the whole notion, or fiction in the case of Somalia, of consent by the host nation. There was simply no reference to it. Then it went close to recognising the legal case for humanitarian intervention, when the preamble stated 'determining that the magnitude of the human tragedy caused by the conflict in Somalia, further exacerbated by the obstacles being created to the distribution of humanitarian assistance, constitutes a threat to international peace and security'. In addition to that it was explicitly accepted that the existing UN peacekeeping force was inadequate; and that the US-led 'coalition of the willing' (for by this time the USA had received a considerable number of offers to participate from other countries, including African ones) would exercise overall command and control. And the Americans of course, rather than acting completely unilaterally as they could have done at no great risk of criticism, had decided to proceed under the authority of the UN. All this was voted by unanimity, the Chinese explaining privately that, for all their misgivings, they would not stand in the way of the wishes of the Africans and in return receiving some grace notes in the preamble about 'the unique character of the present situation in Somalia ...

requiring an exceptional response'. There had never been such a bonfire of shibboleths.

In the event the US deployment went unopposed, the Somali warlords deciding, quite literally, to keep their powder dry for a later day. The distribution of food and aid got underway and the tide of starvation and suffering began to recede. Not much was said at this stage in Resolution 794 about the future except that the short-term and temporary nature of the US deployment was firmly stated, with a reference to 'a prompt transition to continued [UN] peacekeeping operations' and to the need for 'a political settlement under the auspices of the UN aimed at national reconciliation in Somalia'. All that was for another year and another US president. It needs to be remembered, however, in light of the collapse of the subsequent UN operation in Somalia, that this first phase of humanitarian relief was a total success, resulting in the saving of many thousands of lives, and that without the use of force.

Iraq: the cat and mouse game

Iraq did not dominate the Security Council's agenda in 1992 to the extent that it had done in 1991; but that did not mean that it was not frequently discussed and that invariably in the context of failures by Iraq to comply with the terms of Resolution 687 (the mother of all resolutions) and of the subsequent detailed resolutions adopted under it. Twice during the year, in March and then again in November, in response to complaints from the deputy prime minister of Iraq, Tariq Aziz, that Iraq did not really know what was required of it and that the Security Council was forever moving the goalposts, the Council, through its president, set out in extensive detail all the obligations on Iraq and all the areas in which it was so far falling short of complying with these obligations. These debates, which also provided opportunities for the Council to hear from the CHR's rapporteur on Iraq, Max van der Stoel, about the appalling state of human rights in Iraq, had exactly the opposite effect to that intended by Tariq Aziz. He had clearly hoped to open up divisions in the Council and to elicit sympathy, in particular from its non-aligned members, for Iraq's plight. Instead, by forcing the Council to set out Iraq's record in full in factual documents which were agreed by unanimity, he managed to force the members to close ranks and brought out into the open how very far there was to go. Not surprisingly, he thereafter desisted from this strategy.

On sanctions there was no movement at all. The negotiations required to implement Resolutions 706 and 712 (the first version of the oil-for-food scheme) sputtered briefly and then were finally brought to a halt by the Iraqis. The Security Council's response, given that costs were beginning to pile up for weapons inspections, from the first rulings of the Compensation Commission and from the humanitarian aid programmes, mainly in the Kurdish-populated areas of Northern Iraq which were not under Iraqi control and which were being carried out by the UN under Resolution 688, was to expropriate all Iraq's external assets which had originally been frozen after the invasion of Kuwait. This unprecedented measure was, surprisingly, adopted with only one abstention (China) in Security Council Resolution 778 of 2 October. The regular sanctions reviews every two months came and went uneventfully. There were some problems over how to record the conclusions of these reviews given that, technically speaking, no decision was required at all – they were reviews, not, as the media invariably described them, decisions to renew the sanctions – and given also that there were differences within the Council between those who wanted to lighten sanctions in return for partial compliance and those who insisted that the letter of Resolution 687 was clear: it had to be compliance first. Finally with the help of the Ecuadorean permanent representative a formula which subsequently bore his name was hammered out: 'after hearing all the opinions expressed in the course of the consultations, the president of the Council concluded that there was no agreement that the necessary conditions existed for a modification of the regimes established …'. This masterpiece of diplomatic obfuscation then served for every succeeding review through many years, thus saving a great deal of time and papering over of the Council's increasing divisions.

The work on the demarcation of the Iraq–Kuwait frontier went ahead steadily, but not entirely smoothly. The members of the Boundary Demarcation Commission themselves had doubts as to whether their remit covered only the land boundary or also the maritime boundary. The Security Council, in Resolution 773 of 26 August, made it clear that it included the latter. The Council was also required to react strongly to a letter from the Iraqi foreign minister to the Secretary-General which appeared to be a pre-emptive move to avoid having to accept the eventual outcome of the Demarcation Commission's work; and also to Iraq pulling out its representatives from the Commission, no doubt with the same objective in mind. It was made clear that the boundary demarcation provisions were part of the basis for the ceasefire; that the frontier being demarcated was guaranteed by the Council; and that grave consequences would ensue from any breach of that frontier.

But by far the greatest problems arose over the work of the weapons inspectors, which the Iraqis delayed and obstructed every inch of the way. The full, final and complete disclosures which Iraq was required to make for each weapons programme (nuclear, chemical, biological, and missiles of more than 150 kilometres range) were anything but any of those three things. In particular they concealed the existence of some of the more sophisticated chemical agents, VX in particular, and they flatly denied the existence of a biological weapons programme at all. The Iraqi technique was to calculate how much they thought the inspectors actually knew and then declare just that. When they were found out, a new declaration would be proffered, again calibrated to the outer edge of the inspectors' knowledge. It was hardly a technique calculated to inspire trust.

Only the IAEA's nuclear inspections proceeded in a relatively trouble-free manner, offering the prospect that the Director-General, Hans Blix, would be able to report the completion of his work before too long. The inspections revealed a massive programme, the extent of which had been concealed successfully from the IAEA and the intelligence services of the main powers and which, it was calculated, could have given Iraq a useable nuclear warhead – they already had the missiles – by the mid-1990s. Most of it was now in ruins as a result of the attentions of the Coalition air forces; and the only fissile material which the Iraqis at that time possessed, the high-enriched uranium core from the Osirak research reactor, which they had bought from France in the early 1980s and which the Israelis had bombed, was removed and shipped away to Russia.

The extent of this first intelligence failure both alerted the other, non-nuclear, inspectors to the Iraqi capacity for concealment; and it also cast a long shadow forward over the assessment of Iraq's WMD capabilities in the run-up to the 2003 invasion of Iraq. The Council rapidly developed a good working relationship with the Swedish Chairman of UNSCOM, Rolf Ekeus, and gave him full support at every stage. Matters came to a head in February when the Council stated flatly that 'Iraq's behaviour constituted a material breach of Resolution 687' and that 'Iraq must be aware of the serious consequences of continued material breaches'. A high-level Iraqi mission then came to New York for talks with Ekeus and the level of cooperation temporarily improved. But by April the Council was again called on to intervene over Iraqi attempts to interfere with UNSCOM's surveillance overflights. In July a particularly egregious piece of obstruction by the Iraqis took place at the Ministry of Agriculture, where the inspectors were cooped up for many hours in the courtyard while the Iraqis ferried their files out of the rear entrance. This led to another peremptory statement by the Security Council referring to 'a material and unacceptable breach'; but, on this occasion, for reasons no one ever explained, the relatively inexperienced new US ambassador Edward Perkins asked for the usual reference to 'serious consequences' to be removed. The Iraqis were cock-a-hoop, and the risk that things would now get steadily worse was a real one. The Americans summoned a tripartite meeting (France, UK and USA) of senior officials from capitals and from New York to Washington, and it was agreed that the Iraqis must be shown that 'serious consequences' did mean something. Subsequently the three governments announced the extension of the southern No-Fly Zone to include most of the south of Iraq. As with the previous No-Fly Zone decisions this one was promulgated unilaterally and without seeking authority from the Security Council, but there were no complaints there, the objects being pursued clearly being directly related to compliance with Security Council resolutions.

By the end of the year, however, the level of Iraqi cooperation, or rather the lack of it, was as bad as ever; and it became clear that President Bush was not prepared to leave office without demonstrating that there were more serious consequences to this than the extension of No-Fly Zones. The three ambassadors in New York (Merimée, Perkins and I) were instructed to see Ekeus and to say that, unless he could tell us that he was getting full Iraqi cooperation, military action would be taken against a range of targets related to Iraq's WMD programmes. We duly spoke to Ekeus, who asked for 24 hours to see whether the Iraqis would give the necessary guarantees. To this we agreed. When I conveyed all this to Stephen Wall, John Major's Diplomatic Adviser at No. 10, he sounded a bit concerned, saying there was a timing problem; but I pointed out that, having given Ekeus 24 hours to provide us with the answer we had sought, we really ought to stick to that. In the event Ekeus got nowhere with the Iraqis, and a series of missile and bombing raids went ahead 24 hours later than originally planned. Wall said to me afterwards that I really must not ask him again to turn the US Air Force round in mid-Atlantic.

In 1992 I began a series of meetings with Tariq Aziz whenever he came to New York. The Iraqis had made the original move, presumably hoping to find some way of driving a wedge between the British and the Americans, who flatly declined a similar overture. London, however, decided to accept, mainly because we had a number of consular cases we wanted to discuss with the Iraqis (e.g. the case of a British businessman thrown into gaol on trumped-up charges of corruption and a luckless cyclist arrested trying to cross Iraq). So every few months I would find myself sitting in the sepulchral splendour of the Iraqi ambassador's residence in front of a huge, full-length portrait of Saddam Hussein, sipping a glass of whisky. Tariq Aziz, whom I always thought of as the Ribbentrop of the regime, was a skilful, tightly controlled operator who spoke in a sonorous monotone. What, above all, he wanted to know was whether compliance would bring the lifting of sanctions. That, I was not prepared to say. But I made it clear that the only way to find out the answer was full compliance. He would also try to persuade me that the Kurds would do much better to cut a deal with the Iraqis, who knew better how to handle them than we did. Not a view shared by the inhabitants of Halabje (where the Iraqis had killed a large number of Kurds with poison gas), I replied; a small nervous tic appeared in Tariq Aziz's right cheek, but he never lost his temper. Indeed, on one occasion, when one of his accompanying officials – the Iraqi general in charge of their weapons programme – launched into a tirade, he quickly cut in and told him to shut up. My task was to get Tariq Aziz, and through him Saddam Hussein, to understand that the British people whom he had gaoled would not, as he hoped, provide some form of effective political leverage on the British government. Others, King Hussein of Jordan in particular, were conveying the same message. And later, much later, the Iraqis released the prisoners into the custody of Edward Heath, who most nobly made the long land journey across the desert from Amman to Baghdad despite his strong disapproval of the British government's policy towards Iraq.

*   *   *   *

If 1991 was a tumultuous year at the UN, 1992 was a frenetic one. A few figures give the feel of that. The UN's deployed peacekeeping forces rose from 12,000 at the beginning of the year to nearly 60,000 at the end of it (and that excluded the 20–30,000 troops sent under US leadership to Somalia). The cost of peacekeeping rose to $2 billion, more than ten times the annual average before 1990. The Security Council adopted during the year over 70 resolutions, many of them mandatory ones under Chapter VII of the Charter, more than 10 per cent of all the resolutions adopted in the previous 46 years of the Council's existence.

The main milestones of this headlong progress have been set out in this chapter. But considerations of space have not permitted even the mention of a number of other disputes in which the UN became, however marginally, involved. Several of those resulted from hostilities in what had previously been part of the Soviet Union. In Georgia the UN became a partner with the Russian-dominated Commonwealth of Independent States in a small peacekeeping operation in the breakaway region of Abkhazia; in Azerbaijan and Tajikistan it issued statements but did not get directly drawn in. Generally speaking neither the Western members of the Security Council nor the Russians themselves were very keen to see the UN play a leading role in managing the consequences of the breakup of their former empire, although there were tensions between the Russian security apparatus, who preferred to handle these problems themselves, and the progressive Russian foreign minister Andrei Kozyrev, who wanted to be able to demonstrate that the UN could help Russia just as it did other states.

The problems and consequences of state failure continued to trouble and to baffle the UN, while being poorly understood. In 1991 the former Yugoslavia had been a prime example of that phenomenon, and it continued to be so in 1992; to it was now added Somalia; and Liberia and Haiti were waiting in the wings. Afghanistan was perhaps the best example of the relative insouciance of the international community when faced with clear evidence of a state sliding into anarchy. The UN had been much involved in Afghanistan in the late 1980s, brokering and later monitoring the withdrawal of Soviet troops from that country. Subsequently a small, and steadily dwindling, UN presence had attempted to stem the chaos that developed as the successor Communist regime of Najibullah was overthrown. But the warlords who then controlled the country paid little attention to these UN efforts and the Security Council showed no sign of caring much. The mood in the Council was probably quite accurately captured in a contemporary note I made: 'Afghanistan remains resistant to UN treatment, despite the skilful activity of the Secretary-General's Personal Representative [Benon Sevan, a Cypriot, who was to figure prominently much later in the Iraqi oil-for-food scandal]; but the break-up of the Soviet Empire is probably removing it even further from being a focus of international interest or interference and that could well be the only way to bring the Afghans to concentrate on solving their own problems'. How wrong I was. And how heavy was the price to be paid in due course for that neglect.

At the end of the year it was not difficult to spot the biggest challenge to the UN in 1993 and, with Angola, the highest risk of failure. It was of course the former Yugoslavia, which I labelled at the time as 'the UN's own tar baby'. It seemed to me that 'the UN really has no alternative but to wade deeper into the Yugoslav quagmire. . . . it would be less of a cause of concern if its track record and that of its principal member states concerned had been characterised by more unity and firmness of purpose than has been the case'. But Iraq too was obviously going to continue to give rise to plenty of problems: 'As long as Saddam Hussein remains in power he will continue probing the will of the Council and the coalition allies, refusing full compliance and trying to break out of the straitjacket imposed by SCR687; and for just as long the coalition allies and the Council will need to find appropriate responses, backed up by a willingness to use force as a last resort, if the gains made in the Gulf War are not to be frittered away'. The scale of the challenges lying ahead was indeed daunting: 'Saddam Hussein, Pol Pot, Qaddafi, Savimbi and Milosevic are as appalling a collection of international outcasts as even the twentieth century has managed to muster; but the UN is facing them all in 1993 and that is a tall order. Nor does it have many cards in its hand. Sanctions do have a weakening effect but they do not bring about a rapid change in policy by totalitarian opponents. Much therefore will depend on the backing the UN gets from its leading member states'. Thus the fairly sobering view at the time.

This was a period when there was much talk of a new world order – it was, of course, an election year in the USA. I personally never much liked the phrase. There seemed to be too many echoes of Hitler's infamous 'new international order'; and it rather begged the question whether what we were seeing was the emergence of an international community dominated by elements of order or rather one dominated by elements of disorder. What was not in doubt, however, was that we were living in a world dominated by one superpower, the USA, and that the bipolar dimension that had characterised the Cold War period had disappeared. Hence the close attention paid by all at the UN to the outcome of the US presidential election in November 1992. The defeat of President Bush removed a president who had put the UN closer to the centre of US foreign policy-making than any other since Franklin Roosevelt and Harry Truman. What we were going to get in place of that was a source of endless conjecture but little certainty: 'US policy will greatly affect the prospects for the continuation of the cooperation between the five permanent members which has been so influential at the UN over the last three years . . . we will need a good deal of luck, perseverance and patience if P5 unity is not to weaken'. The sense of foreboding was tangible.

As to Boutros-Ghali's first year in office: 'he has', I noted at the time, 'had no honeymoon, rather a baptism of fire. He has so far come through pretty well. He is the most assertive Secretary-General since Hammarskjold. He knows his own mind and is good at getting his way . . . but he does live dangerously . . . . He despises the baser arts of press handling . . . . He may be in for a bumpier ride in 1993 than in 1992'.

Chapter VII

1993: The tipping point

1993 was the year when the balance of the post-Cold War UN's performance began to tip decisively away from success and towards failure. The new US administration, for all its perfectly sincere protestations of support for multilateralism, provided less reliable backing for the UN than its predecessor had done. Peacekeeping disasters in Somalia and Haiti joined intensifying problems in Bosnia and continuing civil war in Angola on the negative side of the ledger, overshadowing the success of the elections in Cambodia and the subsequent installation there of a coalition government. The close working relationship between the P5 of the Security Council began to fray at the edges; and the failure to address in any systematic way the UN's weaknesses in resources and political backing when the going got rough, took its toll.

The year began with the usual transition in the Security Council, five new members joining and five leaving. This year marked no substantial shift in the balance of opinion, although the arrival of Pakistan brought in an eloquent and determined supporter of the Muslim government in Bosnia. But the transition that really held everyone's attention at the beginning of 1993 was the arrival in the White House of President Bill Clinton after his victory over President Bush at the November general election.

The attitude towards the UN and the positions taken up there by successive US administrations had been of central importance since the organisation was established in 1945. Some administrations had tended to ignore the UN, some had been sharply critical of it, and some, among them the outgoing Bush administration, had been strongly supportive of it. In every case those US attitudes had done much to determine the political weather in New York. This was inevitably going to be true in 1993, the first change of US administration since the end of the Cold War. With the USA the only remaining superpower and with the UN at the centre of many of the main international developments, the air of anticipation was tangible. But there was not much to go on in predicting which way the new administration would jump. The election campaign had largely been dominated by economic and domestic issues – Clinton's slogan, 'It's the economy, stupid', said it all. On one foreign policy issue of very great interest to the UN, Bosnia, Clinton had, however, spoken out strongly, criticising the arms-length approach of the Bush administration, promising greater and more active involvement, and taking a tough line against Serb aggression. But even on Bosnia, Clinton's campaign pronouncements were expressed in the most general terms and shorn of all specifics. Nor had the transition period between November and January cast much light on the prospects, the incoming Secretary of State, Warren Christopher, being someone who regarded taciturnity as the ultimate virtue and the incoming National Security Adviser, Tony Lake, being an African expert. Those familiar with previous US transitions and the long period traditionally needed to get through the nomination of new appointees, their confirmation by the Senate and the definition of the new administration's policies were gloomily aware that many of the issues active at the UN – the continued deterioration of the situation in Bosnia, the switch over from a US-led humanitarian intervention in Somalia to a UN peacekeeping operation, the critical election period in Cambodia – simply would not wait while this laborious process played out. Decisions would have to be taken before the new administration had settled down. We were clearly in for a bumpy ride.

The new US ambassador to the UN and a member of the Clinton cabinet, Madeleine Albright, was rapidly confirmed, and she arrived in New York before the end of January. She had had a good deal of foreign policy experience in the Carter White House and as the principal foreign policy advisor to Michael Dukakis, the Democrat candidate for the presidency in 1988, although she had no direct experience of the UN. She made an immediate impact with her strong personality, friendliness and plain speaking. Her media skills were quickly apparent, as was her support for what she described as assertive multilateralism; and she soon filled the vacuum which had existed since Pickering's departure in the late spring of 1992. As a first-generation US citizen, with her roots in pre-Second World War Czechoslovakia, she had a surprisingly 'European' view of the world; for her the seminal foreign policy event of the twentieth century was not Pearl Harbour or the Vietnam War but the betrayal of Czechoslovakia by the policy of appeasement, which she clearly equated with both European and Bush administration policies towards Bosnia. Less positively, at least from a New York point of view, it became clear that she regarded herself as very much a part of foreign policy formulation in Washington and intended to spend a good deal of her time there trying to influence it. And her relationship with Boutros-Ghali, fairly poor from the outset, as much because of his marked tendency to patronise her as because of any policy differences, steadily deteriorated as disagreements over Somalia, Bosnia and policy towards Israel's presence in South Lebanon took their toll.

Bosnia: the Vance–Owen peace plan and the safe areas

The situation in Bosnia at the beginning of 1993 was by far and away the most immediate preoccupation of Britain and other European governments. The decision in the autumn of 1992 to deploy troops there in a humanitarian protection role had clearly in the short term paid off. The major humanitarian catastrophe which the UN's agencies had otherwise predicted for that winter had been avoided. But it had in no way mitigated the viciousness of the three-cornered fighting between Bosnian Muslims, Bosnian Serbs and Bosnian Croats, the latter two with ample support from their motherlands, nor the continuation of ethnic cleansing, nor the outward flow of refugees into Western Europe. It was also clear that much worse fighting would flare up in the spring. So the existing policy mix was not sustainable. It was this analysis which led the British prime minister to call together all those concerned by the Bosnian crisis on the British side, including the ambassadors to the USA and the UN, at a meeting in No. 10 in January. The prognosis of all those present was gloomy, and the prescription was unanimous. What was needed was greater US involvement on the ground and in the peace-making effort. The Vance–Owen peace proposals, which were beginning to take shape, would not be accepted by all the parties and would not bring an end to the fighting unless they received robust and active backing from all the main outside players, the USA in particular; and the inclusion of American troops in the ground effort, whether to protect humanitarian work or to implement a peace settlement, would be essential. These were no longer tasks which could be managed by the Europeans alone. Above all the increased deterrent effect on the warring parties of involving US troops could make a crucial difference. John Major concluded that he would feed these views into the new Clinton White House. In the policy turmoil which prevailed in Washington as the new administration took office, there was no indication that they were ever seriously considered. Certainly the US policy, which eventually, months later, emerged, bore no trace of them.

As Vance and Owen laboriously pieced together their settlement plan, travelling tirelessly and working with the parties in the Geneva conference, no one at first had paid too much attention to the possible attitude towards the plan of the incoming US administration. There was a kind of general assumption that, since most of the main foreign policy players in the new administration had worked under Vance when he had been President Carter's Secretary of State, he would be keeping them fully informed and would enjoy their strong support. Neither assumption turned out to be correct. It gradually began to seep out during January that there was widespread misunderstanding and distrust of the proposals, which were regarded, at least by hawks in the incoming administration, as rewarding Serbian aggression. The proposals were certainly complex, involving the division of Bosnia into a number of cantons with considerable devolved powers and a relatively weak central government. In each canton, as in the central government, there would be a careful balance between ethnic communities and a requirement for power-sharing among the three groups. It was possible to fault this plan on the grounds of excessive complexity and to have doubts about its viability. What is hard to argue is that it did not reflect better the multi-ethnic and multi-cultural nature of the pre-existing Yugoslav state of Bosnia than did subsequent settlement plans, including the one eventually agreed at Dayton in 1995.

Unfortunately the first response to the surfacing of these US doubts only made things worse. Owen, in New York for consultations with Vance and the Security Council, briefed one of the New York Times' leading political correspondents, perhaps inadvertently on the record, and launched into an intemperate onslaught on the new president's pusillanimity, all this at the time of Clinton's inauguration, when he had not yet made any detailed statements on policy towards Bosnia. This provoked a furious response. Albright, always fiercely loyal to her president, virtually refused thereafter to have anything to do with Owen or to support his settlement plan. Discussions began in Washington, to which Albright disappeared at frequent intervals. But when I would ask her in which direction things were moving, she was uncommunicative and would reply that they had just been 'churning about'. That was to continue for many weeks.

Meanwhile, on the ground in Bosnia, the Bosnian Serb forces began an offensive in the east of the country which was clearly designed to eliminate the various pockets of Bosnian Muslim inhabitants there by ethnic cleansing. Bosnian Muslim refugees poured into the main towns and villages concerned: Srebrenica, Tuzla, Zepa and Gorazde; and Srebrenica in particular was soon at risk of falling to General Mladic's forces. UNPROFOR had neither the forces nor the mandate to do anything about this, but its deputy commander, the French General Morillon, went to Srebrenica in an attempt to calm the situation and to persuade the Serbs to cease attacking the town. Pressure mounted in the Security Council, led by the non-aligned members, to do something about the deteriorating situation and their attention gradually focussed on the idea of proclaiming Srebrenica and perhaps other centres of population in the east of the country 'safe areas', a concept which had been discussed in a desultory way in previous months but which had never got very far because of the many difficulties it posed. Neither the troop contributors to UNPROFOR (of whom Britain was one) nor the UN Secretariat were at all keen on it; nor was the USA, which remained as determined as ever not to be drawn into any commitment that would involve their providing troops. For safe areas in places surrounded by territory under Bosnian Serb control, as most of these towns and villages were, to be viable would require full cooperation by the Bosnian Serbs if any UN forces stationed there were to be deployed and supplied; and that was unlikely to be forthcoming unless the Bosnian government was prepared to demilitarise them and to cease any military operations from them, which they were not. Nevertheless in the absence of any obvious policy alternatives, the pressure to move on the safe-area proposal became irresistible. On 16 April, Security Council Resolution 819, adopted unanimously and acting under the mandatory provisions of Chapter VII of the Charter, demanded that Srebrenica and its surroundings be treated as a safe area free from any armed attack. On 6 May, Security Council Resolution 824 extended safe area status to Sarajevo, Tuzla, Zepa, Gorazde and Bihac. And on 4 June, Security Council Resolution 836 extended the mandate of UNPROFOR 'to enable it, in the safe areas referred to … to deter attacks against the safe areas, to monitor the ceasefire, to promote the withdrawal of military or paramilitary units other than those of the Government of Bosnia and Herzegovina and to occupy some key points on the ground'; and at the same time 'authorised the force in carrying out [this] mandate … acting in self-defence, to take the necessary measures, including the use of force, in reply to bombardments against the safe areas by any of the parties or to armed incursions into them or in the event of any deliberate obstruction in or around those areas to the freedom of movement of the force or of protected humanitarian convoys'. To this authorisation was added a second one to the effect that 'Member states acting nationally or through regional organisations or arrangements may take under the authority of the Security Council and subject to close coordination with the Secretary-General and the force, all necessary measures through the use of air power, in and around the safe areas in Bosnia and Herzegovina to support the force in the performance of its mandate'.

This major extension of the mandate and the first explicit authorisation of the use of force in the Bosnian context, including the not very heavily concealed authorisation for the UN to call in NATO air power, was approved by all members of the Council except Pakistan and Venezuela, who abstained, having argued unsuccessfully that the mandate should have included an explicit task of protecting the population in the safe areas. Following that up, Security Council Resolution 844 of 18 June gave the Secretary-General a reinforcement of UNPROFOR to carry out the new mandate. The Secretary-General had suggested two options, which came to be known as the 'heavy' (35,000 troops) and the 'light' (7,500 troops) options; the Council, not too surprisingly, went for the light option, a decision which was later much criticised.

This major shift in the UN's involvement in Bosnia did not occur without considerable misgivings on the part of the UN Secretariat, whose Department of Peacekeeping Operations and whose officials on the ground would have to direct its implementation, and of the European countries, with France and Britain in the lead, who provided a substantial proportion of the forces required and came to represent the backbone of the operation. In addition to the weakness of the safe-area concept itself, the detailed arrangements required in the event of NATO air power being called in – what came to be known as the 'dual key' arrangements – bristled with problems, both technical and political, which were exacerbated by the domination of NATO decision-making by the USA, while it was the Europeans and other troop contributors and not the USA who had troops on the ground exposed to Bosnian Serb retaliation. In addition to these problems two parallel developments in the spring and early summer of 1993 seriously undermined the new policy and made it even more problematic: the first was the collapse of the Vance–Owen settlement plan; and the second was the failed attempt by the Clinton administration to launch a completely different approach to the whole Bosnian problem.

Despite the US misgivings over the Vance–Owen plan, it did look at one stage as if it might be accepted by all concerned. At the end of March the Bosnian Muslim leader, President Alija Izetbegovic, and the Bosnian Croat leader, Mate Boban, both accepted the plan. Slobodan Milosevic, the leader of Serbia (although not of the Bosnian Serbs), also accepted it. But the Bosnian Serb leader, Radovan Karadzic, after looking as if he might do so, rejected it, following a vote in his parliamentary assembly. The majority of the Security Council, with France and Britain in the lead, wanted to give formal, mandatory endorsement to the plan, thus setting it as the benchmark and criterion for the other measures which were under consideration (the safe areas, tightening economic sanctions against the Serbs and the Bosnian Serbs). To general astonishment and great irritation the USA refused repeatedly to endorse the plan. They rejected the word 'endorses' and finally offered 'commends' as the extreme limit beyond which the US Secretary of State personally was not prepared to go. And so it was in Security Council Resolution 820 of 17 April. Whatever one thinks of the fine differences of meaning between the two key words, the all too public scrapping over which one to choose had inflicted major damage to any hope there might be of getting the plan accepted. Not only did Milosevic and the Bosnian Serbs realise that acceptance was no longer a make-or-break issue for the international community, but the Bosnian Muslims too, who had never much liked the plan, rapidly distanced themselves from it; hoping, as they always did, that the USA could be brought in on their side militarily. Attempts by the UN and the Europeans to keep the plan alive suffered further damage when the US, Russian, French and British foreign ministers met in Washington in late May and made only passing reference to it. In reality it was dead. And the safe-area policy, which might have proved viable as a short-term expedient to hold the line in the run-up to a settlement, was left without any political underpinning.

The second development, the agonisingly slow gestation of the Clinton administration's own Bosnia policy, took place exclusively in Washington and was never even discussed in New York; but it hung like a heavy cloud over the Security Council, particularly once enough of the outline of the new policy had leaked into the public domain to reveal that it was fundamentally inconsistent with everything which was being decided day by day around the Council's table. The new US policy was soon given the soubriquet of 'lift and strike' – which signified lifting the UN-imposed arms embargo on all combatants other than the Serbs and deploying NATO air power (but no ground troops) against the Bosnian Serbs. In New York it came to be known as 'lift and pray', since implementation of the policy was likely to encourage the Serbs to more aggressive military efforts so as to take advantage, while it lasted, of their superiority in military material over the Bosnian Muslims, and would have necessitated the extraction from Bosnia in extremely difficult circumstances of the UN troops deployed there, as they could not have been sustained there once the international community had clearly taken sides. In late April 1993 the US Secretary of State set off to sell this policy to the main European capitals. Christopher was met by a barrage of objections unprecedented in the annals of the transatlantic alliance and symptomatic of the loosening of ties since the ending of the Cold War. The Europeans – and for once there were few shades of difference between them, with the British government, traditionally inclined to bend as far as possible to accommodate American policy, as hostile as the others – were horrified at the prospect of such a swerve in policy. They foresaw major difficulties in extracting their lightly armed troops, by now scattered over many parts of Bosnia under, or close to areas under, Bosnian Serb control; they predicted massive increased flows of refugees into Western Europe, where some countries, Germany in particular, were already buckling under the strain; they anticipated a sharp upsurge in the fighting in Bosnia, with the Bosnian Muslims unable to stand their ground until they were better armed and trained and thus being subjected to more atrocities and ethnic cleansing, the blame for much of which would end up on the shoulders of the European countries which would have withdrawn;

and they had no confidence at all that the use of NATO air power would on its own prove sufficient to halt the Serbs. Less defensibly, given the aggressive behaviour of the Serbs, they remained unwilling to be drawn into the dispute on one side.

The upshot of this European reaction was that the USA dropped 'lift and strike' like a hot potato. But much damage had been done, and not only to the Atlantic Alliance. The Serbs concluded that these divided counsels meant that they had little to fear from pushing ahead militarily; the Bosnian Muslims that there was still hope that a bruised but unconvinced US administration could be brought in on their side and that this was a better option for them than trying to cut a deal at the negotiating table. Little more was heard of the policy except that a few months later Albright was allowed to join with the non-aligned members of the Security Council in proposing a resolution to lift the arms embargo. This rather half-hearted effort ended in humiliation with only six votes in favour (the USA and the five non-aligned countries) and with nine abstentions (four out of the five permanent members, and countries as diverse as Japan, Brazil, Hungary and New Zealand). The question of vetoing the resolution thus never arose.

This long and tangled series of developments should, but did not in the short term, have convinced both Europeans and Americans that they had no hope of getting an effective grip on the Bosnian crisis if they could not hammer out a joint policy. Ironically the Clinton administration, which had come to office determined to be more active than their predecessors, ended up by the summer of 1993 almost as semi-detached from the day-to-day handling of the crisis as the Bush administration had been. Meanwhile, in Bosnia, Serb bombardment of the safe areas and in particular of the capital, Sarajevo, continued; but no further major military developments occurred during 1993.

International justice: the end of impunity

The two tribunals established by the victors at the end of the Second World War to try German and Japanese officials for war crimes remained throughout the 45 years of the Cold War, developments which seemed to have created no precedent and which few believed would be replicated. This was not because no war crimes were committed during that period. Plenty were; and there were massive breaches of international humanitarian law. But in many cases the party or parties involved were either operating within their own domestic jurisdiction (as was the case in Cambodia, Bangladesh or Uganda) or there was a Cold War dimension to the disputes which made it inconceivable that any international machinery equipped to bring the culprits to justice would ever have been approved. And then how was such machinery to be established? Did the Charter give the Security Council the authority to do that? Or would a laboriously negotiated international convention, with the need for ratification by each signatory, be required? These questions had neither been posed nor answered.

At the time of the Gulf War, following Iraq's seizure of Kuwait in 1990, consideration was given to the idea of some method being found to bring Iraq's rulers to book for their crimes. A Security Council Resolution (674 of 29 October 1990) had invited member states to collate substantiated information of breaches of international law and pass this to the Security Council. But, following the hostilities and the expulsion of Iraqi forces from Kuwait, once it was decided that Coalition forces would not occupy Iraq, with the consequence that Saddam Hussein would remain in power, nothing further was done about the matter. If a tribunal had been established it was hard to see how it could have operated effectively or how such operations could have been compatible with the implementation of the post-war settlement (Security Council Resolution 687), which required the extensive cooperation of the Iraqi government.

But, as the evidence began to flood in during 1992 of the atrocities being committed by all parties to the conflicts in the former Yugoslavia (although preponderantly by the Serbs), opinion began to shift, and what had previously been unthinkable became the object of closer scrutiny and active negotiation. The Commission of Experts, which had been set up under Security Council Resolution 780 of 6 October 1992, produced an interim report recommending that an ad hoc international tribunal be established in relation to events in the territory of the former Yugoslavia. The Secretary-General supported this recommendation, as did the US government with enthusiasm. Several European governments threw their weight behind it too, as did the non-aligned members of the Council. In many cases there was an element of compensating for the lack of effectiveness of the UN's efforts in Bosnia and Croatia, but there was also a genuine determination to respond to the horrendous media reporting coming out of the former Yugoslavia.

There was not a lot of enthusiasm in London for the establishment of a tribunal, partly due to legal doubts about whether the Security Council had the powers to take such a decision and partly because David Owen, the EU's peace facilitator, was concerned that indictments, for example of Slobodan Milosevic, would render the task of negotiating a peace settlement even more problematic. But it soon became clear, to my own considerable relief since I was personally convinced of the case for setting up a tribunal, that there was no question of our standing out against the overwhelming weight of opinion in the Council, let alone of vetoing it, as was our theoretical right. So Security Council Resolution 808 of 22 February decided that an international tribunal would be established 'for the prosecution of persons responsible for serious violations of international humanitarian law committed in the territory of the former Yugoslavia since 1991'. The very wide geographical scope of this determination, covering much of the country where at that stage no hostilities had occurred, proved, perhaps fortuitously, a sound decision, since it meant that crimes committed much later in Kosovo fell within the tribunal's remit without any need to change it. Then a second resolution (827 of 25 May) firmed up various aspects of the first decision. It was made explicitly clear that the tribunal was being established on the basis of Chapter VII of the UN Charter; the work of the tribunal would cover all violations of law after 1 January 1991 until a date to be decided by the Security Council 'upon the restoration of peace'; and the tribunal would normally sit in The Hague (where the quite separate International Court of Justice already had its headquarters). A third resolution (857 of 20 August) appointed the judges for the tribunal. And a fourth (877 of 21 October), following a somewhat unseemly squabble, with two earlier candidates being blocked by different groups within the Council, appointed the key official – the Tribunal's Prosecutor. Every one of these resolutions was adopted by unanimity. Considering the ground-breaking nature of the decisions taken and the massive intrusion they represented into what had previously been the domestic jurisdiction of a sovereign member of the UN, this was quite remarkable.

Macedonia: UN membership at last

Despite the stabilising effect of the preventive deployment of UN peace-keepers to Macedonia in 1992, the country remained fragile, denied membership of the UN by the continuation of the dispute with Greece and being severely damaged economically by the effect of the UN sanctions against Serbia and even more so by the unilateral blockade imposed by Greece which also cut it off from its main trade route through Thessaloniki. But, little by little, Vance, who continued his peacemaking activities in the Greek/Macedonian area even after he handed over overall responsibility for peacemaking in the former Yugoslavia to Thorvald Stoltenberg, the former Norwegian foreign minister, helped by a change of government in Greece which brought to office a team who realised that the destabilisation of Macedonia could well end up damaging Greece more than any other country, began to make progress in reconciling the two parties. Gradually he found language to deal with most of the problems, those relating to the sanctity of existing borders and the abandonment of irredentist claims in particular. But one problem he could not solve was that relating to the name of the new country. Any number of different variants were tried, ranging from the ingenious to the grotesque. But in the end the Macedonians would accept nothing less than 'Republic of Macedonia' and the Greeks would only accept anything but that. It became clear that leaving the name aside for the moment for later solution, while using the temporary placebo of 'The Former Yugoslav Republic of Macedonia', was going to be the best way of establishing a substantial but incomplete agreement, of which accession to the UN was to be an integral part.

The situation within the Security Council, which had to recommend any new state for membership to the General Assembly, was bizarre and unsatisfactory. Because the Greek/Macedonian dispute was regarded as a primarily European matter, the non-European members of the Council (including the USA) said they would be guided by the views of its EU members (at that time France, Spain and the UK). But the EU members were not of one mind (like the EU as a whole): the French leaned towards the Greek point of view and had instructions not to override the wishes of the Greek government, while Britain strongly supported the case for Macedonian membership, and the Spaniards had instructions to go along with whatever the other two EU members could agree on, which was, in the circumstances, not much use. An early attempt, right at the beginning of 1993, to bring Macedonia in had run into the sands when the Council, vigorously lobbied in contrary directions by the two parties, had fallen into a state of paralysis. Now, in April 1993, the pieces of the jigsaw began to fall into place and it was time for another try. Both Greek and Macedonian foreign ministers took up semi-permanent residence in New York and bent the ears of anyone who would listen. The Macedonians were particularly grumpy over the placebo name, even though, as I pointed out to them, they would over time be bound to win out from a postponement of the decision on the country's name – most people would simply call it Macedonia and those who used the absurd acronym of FYROM would gradually dwindle.

By the end of 6 April all was ready for the adoption the next day of what was to become Security Council Resolution 817. But it was not to be as easy as that. After dinner that evening I had a telephone call from the Secretary-General asking me to go round to his Sutton Place residence immediately. I walked over (it was only four blocks or so away) and found the French and Spanish ambassadors already there. Boutros-Ghali said a new and insuperable problem had arisen. The Greek foreign minister had told him that it would be quite unacceptable if the Macedonian flag (whose design was one of the contentious issues in the dispute) were to be run up the flagpole on First Avenue alongside the flags of the other members. Boutros-Ghali said he had consulted his Legal Counsel who had told him he had no flexibility in the matter; the flag had to be raised. So Boutros-Ghali asked us to postpone the decision. The three of us were filled with gloom, if for rather different reasons, Merimée because his instructions required him to support postponement, Yanez because the EU was about to be split again and I because our main objective of getting Macedonia into the UN risked being thrown back into the morass of tortuous negotiation from which we had only just extricated it. So I challenged the advice given by the Legal Counsel (fortunately not present). I said I had read the Charter many times and had never yet seen a provision requiring the Secretary-General to raise the flags of the member states on First Avenue; nor did the various resolutions or decisions admitting countries to membership say anything about flag raising. Surely the best response would be for the Secretary-General to decide, on his own authority and acting under his responsibility for the furtherance of peace and security, that the Macedonian flag would not be raised for the meantime. No doubt the Macedonians would be pretty fed up with this last-minute, and successful, Greek try-on. But they were, after all, getting what they really wanted, UN membership. These arguments received enthusiastic endorsement by my EU colleagues whose instructions fitted that situation well. And Boutros-Ghali, in that flexible and decisive way that was one of his strengths, agreed to proceed. The resolution was adopted the next day with no reference being made to flags. And the UN had taken another step through the only part of the Yugoslav labyrinth that it was to navigate with almost complete success.

Cambodia: a job well(ish) done

By the beginning of 1993 the main task for the Security Council in Cambodia had been done. The crucial decision, whether or not to let the Khmer Rouge armed resistance wreck the peace process, had been taken when it had been agreed unanimously that the elections for a constituent assembly should go ahead in those parts of the country not under Khmer Rouge control. Now it was a question of whether that decision could be sustained in the face of increasing violence or whether the elections would need to be postponed. That question too was answered when, in Security Council Resolution 810 of 8 March, the Council endorsed the decision of the Cambodian Supreme National Council that the elections should be held from 23 to 27 May. This decision was made a good deal easier by the remarkable success of the voter registration campaign in the face of the Khmer Rouge's efforts to disrupt it. Despite one or two wobbles as the incidence of violence mounted and UN officials, both military and civilian, began to take casualties, the determination to move ahead on the agreed timetable held up, for which Boutros-Ghali, his special representative in Cambodia, Akashi, and the UN's Australian military commander General Sanderson, deserve a good deal of credit. The Chinese, despite their long patronage of the Khmer Rouge, never did wobble; and, when the Khmer Rouge made the mistake of shelling the Chinese engineering battalion, which was part of the UN force, their determination became positively steely. On the eve of the elections, Security Council Resolution 826 of 20 May stated flatly the Council's 'determination to endorse the results of the election for the constituent assembly provided that the UN certifies it free and fair'.

In the event the election went off far better than anyone had dared to hope. Not only was the participation very high in every part of the country not controlled by the Khmer Rouge (the large majority of the populated areas), but there was anecdotal evidence of Cambodians walking or bicycling out of the Khmer Rouge areas to cast their votes. Moreover the outcome revealed a stronger showing by the main royalist party (National United Front for an Independent, Neutral, Peaceful and Cooperative Cambodia – FUNCINCEP) and a weaker showing by Hun Sen's Communists (Cambodian People's Party – CPP) than had been expected. The vote was virtually split down the middle, which made the formation of a government of national unity unavoidable. Following the certification of the results of the election by Akashi on 29 May as free and fair, the Council endorsed them in Security Council Resolution 835 of 2 June and urged the assembly to get on with the task of drawing up a constitution and establishing a government. In the next resolution, 840 of 15 June, the Council was already beginning to think of withdrawing the peacekeepers and the transitional administration, and asked the Secretary-General for his recommendations on the possible role of the UN and its agencies after the expiry of the peacekeeping mandate. Security Council Resolution 860 of 27 August approved the Secretary-General's withdrawal plan and confirmed that the transitional administration's functions would end with the formation of a new Cambodian government in September.

On 5 October the Security Council, not much given in the normal order of business to pomp and ceremony, did stage a quite effective piece of political theatre. By this time the constitution had been adopted and Prince Sihanouk had re-emerged as the constitutional monarch and Head of State of the new Cambodia. A government of national unity had been formed, with Prince Norodom Ranariddh as its rather quaintly named 'First Prime Minister' and Hun Sen as Second Prime Minister. This oxymoronic duo of prime ministers came to New York for a valedictory session with the Council. They were an odd pair: Ranariddh was all smiles and giggles, shaking hands with everyone in sight, fulsome in his rhetoric; Hun Sen was dour, even grim, and his rhetoric was hewn from good Marxist–Leninist rock. It did not, unfortunately, take the gift of second sight to work out which of the two was likely to have the longer staying power. Then, in Resolution 880 of 4 November, the curtain was rung down on the peacekeeping operation.

It was never supposed by anyone involved that this superficially seamless completion of what, up to then, had been the UN's biggest peacekeeping operation was going to produce perfect results. Even in the euphoria of the moment my own assessment was well short of ecstatic: 'whatever happens in Cambodia, and no one in their right mind would seek to argue that the UN has somehow inoculated the country forever against the ills that plagued it for so long, this was a real achievement'. Interestingly enough the problem that loomed largest at the time, the continuance of the Khmer Rouge insurrection, proved the shortest lived of the many unsolved issues. Within months the Khmer Rouge structures began to crumble and the Cambodian people, for so long held in thrall by them, ceased even to fear them in the way they had. High-level defections occurred; and eventually the new government controlled the whole of its territory. More worrying was the state of Cambodian democracy, which often teetered close to becoming an authoritarian regime controlled by Hun Sen's CPP, mainly restrained by the ever tactically agile King Sihanouk. There were many concerns about respect for human rights. It took more than ten years before a judicial process against the Khmer Rouge's leaders got under way. But the economy gradually picked up from the nadir in which it had been left by so many years of civil war, and investment, particularly in tourism and textiles, began to flow in. Cambodia became, for all its imperfections, just another South-east Asian country.

Somalia: an avoidable disaster?

The pressure to take early decisions on Somalia in the first months of 1993 was very strong. The large, US-led multi-national force, whose deployment had been authorised by the Security Council in December 1992, had carried out its sole mandate 'to establish a secure environment for humanitarian relief operations' with commendable success and without the need to use force. In its wake relief supplies poured into Somalia and the UN's civilian agencies were able to resume their work. Many tens of thousands of Somalis who would otherwise have died of hunger and disease were saved. But the multi-national force had neither the mandate nor the capacity (it had no civilian peacemaking and peacebuilding capacity) to conduct a complex peace operation in the most comprehensively failed state which the international community had yet encountered.

The question was, what should be put in its place? Clearly the pre-existing UN peacekeeping operation, which had been suspended at the time of the multi-national force's deployment, was not the answer, having proved quite unable to cope with the complexities of the situation and with the Somali warlords. Nor was the simple withdrawal of all UN and UN-authorised forces even remotely defensible; in such circumstances it could be assumed that the warlords would resume their depredations and another major humanitarian crisis would be just around the corner. So the negotiations both inside and outside the Security Council (whose main protagonists were Boutros-Ghali and his officials and the incoming US administration) focussed on the option of replacing the US-led multi-national force by a major UN-led, blue-helmeted peacekeeping operation with substantial civilian elements, designed to help the Somalis rebuild their shattered state institutions. In many ways it resembled the Cambodian peace operation, although the UN did not purport to provide a transitional administration itself; but it lacked both the pre-established agreement amongst all the parties as to the shape and content of the future state of Somalia and also any functioning Somali state machinery through which day-to-day administration could be conducted.

The large peacekeeping force, which in many cases consisted of the same troops as had composed the multi-national force, was to be commanded by a Turkish general, Cevek Bir, and the key role of the Secretary-General's special representative went to a former US naval officer who had held senior posts in the Bush State Department and the National Security Council, Jonathan Howe. The US military element was smaller than in the multi-national force, but a US-commanded, over-the-horizon capability was provided in case things went badly wrong. Agreement was not reached on this structure and on the detailed mandate without a good deal of tension both within the UN and the US camps and between them. Boutros-Ghali parted in acrimony with his previous special representative when Sahnoun warned that the whole approach was too heavy and too centralised and that it took insufficient account of the need to bring about a consensus among the main Somali clans. On the US side, expert voices were raised in particular against giving the peacekeeping force a mandate to disarm the Somali armed factions. But the fact that so far there had been no hostilities and no need to use force lulled many into a false sense of complacency. On 26 March, Security Council Resolution 814 was adopted unanimously; it laid down a comprehensive mandate for the peacekeeping operation.

Britain played virtually no role in any of these developments. We had declined a US invitation to provide a contingent for the multi-national force and maintained that refusal when the full UN-led operation was constituted. We even refused a further US request, when things went badly wrong, to deploy some special forces to work with their own over-the-horizon troops. This adamantine refusal to have anything to do with relieving a major humanitarian catastrophe, in a region where we had traditionally, as a colonial power, been much involved, left me feeling pretty uncomfortable. But my arguments for participation were given short shrift by London and, since there was no serious difficulty in assembling the troop contingents for either force, there was no leverage behind them. I never did get a full explanation of our attitude. Long after everything had gone wrong, there was a tendency towards self-congratulation that we had avoided involvement in a nasty mess, but just how prescient we were I am not too sure. One element which was not given any prominence was the fact that the former British Somaliland, which had become part of Somalia when they were both given independence, was trying to secede from the failed state, and there was some concern that involvement in the UN peacekeeping operation would be bound to pull us into resisting that secession, a position we wished to avoid. Whatever the reasoning behind our position, the consequence of it was that we were condemned to act the role of an appalled but powerless spectator as the operation slipped towards failure. It is sometimes thought (even by some members of the Council itself) that the Security Council is like some kind of divine Areopagus whose members are there to opine on anything and everything. But that is not so. They are there to carry out the instructions of their governments; and, if their governments instruct them to play no role in a particular matter, that is what they have to do.

Trouble was not long in coming. On 5 June one of the Somali factions, the United Somali Congress/Somali National Alliance, whose leader General Mohammed Aideed had, somewhat bizarrely, long before served in the US armed forces, deliberately ambushed a unit of Pakistani peacekeepers and killed more than 20 of them in cold blood. Two aspects of the UN mandate particularly worried Aideed: the disarmament provisions; and attempts by the UN to neutralise the various factions' broadcasting systems which were contributing to violence. The Security Council's reaction was tough. Security Council Resolution 837 of 6 June condemned the killings in strong terms, strengthened the parts of the mandate which particularly riled Aideed (disarmament and broadcasting) and gave Boutros-Ghali the authority to take all measures necessary against those responsible for the attacks, an authority which his special representative shortly after interpreted as permitting putting a price on Aideed's head. It also authorised supporting operations by over-the-horizon troops (effectively the USA). The resolution was in effect a declaration of war on one of the Somali factions, a development naturally greatly welcomed by all the others.

The situation on the ground then deteriorated steadily, and second thoughts led slowly towards some questioning of the wisdom of the very strong reaction to the June attack on the Pakistani peacekeepers. Security Council Resolution 865 of 22 September represented a first shift of emphasis back towards political negotiations, with the Secretary-General being urged 'to redouble his efforts at the local, regional and national levels to continue the process of national reconciliation and political settlement'. But before this had any chance to take effect, early in October, a military operation by the US over-the-horizon force against Aideed ended in disaster, with two American helicopters being shot down, 18 US military personnel killed, as well as hundreds of Somalis. The subsequent television pictures of a US helicopter pilot's body being dragged through the streets of Mogadishu triggered off a wave of revulsion and anger across the USA and strong demands in Congress that the US troops be brought home. The Clinton administration, which had in truth done little to explain to the public the rationale for the US involvement in Somalia, was simply swept off its feet. The president, who left a strong public impression that the debacle was in some way the fault of the UN, despite the fact that the operation was planned and carried out by US troops under his own ultimate command, announced on television that all US troops would be withdrawn within six months. From that moment on, although the peacekeeping operation lingered on for another 18 months, its ultimate fate was sealed.

The knock-on consequences of the debacle in Mogadishu were not long in being felt and they were seriously negative. While no one had ever expected the USA, with its considerable worldwide, non-UN military commitments, to be a major UN troop contributor, it had been hoped that they would get more involved than they had done in the past. That was the sense of their participation in the Cambodian peace operation and indeed of the operation in Somalia itself. That hope now died; and, apart from providing a contingent for the preventive deployment in Macedonia, US troops were from then on entirely absent from the rapidly expanding UN operations. Moreover the fact that the

Clinton administration chose, for domestic political reasons, to present Mogadishu as a UN failure and not a US one contributed to Congressional criticism of the UN and to reluctance to finance the bills arising from the lengthening list of peace operations for which the USA was voting in the Security Council. In addition it meant that the US military, with little or no experience of peacekeeping, which required the minimum use of force, remained in that state of ignorance.

More widely the Mogadishu disaster instilled a general sense of risk aversion in the Security Council and among the pool of potential troop contributors, which made itself felt with extremely damaging consequences in the cases of Haiti and Rwanda. And it gave birth to two rather dubious pieces of conventional wisdom, the need for an exit strategy and the concept of what came to be called 'the Mogadishu line'. It is certainly the case that any peacekeeping operation requires a strategy for bringing the operation to a successful conclusion and thus for withdrawing peacekeeping troops; but that is quite different from what came to be meant by the term 'exit strategy', which was taken to signify an externally driven, time-limited commitment to UN troop deployments in a particular operation, irrespective of developments in the country in question, often a more or less completely failed state. This kind of exit strategy provided an invitation to the 'spoilers' either to bide their time or to try to precipitate the circumstances which would trigger implementation of the exit strategy. As for the Mogadishu line, no one contested the fact that serious mistakes were made in Somalia and that it had been unwise to be drawn into a direct military confrontation with one of the factions, even when that faction had precipitated the confrontation; but to derive from that experience a general and extremely restrictive doctrine governing the use of force in peacekeeping operations was, yet again, an invitation to the spoilers to push their luck and also ignored the fact that the circumstances under which a peacekeeping operation needed to be judged as impossible to carry on were likely to differ quite a lot from operation to operation. The ghost of the Mogadishu line was to come to haunt the UN operation in Bosnia.

North Korea: a nuclear impasse

When the Security Council recommended the admission of North Korea to the UN in August 1991, it was certainly not in the expectation that that country would be back on the Council's agenda again within 18 months. North Korea's past record in respect to international peace and security had not been a happy one, involving as it had a war of aggression against its neighbour to the south in June 1950 and a later campaign of terrorism against the leaders of that country. But the hope was that, with the ending of the Cold War and the many signs of increased international cooperation between the leading members of the two camps, North Korea would become more cautious and circumspect; North Korea's earlier signature of the NPT, and negotiation of a full-scope safeguards agreement with the IAEA, involving the acceptance of the Agency's inspectors at their nuclear installations, had been seen, wrongly as it turned out, as a welcome step in that direction.

By early 1993, however, the IAEA had become seriously concerned at evidence that some of the spent nuclear fuel from a North Korean reactor could not be accounted for. This spent fuel contained plutonium, which, if separated out through reprocessing, could provide material for a nuclear weapon. The Agency discussed their concerns lengthily with the North Koreans themselves and then, when satisfactory explanations were not forthcoming, with the Governing Board of the IAEA, which authorised the Director-General, Hans Blix, to bring the matter to the attention of the Security Council, as they were bound to do under the NPT. The North Korean response was to notify their intention to withdraw from the NPT after the required six months' notice had expired. Blix came to New York and gave the Security Council a full and careful briefing on the technical aspects of the case, after which no one could be in any doubt as to the seriousness of the challenge nor as to the difficulty of responding to it.

The Security Council Summit meeting in January 1992 had stated flatly that nuclear proliferation was a threat to international peace and security. North Korea's threatened withdrawal from the NPT, the first ever such withdrawal, merely aggravated the situation without in any way helping their cause, since the suspected violation of the treaty had taken place when they were bound by its terms. Indeed one great enigma throughout the proceedings, which the North Koreans naturally did nothing to clarify, was why on earth they had signed the NPT in the first place if (as proved to be the case) they were embarked on a weapons programme. The most likely explanation seemed to be that, having seen how successful one or two other countries (Iraq and South Africa for example) had been at eluding the vigilance of the IAEA's inspectors, operating under their then very restrictive terms of reference, they had concluded that they could do the same while improving their international standing.

The response to Blix's briefing was immediately taken up by the P5 of the Security Council and led to a long, frustrating and eventually unproductive series of discussions amongst them. The USA, France and the UK were in favour of taking tough action, setting out clearly what was required of North Korea to bring it back into line with its obligations under the NPT and its safeguards agreement with the IAEA, and being prepared to envisage sanctions in the all too likely event of North Korea not cooperating, although no specific measures were at this stage put forward. Russia took a position which was not that much less firm, although their anxiety about the possibility of an aggressive response by North Korea was evident. The Chinese, while making it clear that they supported a de-nuclearised Korean Peninsula and that they were well aware of their own national interest in avoiding nuclear proliferation in the Northeast Asian region, argued strenuously against any Security Council action at all. They believed the issue was best handled through bilateral and regional dialogue. Action by the Security Council would merely make things worse. They certainly could not contemplate UN sanctions against North Korea. Out of this deadlock finally emerged, first, a remarkably feeble presidential Statement on 6 April which did little more than ask the IAEA to resume their discussions with the North Koreans over the verification of the missing spent fuel, and then, secondly, a hardly less feeble Security Council Resolution 825 of 13 May on which, even then, China (and Pakistan) abstained. The resolution merely called upon North Korea to 'reconsider' the announcement of its intention to withdraw from the NPT and to honour its obligations under the treaty and its safeguard agreement with the IAEA; it requested Blix to continue to consult North Korea with a view to resolving the spent fuel problem and to keep the Security Council informed; and it urged all UN members to encourage North Korea to respond positively to the resolution. The North Koreans naturally did nothing of the sort and continued with what subsequently transpired to be a fully-fledged nuclear weapons programme.

This sequence of events was a clear indication of just how difficult the Security Council would find it to furnish the underpinning to the NPT which it was its allotted task to provide. The IAEA emerged with considerable credit, its often maligned inspectors having spotted at a relatively early stage the tell-tale signs of an effort by North Korea to get round its international obligations. But the deadlock among the P5 and more widely in the Security Council rendered that success nugatory. Of course in theory it would have been possible to bring forward to the Council a stronger resolution but, while such a resolution would have almost certainly been approved by a majority, the risk of a Chinese veto was a real one and in any case the option of proceeding without full Chinese support was not attractive. The conclusion drawn by the USA was that the Security Council route to dealing with North Korea's nuclear programme was unusable and they turned towards the Chinese prescription of bilateral and regional action to achieve this end, making no further attempt to bring the matter back to the Security Council. We and the French argued with them in favour of keeping both tracks open and running in parallel; since both the North Koreans and the Chinese seemed to attach great importance to avoiding any action by the Security Council, it surely made sense to keep that track open if only to create pressure to achieve results on the other one. But neither of us had a major stake in the issue and the US administration ignored the advice. It was only 13 years later that a twin-track approach re-emerged.

Haiti: yet another case of state failure

The problems of Haiti, the poorest country in Latin America and one which, until quite recently, had been under the heel of the authoritarian dictatorship of the Duvaliers, had been teetering on the brink of the Security Council for several years. With the departure into exile of the younger Duvalier in 1986, an effort was made by the international community to help the country, in particular to organise free and fair elections which, it was hoped, could provide a more stable basis for its future development. The USA, which had close links with Haiti, not least as a result of its being the haven of choice for Haitians fleeing from persecution or poverty, had strongly supported this effort.

In June 1990 the president of the Interim Government of Haiti appealed to the UN Secretary-General to send an observer mission to assist with the elections and asked that this contain both civilian and security personnel. Perez de Cuellar's response was positive and, since he proposed that 150 military personnel should be deployed, he quite rightly sent his proposal on 7 September both to the Security Council and to the General Assembly, which had responsibility for electoral support missions of a non-military nature. This triggered off a truly vintage filibuster in the Security Council by the Cuban ambassador, whose country was at the time an elected member. Ricardo Alarcon was a talented, if infuriating, person, as likely to quote from 'Alice in Wonderland' or Dickens as from Spanish literature. He was a senior figure in the Castro regime (and went on to be a long-serving president of the National Assembly). He regarded any involvement of the Security Council in Haiti as completely improper and as likely to represent the thin end of a (US) interventionist wedge in the affairs of Latin America in general and the Caribbean in particular. He enlisted some support from the other Latin America member of the Council (Colombia), and the debate raged through several sessions of informal consultations with scant regard being paid to the needs of the Haitians in all this. Eventually (I was in the chair that month) I was able to wring out of Alarcon acceptance of the text of a letter of reply to the Secretary-General on 5 October, which stated that the Council 'concurred' in the importance of giving a positive reply to the Government of Haiti. The formulation thus stopped short of any formal Security Council involvement but it was enough for Perez de Cuellar. The assistance, civilian and military, was provided. A free and fair election was held and it was won by Jean-Bertrand Aristide, a former priest and a populist politician of great charisma but rather less soundness of judgement.

This brief foretaste of things to come had demonstrated just how difficult it was going to be if ever it proved necessary for the UN to get more deeply involved. That Haiti was a failing state was not in doubt. But it was not easy to describe its failure as a threat to international peace and security, which was the yardstick by which Security Council involvement had to be measured. The same problems as before arose when in October 1991 Aristide was overthrown by a military coup led by the head of the armed forces, General Raoul Cedras. Aristide, who was in the USA at the time, came straight to New York and asked to address the General Assembly and the Security Council to appeal for support for his reinstatement. There was no problem so far as the General Assembly was concerned, but there was much sucking of teeth in the Security Council, which was chaired that month by the strongly anti-interventionist Indian ambassador. Might not it create a dangerous precedent if the Council were to provide a platform for heads of state or government displaced in internal coups? Would it not create a presumption of some Security Council action to follow? In the end these doubts were overcome, but only at the price of agreeing that the Council, through the mouth of its president, would say absolutely nothing of substance after Aristide had spoken. And so it was. This distinctly feeble response was acquiesced in by the USA and other members of the Council, who would have liked more to have been said and done, on the grounds that it was too soon to bring matters to a head in the Council by trying to improvise a substantive response.

In the months that followed, pressure for the reinstatement of Aristide grew and resulted in a series of resolutions by the OAS proposing a trade embargo on the Cedras regime in Haiti. It was on this basis that, in June 1993, the Security Council became fully and formally involved (by then Cuba was no longer on the Council and the doubts of its Latin American members – strong in the case of Brazil, nonexistent in the case of Venezuela – were reduced by the prior action of the OAS). So Security Council Resolution 841 of 16 June endorsed and gave mandatory effect to an embargo on the export of arms and petroleum products to Haiti. Perhaps the most surprising aspect of this resolution was the language used in the preamble to justify recourse to Chapter VII of the Charter. The OAS request was described as defining 'a unique and exceptional situation warranting extraordinary measures' and the Council therefore determined that 'in these unique and exceptional circumstances the continuation of their situation threatens international peace and security in the region'. Never mind that much the same had been said, admittedly in somewhat different circumstances, about Somalia only a few months before. But no one doubted that this intervention by the Security Council to take forceful measures to uphold a democratically elected leader displaced by a domestic coup had crossed yet another hitherto uncrossed line.

The imposition of sanctions quickly produced the desired result of bringing Cedras to the negotiating table to discuss the re-establishment of constitutional order. A conference was convened by the UN Secretary-General on Governors Island (the headquarters of the US coastguard just off the southern tip of Manhattan, in New York harbour) involving both Aristide and Cedras; and after much haggling an agreement was reached on the reinstatement of Aristide, together with the deployment of UN military and police contingents. This was not achieved without considerable difficulty and not all of that caused by Cedras. Aristide managed to infuriate both of his main sponsors, the

USA and the UN Secretary-General, by making excessive demands and by his fickleness of purpose. At one stage in the negotiations, which he was attending daily, Boutros-Ghali said to me bitterly: 'Aristide is as bad as Joan of Arc. He keeps hearing voices'. But in the end a deal was done. The Security Council then, on 27 August in Resolution 861, suspended the economic sanctions; on 31 August in Resolution 862, it authorised the despatch of an advance team to prepare for a military and civilian police deployment; and on 23 September, Resolution 867 authorised that deployment; a US Colonel was appointed to command the military contingent, a Canadian the police one, all to be under the authority of the UN Secretary-General's special representative Dante Caputo, who had been active and effective in brokering the Governors Island agreement. All seemed to be going according to plan.

But it was not to be. On 11 October, just a week after the events in Mogadishu described earlier in this chapter, a US military vessel was due to dock at Port-au-Prince with the advance elements of the UN military and police personnel. The ship was met by an angry and threatening mob, which the Cedras regime did nothing to control. Without more ado the commander decided not to disembark his troops and the ship sailed away; with it went any prospect of honouring the Governors Island agreement. This astonishing sequence reflected if anything an even greater, and less justified, loss of nerve than had occurred in Mogadishu. Taken together the two events had dire consequences for UN peacekeeping. On 13 October the Security Council in Resolution 873 reimposed the earlier economic sanctions and in Resolution 875 of 16 October called on member states to give them full backing. Attempts were made during the rest of the year to revive and reschedule the Governors Island agreement but they were to no avail.

Enlargement of the Security Council: the Great White Whale of international diplomacy

Pressure to enlarge the Security Council had been pretty well constant throughout the existence of the UN. The powers allocated to the Security Council under the Charter, even if they were not often, during the long years of the Cold War, properly exercised, made membership an alluring target for governments and their diplomats (although, as some of them were to discover, membership was not always a comfortable experience when matters of great moment to the super-powers were to the fore). At the same time the steady increase in the overall membership of the UN made getting a seat through election a more demanding process, often necessitating a major, world-wide diplomatic campaign to win support. In 1965, in response to this pressure, the Security Council was enlarged from 11 to 15 members, bringing the number of rotating members elected for two-year, non-renewable terms from six to ten. Since then no further change had been made.

With the ending of the Cold War and the subsequent increase in both the authority of the Security Council and the scope of the business it transacted, the pressure to enlarge rose rapidly. There were indeed a number of compelling arguments in favour of enlargement. In purely numerical terms the overall membership had more than tripled since 1945, but the membership of the Security Council had grown by a much smaller proportion. The representation on the Security Council of Asia, Latin America and Africa, that is to say of the developing countries, was disproportionately small, while that of Europe in particular and the West in general was disproportionately large. And the 1945 allocation of permanent seats on the Council had reflected the victors of the Second World War's allocation of post-war responsibilities rather than the international community as it was now, as the end of the century approached. All this, it was argued, undermined the legitimacy and representativity of the institution. Of course there were arguments in the other direction, that a larger council might mean a less efficient one, that the creation of new permanent member seats, particularly if accompanied with the power of veto, might lead to the undesirable creation of regional hegemonies. These arguments were pushed hardest by middle-ranking powers which had no chance of getting permanent seats; they favoured enlargement, but only, as in 1965, by the creation of new rotating seats. On balance the force of rational argument pointed towards the addition of both some new permanent members and some new elected seats, but this negotiation was about raw power and the force of rational argument did not hold sway.

By 1993 the pressure at least to begin a process that might lead to an enlargement of the Council was irresistible. But that process had plenty of catches in it. Enlargement of the Security Council was not a matter to be decided, or even discussed, by the Council itself; it was a matter for the whole membership. So it was bound to be time-consuming and divisive. To amend the Charter, and enlargement of the Security Council required that, a two-thirds majority of the General Assembly was needed. But Article 108 of the Charter, which provided for such amendment, effectively recreated the veto power of the permanent members, specifying that any change would need to be ratified 'in accordance with their constitutional practices' by all the P5; and that reference to ratification was a reminder that behind all this lay the power of the US Senate.

So what was described as an 'open-ended working group' of the General Assembly was established to take up the issue of enlargement and also to look into other aspects of the rules and procedures of the Security Council. There was in fact plenty wrong with these, the Council never having been able throughout the Cold War to adopt formal rules of procedure. Moreover there were legitimate complaints from the rest of the membership about the lack of transparency in Security Council proceedings, particularly those of meetings held in the 'informal consultations' format, and about the difficulty troop-contributor governments had in influencing decisions over mandates and over the reaction to crises in peacekeeping operations, which could be of vital concern to the troops they had contributed. These important procedural issues unfortunately remained something of a sideshow to the main game of membership of the Council. They could in fact have been settled relatively expeditiously if there had been the will to do so. But the principal protagonists of enlargement, particularly those who wanted to attain permanent seats, saw no interest in allowing various anomalies and grievances about Security Council practices to be settled in advance of the membership issue and indeed sought to harness these to their own case. So, over time, the Security Council, tiring of waiting for an agreed outcome, began to introduce off its own bat procedural changes designed to meet the most glaring complaints.

At the time the open-ended working group was set up, no one had any illusions that progress towards an agreed or two-thirds majority outcome would be rapid. Indeed the group soon came to be known in the New York parlance as 'the never-ending working group'. My own contemporary view was 'this show is set to run and run and only a very foolhardy person would seek at this stage to predict its duration. The divisions between those who sincerely want to be permanent members

(Germany, Japan, Brazil, Nigeria, India) and those who sincerely do not want them to be, between those who want to keep the Security Council effective and those who want it less so, between "satisfied" members (roughly the P5 and many states with no real aspirations to even non-permanent Security Council membership) and those who want change at almost any price, run very deep, masked though they currently are behind a façade of consensus [in favour of enlargement]'.

New York was soon divided into competing cabals. The P5 discussed the matter from time to time amongst themselves but these were from the outset exchanges of views, not an attempt to arrive at a common approach or position. All five were cautious and disinclined to reveal their hand at an early stage. The USA were the most reserved towards any enlargement, the French and British the least so. Russia was clearly hesitant about any move which would reduce further its already much diminished international status. The Chinese were typically enigmatic, not yet revealing the extent of their hostility towards Japan's bid to become a permanent member which was to emerge so clearly when the issue once again came alive in 2004–5. The most active group was that opposed to new permanent members, known at the time as the Coffee Club, and led by the hyperactive Italian ambassador Paolo Fulci, who took it as his life's vocation to prevent Germany achieving permanent membership. The aspirants to permanent membership were at this early stage less well organised, the Japanese and the Germans still nursing the illusion that they could achieve some priority for their candidatures over the others; and there was a real snag over a possible African permanent seat, given that the then military regime in Nigeria, the most populous African country, led by the unsavoury General Abacha, was not acceptable to a wide spectrum of the membership as the occupant of such a seat.

All the ingredients for deadlock were there, and deadlock was what was achieved. This might not have mattered too much had failure to make any progress on Security Council enlargement not served to undermine the legitimacy of an institution which was already struggling to maintain its authority and to carry out a multitude of tasks, not all of which were proceeding satisfactorily. As it was, perceptions of the UN and of its Security Council in the wider international community and in the media were adversely affected by the view, vigorously promoted by those who wanted change, that the existing arrangements were in some way unrepresentative and unfair.

Libya: a further turn of the sanctions screw

Following the initial outburst of defiance and the burning of the Venezuelan Embassy when sanctions were originally imposed in March 1992, not much happened; and certainly no significant progress was made towards handing over the two indicted Libyans for trial. The targeted sanctions against Libya's civil aviation links with the outside world worked pretty effectively. As intended they impacted particularly on Colonel Qaddafi himself and on Libya's elite who had valued opportunities to travel abroad to international meetings and for pleasure. Now all travel had to begin with time-consuming and uncomfortable journeys by land (through Egypt or Tunisia) or by sea (through Malta); and the same was the case for inward visits, thus discouraging trade links and investment.

There were some very faint signs that Libya wanted to extract itself from the predicament into which its reckless support for and practice of terrorism (including arms shipments to the Irish Republican Army) had dropped them. The Libyan Ambassador in New York wrung his hands and told the Secretary-General he was sure some way out of the impasse could be found, but he never received any instructions which offered a way forward. Boutros-Ghali and the Egyptian government, which needed little encouragement by him to work actively to end a situation which was causing tension on their frontier and threatening the livelihoods of the many Egyptians who worked in Libya, each used every possible opportunity to bring home to the Libyans that the surrender of the indicted men was an essential first step towards the ending of sanctions. It was clear that Qaddafi was constrained not only by the humiliation of handing over the two men directly to be tried in the courts of one of his great enemies, the USA or the UK, but also by concern that any trial would lay bare a trail leading back to the highest levels of the Libyan regime, thus resulting either in more sanctions or even in military action.

The US and British governments were not at that stage minded to make things any easier for Qaddafi. Under continual pressure from the relatives of the bereaved families of the victims in the air disasters, they declined to contemplate the sort of imaginative solutions which eventually, much later, led to a trial taking place before a Scottish court sitting in the Netherlands. Meanwhile it was decided to strengthen the sanctions regime by extending it to cover the freezing of Libyan financial assets abroad and the export to Libya of equipment for oil pipelines, export terminals and refinery operations. Security Council Resolution 883 of 11 November was adopted by 11 votes (one more than the original sanctions), with four abstentions (China, Djibouti, Morocco and Pakistan). On this occasion the resolution spelled out in some detail what Libya needed to do to escape from the sanctions net. If the indicted men were handed over, the Council 'expressed its readiness to review the measures … with a view to suspending them immediately, and to do so with a view to lifting them immediately when Libya complies fully with the requests in SCR's 731 and 748 [on support for terrorism]'. Once again the Libyans' immediate reaction was one of defiance. But the new measures gradually had a substantial negative impact on Libya's oil industry which was virtually its sole means of financing its import requirements in other fields.

Iraq: a (slightly) quieter year

Following the air attacks on Iraq in the dying days of the Bush Presidency, triggered by a whole series of incidents in which the Iraqis blocked or impeded the work of UNSCOM, the process of ridding Iraq of all its weapons of mass destruction settled into a steadier and less troubled rhythm. In particular UNSCOM destroyed huge quantities of chemical warfare munitions and accounted for most but, it was believed, not quite all of the Scud missiles which had been used to bombard Tehran during the Iran–Iraq war and Riyadh and Tel Aviv in 1991. They also began the task of installing monitoring systems and equipment in potential dual-use facilities which would be essential if the point was ever reached when it was concluded that all Iraq's past weapons programmes had been destroyed or rendered harmless. The IAEA's work on the nuclear programme was well ahead of UNSCOM's, given the degree of destruction wrought by the coalition air forces during the hostilities. It seemed clear that Saddam Hussein was trying, through relatively full cooperation with UNSCOM, to test the intentions of the incoming US administration, perhaps encouraged by some very slightly less hawkish remarks made by Clinton in the course of his election campaign. But all was by no means straightforward. There were increasing suspicions that Iraq was concealing the most sophisticated of its chemical weapons programmes, for the production and weaponisation of VX (nerve) gas; and the Iraqis remained in a state of total denial over the biological research activities they had undertaken and the existence of a programme for biological weapons.

Nor were Iraq's other activities particularly encouraging of the view that the regime had turned over a new leaf. In the spring an Iraqi-sponsored assassination plot against former President Bush, who was on a visit to Kuwait, was uncovered, and damning evidence of Iraqi involvement was pieced together. In June the USA retaliated unilaterally by launching missile attacks against the headquarters of Iraq's intelligence services in Baghdad. The USA did not seek any UN authority for this retaliation, but they did brief the Security Council in detail on 27 June about the information on the basis of which they had acted and the limited nature of the action they were taking. It was generally accepted in the Council that they had acted properly and proportionately within the Charter provisions for self-defence. More worryingly there were a series of incidents on the Iraq–Kuwait border, which led to a strengthening of the peacekeeping force there (UNIKOM) and a stern reminder in Security Council Resolution 806 of 5 February of the Council's guarantee of the inviolability of that border and of its commitment to take 'all necessary measures to that end'.

Then in May (Security Council Resolution 833 of 27 May) the Council welcomed the final report of the Boundary Demarcation Commission, which had now identified the entire land and maritime borders, reaffirmed that this demarcation was final and encouraged the Secretary-General to proceed with the physical marking of the boundary. This provoked an Iraqi response challenging a number of aspects of the Demarcation Commission's work and clearly indicating an unwillingness to accept its findings. The Council reminded Iraq (presidential Statement of 28 June) that everything the Demarcation Commission had done had been based on the post-war settlement (Security Council Resolution 687) which Iraq had formally accepted; that it had not, as the Iraqis alleged, re-allocated any territory between Iraq and Kuwait but had merely demarcated the line agreed between Iraq and Kuwait in 1963; and that Iraq's acceptance of all this provided the basis for the ceasefire at the end of hostilities. There the matter rested for the meantime, not entirely satisfactorily, since Iraq had not yet accepted the demarcation outcome.

*   *   *   *

1993 was therefore a difficult, patchy and ominous year for the UN. It was not that nothing went right. Quite a lot of things continued to do so: the UN's biggest peacekeeping operation to date, in Cambodia, was reasonably successfully concluded; another substantial peacekeeping operation, in Mozambique, made steady progress towards the presidential and parliamentary elections which were due to be held in 1994; the ending of the civil war in El Salvador remained on track; and the disarming of Iraq's weapons of mass destruction continued. But a lot of things had begun to go wrong: two big UN operations, in Bosnia and Somalia, were by the end of the year in serious difficulties with no sign that the political will and resources were there to get them back on the rails; another one, in Angola, remained on life support, with a renewed civil war ongoing despite the imposition of sanctions on Jonas Savimbi's UNITA movement; the attempt to get the democratically elected president of Haiti restored after a military coup had ended in a fiasco; and the first brush with the problem of nuclear proliferation had not proved a success. Above all, no systematic attempt was being made to address the problems of overstretch and to think through and apply the lessons of the various setbacks the organisation was undergoing. As the list of failed states totted up, no effort was being made to analyse the phenomenon, to seek to prevent it before it occurred and to remedy it once it had occurred. And so that priceless but intangible commodity of credibility, of which the UN had had a considerable supply following the successes of 1990–2, began to leach away and be replaced by lack of respect leading even to contempt. As it seemed at the time, 'the CNN factor', having in 1990–2 boosted the UN's reputation and credibility beyond its capacity to sustain them, in 1993 turned and rent it, while continuing to fuel the 'something must be done' sentiment.

Much of the malaise stemmed from the uneven performance of the new US administration. In the unipolar world – even though it was not yet called that – which had existed since the Cold War had ended, that mattered a lot. Characterising that performance at the time, I drew a rather unkind analogy from Dryden's description of a seventeenth-century Duke of Buckingham: 'everything by starts and nothing long'; and I noted that the Secretary-General 'sought, but, to his frustration, failed to establish the crucial relationship of trust and confidence with the Clinton Administration which he and the organisation need'. And, despite all the fair words about support for multilateralism, I registered 'it is sobering to note that the new US administration, with majorities in both Houses of Congress and a platform of strong support for the UN, is actually pulling its weight less well in the financial field than its predecessor'.

1993 also was the year in which the solidarity of the five Permanent Members began to fray and weaken. It is not possible to put one's finger on one particular episode or item of business which marked this weakening, but there was no doubting the trend, which occurred as much through neglect as through deliberate intention. Some of the elements which contributed to it were fortuitous. Two of those who had made up the New York quintet and who had worked so closely together over Iraq and Cambodia, Pickering and Li, had moved on to other posts. The issue of Cambodia which had been such a remarkable example of P5 cooperation was slipping off the agenda, with nothing of a similar nature to replace it. On Bosnia, which now took up such a large part of the Security Council's time, the Chinese had politely indicated that they would rather this was not discussed at P5 meetings. There proved to be nothing particularly sinister about this development, since the Chinese did not in fact make any serious difficulties about the many resolutions and presidential statements on Bosnia that came before the Council. But it did weaken habits of cooperation. Moreover other, political factors were at work. Discussions on Bosnia were invariably difficult and often tense, and Madeleine Albright resented the fact that she tended to be in a minority of one in such restricted group meetings, whereas in the Council itself she could count on support from the non-aligned members for her more hawkish views. On Iraq too, following the election of a Gaullist-led government in France, instinctively more friendly towards Saddam Hussein's Iraq than its predecessor, tensions began to surface, although for the time being these were kept under control.

Above all, the new US administration seemed to set no great value on P5 cooperation. Nothing better epitomised that than the annual lunch of the five foreign ministers with the Secretary-General in September 1993. These lunches had been instituted by Perez de Cuellar back in the 1980s, when P5 cooperation had first become a reality over efforts to end the Iran–Iraq war. Their significance was as much symbolic as substantive, with a lengthy communiqué issued afterwards which, while it was never used to innovate, did demonstrate over the years the increasing scope of the cooperation. Discussion at the lunches tended to be guarded and a bit stilted – after all this group of five ministers never met on any other occasion in this format – but a wide agenda used to be covered. 1993 was the new US Secretary of State Warren Christopher's first appearance at such an occasion. Throughout the one-and-a-half hour's proceedings in the intimacy of the Secretary-General's small dining room on the 38th floor of the UN Secretariat building, he never spoke once. Nor for that matter did the Chinese foreign minister Qian Qichen, who habitually only spoke on matters of direct interest to China, of which there were none that year. Which left an increasingly despairing Boutros-Ghali to initiate a series of fairly inconsequential discussions with Alain Juppé, Douglas Hurd and Andrei Kozyrev. No one could possibly have supposed after that experience that cooperation with the P5 came high up the US agenda.

It was clear therefore that 1994 was going to be another difficult year and the auguries were not particularly good. The number of active peacekeeping operations had risen from 13 to 18, the number of peace-keepers deployed to around 80,000. My contemporary observation was 'at least the UN should by now have put behind it the era of excessive expectations and be better placed to take a cautious and hard-headed approach to the handling of peacekeeping commitments, both politically and managerially. But a policy of cut and run or of turning a blind eye to regional mayhem will undermine the UN's credibility every bit as surely as one of overcommitment and intervention. What is needed is to establish some mean between the excessive swings of elation and despair which have characterised recent years'; and I added: 'if the UN had one wish to put to Father Christmas, I imagine most practitioners [in New York] would opt for a solid and supportive contribution from the USA'. Alas, neither of those wishes was to be granted.

Chapter VIII

1994: The heart of darkness

The atmosphere at the UN at the beginning of 1994 was very different from the three previous years. In 1991 the organisation was about to put to the test the ultimatum it had given Saddam Hussein's Iraq to reverse its seizure of Kuwait and thus to demonstrate whether or not the concept of collective security in the new post-Cold War world would be to some extent centred on the UN. In 1992 the UN had been on the crest of a wave, Iraq's aggression successfully reversed and a number of other peacekeeping missions settling relics of the Cold War well under way, and the struggle with South Africa over apartheid successfully accomplished or on the way to being so. The Security Council summit meeting in January that year placed the UN even more demonstrably at the centre of international affairs. In 1993 all eyes had been turned on Washington, where the new Clinton administration had been about to take office, committed to finding multilateral solutions to the world's problems; while the first signs of overstretch were clearly visible, the optimists still clearly outnumbered the pessimists. Now, in 1994, all that had changed, and the mood was more sombre, although not yet despairing. The mountains to climb seemed more daunting; the doubts about the organisation's ability to climb them more real; and 1993 had been a bruising year, when the immediate post-Cold War unity among the main powers showed signs of cracking – between the USA and the Europeans over Bosnia and between the US and the UK and the other three permanent members of the Security Council over Iraq.

By the end of the first four months of the year, a complex series of crises in the Bosnia peacekeeping operation, which had at first seemed to offer a genuine opportunity of making progress, had left matters much as they were, if not worse. And in Rwanda the catastrophe of the genocide had found the UN with no capacity or will to respond adequately.

As usual in the post-Cold War world, the changes in the membership of the Security Council at the beginning of the year did not herald any very great shifts. The arrival of Argentina, where the Menem administration hewed to a very pro-US foreign policy, meant that the USA and the UK felt less lonely in promoting a tough line over Iraq. One Arab moderate (Oman) succeeded another (Morocco). The one real oddity, which at first remained just that, but which soon became a source of crippling embarrassment, was the arrival of Rwanda in one of the three African elected seats. This was odd because Rwanda was already then on the receiving end of a UN peacekeeping mission designed to help bring an end to the civil war which had been raging there with varying degrees of intensity for several years, and it became much worse than odd when the government of Rwanda became involved in genocidal massacres following the killing of its president and the collapse of the peace process. Rwanda's presence was a consequence of the rigorous automaticity with which the African group at the UN applied the rotation among their members of the three seats allocated to them. In this way, during the early 1990s, Africa's representation was provided by micro-states such as Cape Verde and Djibouti, as well as another, Rwanda, which should never have been chosen at all since it was the subject of a dispute already on the Security Council's agenda. Later, in 1995, this automaticity was to give rise to the threat of Libya getting one of the three African seats when it too was in dispute. Only when the Africans failed to agree amongst themselves on a clean slate of three names did other non-Africans get a say in the elections for the Security Council, and that was unusual, although not unprecedented. Boutros-Ghali was not the only person who felt that this automaticity was crippling the Africans' ability to play a full role at a time when the problems of their continent were becoming an evermore prominent part of the UN's agenda.

Bosnia: an ultimatum, and opportunities missed

As we have seen in the previous chapter, the establishment of the UN's so-called safe areas did to some extent stabilise the situation, in eastern

Bosnia in particular, and bring at least a temporary halt to the Bosnian Serbs' offensive there. But it did not put an end to the fighting either between the Bosnian Serbs and the Bosnian government, nor between the latter and the Bosnian Croats; nor did it halt the practice of ethnic cleansing which continued in full swing in many parts of the country, almost wherever one party had real supremacy; and, above all, it did not put an end to the daily bombardment of Sarajevo by Bosnian Serb artillery and tanks positioned on the hills around the city, under the noses, and to the entirely justified outrage, of the world press, which was heavily represented in the city. Meanwhile the two peace facilitators, David Owen for the EU and Thorvald Stoltenberg, the Norwegian who had taken over from Vance as the UN part of the duo, were painfully picking up the pieces after the failure of the Vance–Owen plan, but this was slow going and no agreement was yet in sight. There was no question that the situation was not sustainable and that the shelling of Sarajevo was leaching away the credibility of the UN and its current policies. But, as usual, there was no agreement about what needed to be done. The Americans had retired hurt after the rebuff of their lift-and-strike initiative and were not playing a very active role, apart from repeating to anyone who wanted to hear that they had no intention of participating in any UN operation on the ground. The Europeans were clinging on desperately to the doctrine of impartiality and to their unwillingness to be drawn into the fighting as a protagonist while all the time being compelled to increase their presence on the ground even to half carry out the not very satisfactory mandate they had. Some (Owen and the UN High Commissioner for Refugees Sadako Ogata, who was the UN's overall humanitarian coordinator in Bosnia) were inclined to believe that the humanitarian relief operations were either (Owen) prolonging the hostilities, since they provided ample opportunity for the warring parties to resupply their troops, or (Ogata) were not sustainable in the maelstrom of civil war and should be withdrawn. But neither the USA nor the Europeans believed that that was necessary or politically defensible. Meanwhile the non-aligned members of the Council called ceaselessly for more action to defend the Bosnian Muslims.

Such, broadly speaking, was the situation when, on a Saturday morning early in February (5 February), the news came through that a shell or shells had fallen on a crowded market place in Sarajevo killing some 60 or more innocent civilians. Horrendous news photographs followed.

This was by a long way the worst single incident that had occurred so far. Douglas Hurd ran me to earth that morning in Southampton, Long Island, where we were spending a snowy weekend with Felix and Liz Rohatyn (an investment banker of great distinction, at one time trailed as a possible Secretary of the Treasury in a Clinton cabinet, he was later to be sent to Paris as President Clinton's ambassador there). Bosnia had already taken over the weekend, since John Warner, the experienced and moderate Republican Senator and member of the Senate's Armed Services Committee, who was staying in the Rohatyn's guesthouse, had given me a hard time the evening before about the indefensibility of European policy. Hurd asked me what it was feasible to envisage doing in UN Security Council terms. I said that depended on us. Hurd was a bit surprised by this and asked me to explain. I pointed out that the Americans were unlikely again to propose a course of action which would put them at loggerheads with the Europeans. The French and ourselves were operating in Bosnia in lockstep and they would certainly not break with us, even though their instructions were somewhat more robust than ours. And Boutros-Ghali would not propose anything without the prior agreement of his two main troop contributors, France and Britain. So, what Britain was prepared to do was likely to be determinant. So far we had always kept our foot on the brake.

As to the Security Council, I advised against starting a discussion there. The Russians were certain to filibuster against any robust response and we would end up with one of those 'on the one hand ... on the other hand ...' presidential statements of which there had already been far too many. In any case the UN already had all the authority from the Security Council under Security Council Resolutions 824 and 836 that was required to cover a strong response to the market-place shelling if the will was there. Hurd agreed with this analysis; and told me to proceed accordingly. As a first step I agreed with Albright and Merimée that we should meet at my apartment on the Sunday evening (to avoid exciting the interest of the press who were already staking out our missions' premises). When we met we found that there was agreement between us that a robust response was essential and that we should go to the Secretary-General to urge action, not to the Security Council. We also agreed (again to avoid exciting premature press interest) that Merimée alone should go round to see Boutros-Ghali at home that evening and speak on our behalf. This he duly did and reported back that the Secretary-General was sending a message to NATO asking for NATO air power to be deployed to prevent any recurrence of the market-place shelling.

The response from the Secretary-General of NATO (Manfred Woerner) was prompt. He proposed to the NATO Council that the Bosnian Serbs be given a time-limited ultimatum to cease all shelling of Sarajevo and to put their artillery and tanks around the city under UN monitoring. At this point there was a hiccup in London, since several members of the cabinet, with the Chancellor of the Exchequer, Kenneth Clarke, in the lead, were reluctant to follow the Prime Minister and the Foreign Secretary's proposal to approve the ultimatum. But, faced with the evidence that there was otherwise a consensus in NATO, this opposition was overcome. The period up to the 21 February expiry of the ultimatum was an anxious time. The Bosnian Serbs breathed defiance and showed no outward sign of compliance. The Russians grumbled loudly but not too forcefully at the way the Security Council had been by-passed, but were unable to point to any action which had gone beyond the existing authority. Shortly before the expiry of the ultimatum, Boutros-Ghali approached me in the margin of a Security Council session on some other matter to say that the UN ballistic experts in Sarajevo were beginning to have doubts as to whether the market place shelling had necessarily originated with the Bosnian Serbs, i.e. that it might have been staged by the Bosnian Muslims themselves. What should he do? Should he inform the Security Council of these doubts? I said I would advise against that. Such a course would sow confusion and encourage the Bosnian Serbs to defy the ultimatum. In any case things had moved on. The central issue was no longer who had fired the market-place shells, but rather whether or not the Bosnian Serbs were prepared to accept the properly formulated views of the international community and verifiably cease the bombardment of Sarajevo. Boutros-Ghali must have received similar advice from others because no more was heard of it. And then the Bosnian Serbs blinked. The ultimatum was accepted. The bombardment of Sarajevo, for the time being at least, ceased. UN monitors were positioned at the various gun and tank positions around Sarajevo. Within the city there was euphoria; and the UN military commander in Bosnia, General Sir Michael Rose, who had taken over at the end of 1993, moved rapidly to consolidate the improved situation and to boost the morale of the still almost totally beleaguered population. And in Security Council Resolution 900 of 4 March the appointment of a senior official to work on the restoration of public services in Sarajevo was approved.

Within weeks of the Sarajevo ultimatum a further positive development occurred. Under heavy US pressure, the Bosnian government and the Bosnian Croats agreed a ceasefire and also agreed on federal arrangements for the government of the parts of Bosnia they controlled. This agreement was implemented and monitored by the UN forces deployed around the country, and it resulted in a considerable diminution in the overall level of fighting. It also prefigured the shape of the new peace plan which Owen and Stoltenberg were to work up, which, in place of the many multi-ethnic cantons envisaged in the Vance–Owen plan, broadly divided the country into two roughly equal (49 per cent–51 per cent) parts, one part under a Bosnian Muslims/ Bosnian Croat federation and one part under the Bosnian Serb authorities (which might or might not be called, as the Bosnian Serbs desperately wanted, 'the Serb Republic'), the central government having limited authority and the two parts extensive regional autonomy. This was in fact the structure which finally emerged at Dayton in 1995 as the agreed peace settlement, but a long and weary road lay ahead before this point was to be reached.

Meanwhile the Bosnian Serbs were in no mood and no hurry to accept any peace settlement at all. Having blinked at Sarajevo they soon set about testing the strength of the UN/NATO position. The first pressure point was Gorazde, a safe area in eastern Bosnia and one of the main objects of the Serbs' determination to complete the ethnic cleansing of that part of the country which was contiguous to Serbia (known either as the Federal Republic of Yugoslavia or later as the Federal Republic of Yugoslavia (Serbia and Montenegro)). Fighting raged around the town, in which a heavily outnumbered Bosnian Muslim garrison and an exiguous UN observer force were beleaguered. There was another, somewhat less convincing, NATO ultimatum, and one or two individual air sorties were flown by NATO against the Bosnian Serb attacking forces. In the end the Bosnian Serbs backed off and allowed Gorazde to survive as a Bosnian Muslim outpost surrounded by Serb-controlled territory. But they had discovered that the NATO threat which lay behind the ultimatums was more likely to involve relatively ineffective, pin-prick air attacks and not the major onslaught they clearly feared. They had also discovered a new pressure point on the UN in the shape of taking hostage unarmed UN military observers who were widely deployed around Bosnia performing many parts of the increasingly complex Security Council mandates. Security Council Resolution 913 of 22 April helped on this occasion to bring about the release of all those seized. But the threat of this sort of Serb response sapped the will of the UN commanders on the ground to call for NATO air support.

By the late summer the duo of UN and EU peace facilitators, backed up now by a Contact Group composed of the Political Directors of the USA, Britain, Germany, France, Italy and Russia, a grouping which came to play an increasingly prominent role in efforts to broker an overall political settlement, put to all parties a comprehensive package which came to be known as the 'Illustrious' terms (the name of the British aircraft carrier located in the Adriatic which provided the venue for the final round of negotiations). On this occasion the Security Council, in Security Council Resolution 942 of 23 September, did a little better than the previous year by stating that it 'expresses its approval of the proposed territorial settlement for the Republic of Bosnia and Herzegovina which has been put to the Bosnian parties as part of an overall peace settlement' and 'strongly condemns the Bosnian Serb party for its refusal to accept the proposed territorial settlement'. But this formulation still masked, not entirely successfully, a lack of firmness and unity of purpose in the Council in that it failed to endorse the other elements of the settlement plan which were being resisted by the Bosnian Muslims, on whom the USA were unwilling to put serious pressure; and in that it also failed, on European insistence, to threaten the Bosnian Serbs and their backer in Belgrade, Slobodan Milosevic, with any consequences of continuing rejection going beyond a further package of economic sanctions directed explicitly against the Bosnian Serbs and which was set out in the same resolution. So these peace proposals, like the Vance–Owen plan of 1993, gradually withered on the bough until they were much later incorporated in the Dayton peace settlement of 1995.

Meanwhile on the ground in Bosnia a steady deterioration took place from the high-water mark reached following the NATO ultimatum to the Bosnian Serbs over the shelling of Sarajevo and the successful conclusion of a Bosnian Muslim/Bosnian Croat ceasefire and political settlement in the spring of the year. The Bosnian Serbs nibbled away at the safe area policy and resumed their efforts to strangle Sarajevo by tightening their grip around the city and by resuming shelling, to which steady attrition the UN and NATO proved unable to find an effective response beyond the issuing of ever more Security Council presidential statements. Towards the end of the year heavy fighting broke out in and around the safe area of Bihac in the extreme north-western tip of the country, where the local Bosnian Muslims, in any case of doubtful loyalty to the government in Sarajevo, were surrounded by Bosnian Serb territory and by the Serb-controlled enclaves in Croatia known as the Krajina. While the Bihac safe area was not completely overrun, the UN attempts to safeguard it led to more humiliation than success. And even a NATO air attack on a Serb-controlled airfield in the Krajina, which was being used against the defenders of the Bihac safe area, explicitly authorised by Security Council Resolution 958 of 19 November, was more of a pinprick than an effective response.

Throughout 1994 the shortcomings of the arrangements for cooperation between the UN, with forces on the ground, and NATO, with its air power but with no direct exposure on the ground, the system known as the 'dual key', were gradually being laid bare. It was difficult to escape from the logic of the need for dual authorisation of any use of air power. But the practical application of such a bifurcated system of command and control bristled with problems. Moreover the operation of the UN leg of the decision-making process, entailing, as it did, a series of decisions running through layers of UN bureaucracy from the UN military commander in Bosnia through the UN overall military commander in the former Yugoslavia in Zagreb, through the Secretary-General's special representative Yasushi Akashi, also in Zagreb, to the Department of Peacekeeping Operations in New York and, eventually to the Secretary-General himself, was a potential and, in practice, an actual nightmare. Attempts made by the UK and other troop contributors to shorten and to depoliticise this chain got nowhere until 1995. In any case the problem was not just one of bureaucratic methodology. There was a permanent tension between NATO, dominated by the USA, where substantial strategic deployment of air power was favoured, and the UN hierarchy, which listened more to the concerns of the main troop contributors (France and Britain) and which favoured limited tactical use of air power in narrowly defined circumstances. Whatever the rights and wrongs of these two approaches, the existence of this tension and the failure again and again to resolve it in a consistent way merely encouraged the Bosnian Serbs and Milosevic to continue with their defiance.

It was hard to believe, even at the time, that serious opportunities to bring the Bosnian conflict to a conclusion in 1994 were not being missed. The fact that the Serbs had blinked when faced with the NATO ultimatum in January of that year had demonstrated that there were limits to how far Milosevic would let the Bosnian Serbs go in their defiance of the international community, particularly when the possibility of a massive response remained a real one. But that threat was subsequently frittered away at Gorazde and Bihac. Moreover the effects of economic sanctions on Serbia itself were becoming more and more crushing, resulting in astronomical rates of inflation, and led in the late summer to Milosevic agreeing to enforce the new package of economic sanctions against the Bosnian Serbs in return for some alteration of the sanctions against Serbia itself (Security Council Resolution 943 of 23 September). Whatever the doubts about how strictly Milosevic was applying these new sanctions on the borders between Serbia and Bosnia – and the Americans for one had plenty of doubts – this move was clearly a sign of stress which could have been built on but was not, or at least not yet. The Europeans, Britain prominent amongst them, must share a good deal of the responsibility for failing to take those opportunities.

I found myself increasingly uneasy about the way we almost invariably backed down and counselled caution whenever an act of Bosnian Serb provocation around a safe area occurred. My refrain on the telephone to London was that we needed to find a way of frightening the Serbs, not yet another way of frightening ourselves about the possible consequences of firm action. But this had little impact in London, where the government's weak parliamentary situation – there were a substantial number of the government's supporters who criticised the extent of our involvement in the former Yugoslavia – and the spine-chilling intelligence assessments they were receiving all pushed in the opposite direction. The year before (1993), I had felt driven finally to criticise the way in which these intelligence assessments were discouraging firm action. Rodric Braithwaite, who was both the prime minister's diplomatic adviser and the Chairman of the Joint Intelligence Committee, sent me a magisterial rebuke at the mere suggestion that these intelligence assessments, which I argued – although not in those words as the concept was not then so described – were overstating the risks of taking a tougher line and were creating a kind of 'group think' in which the politicians drew on the assessments of the intelligence analysts to justify their caution and the intelligence analysts felt encouraged to ensure they did not understate the risks, might in any way have been influenced by political factors. The events of 1995, when NATO and the UN did finally adopt a more robust policy, on the whole justified my complaint more than the rebuke I received.

The appearance of disarray over Bosnian policy at the UN was further deepened towards the end of the year when the Clinton administration, under mounting congressional pressure, pulled out of the NATO patrols in the Adriatic enforcing the arms embargo against the whole of the former Yugoslavia. This, together with mounting rumours that the Americans were themselves clandestinely encouraging evasion of the arms embargo for the benefit of both the Croatian and Bosnian governments, substantially raised the tension between the Europeans and the USA and increased the damage being inflicted by the Bosnian crisis on the UN, on NATO and on the EU. The stage was being set for the disaster at Srebrenica.

Rwanda: the heart of darkness

The UN's involvement in Rwanda was, from the outset, reluctant and half-hearted. For some time there had been fighting going on in the north of the country between the Hutu-dominated government, supported by the former colonial power Belgium and by a small French military and training contingent, and Tutsi-led rebels, mainly based in the neighbouring Uganda where many of them had been living in exile since the overthrow of the previous Tutsi-led regime, shortly after the country became independent in 1962. Attempts to bring these hostilities to a close, in which the UN played no direct role, gradually gathered pace. Other countries in the region were disturbed by the instability in Rwanda and sponsored a series of negotiations which took place at Arusha in Tanzania; President Habaryamana of Rwanda became convinced of the need for a peace settlement involving the formation of a government of national unity including both Hutus and Tutsis; pressure mounted on the Tutsi-led Rwandese Patriotic Front to compromise; and the French were looking for a way out of their military commitment in Rwanda which would avoid the collapse of President Habaryamana's regime. These pressures led to the conclusion of a ceasefire agreement between the government of Rwanda and the

Rwandese Patriotic Front (RPF) which came into effect on 9 March 1993; and immediately thereafter pressure mounted on the UN to become involved in the implementation of the ceasefire and of any peace settlement which might emerge from the negotiations in Arusha.

The first step taken by the Security Council was the adoption of Security Council Resolution 812 of 12 March 1993, which called on the two Rwandese parties to respect the ceasefire and invited the Secretary-General to examine, in consultation with the OAU, the contribution the UN could bring to strengthen the peace process. It also asked him to examine the request made by the governments of Rwanda and Uganda for the deployment of observers along their mutual border, the aim being to reassure the government of Rwanda that the RPF was not bringing in military supplies across that border. This latter part of the remit led, in Security Council Resolution 846 of 22 June 1993, to the establishment of a small UN observer mission on the Ugandan side of the border. This resolution also requested the Secretary-General to begin contingency planning on the contribution which the UN might make to assist the OAU in the implementation of any comprehensive peace agreement that might emerge from the Arusha peace talks. Such a comprehensive agreement was, in the event, signed in Arusha on 4 August 1993, and it called for the deployment of an international neutral force in Rwanda to help to implement the settlement. It was by now clear to all concerned that the OAU did not have the capacity to mount such a deployment itself and so the buck passed to and stopped with the UN.

Security Council Resolution 872 of 5 October 1993 authorised the establishment of a peacekeeping mission in Rwanda. Its mandate was a classically consensual one, concentrating on monitoring various aspects of the Arusha agreements, in particular in Kigali, the capital, with no reference of any kind to enforcement or to the protection of the civilian population. Uncertainty about the will of the parties to implement the Arusha agreement in good faith was reflected in a provision that the Secretary-General should report to the Council half-way through the first six-month period of authorisation as to whether or not substantive progress was being made towards such implementation. And the general problem of UN overstretch was reflected in a provision for staged deployment (and eventual withdrawal after national elections foreseen for 1995) of the pretty exiguous force (three small battalions to be provided by Belgium, Bangladesh and Ghana). Behind these bare facts lay a distinct lack of enthusiasm in the Council for undertaking yet another operation, which some believed had been landed on the UN's doorstep without adequate preparation or consideration; but the pressure within the Council of the French and from outside it by the African countries in the region was sufficient to overcome these qualms.

By the early months of 1994 the peacekeeping force had been deployed to Kigali, but progress in implementing the Arusha agreement, in particular in the installation of a government of national unity, had stalled. The force was thus in place, but with little to do. The Security Council's impatience with this unsatisfactory state of affairs was made very clear in Security Council Resolution 893 of 6 January, following the mid-term review of the peacekeeping mission's authorisation, which stressed that continued UN support for the mission would depend on full and prompt implementation of Arusha. It was this impatience which dominated Security Council discussions at the time and not any concern about the underlying security situation in Rwanda. The same was true of the UN Secretariat's regular reporting to the Council, which made no mention even of such information as they did have about Hutu plotting for a break-out from the Arusha agreement. In truth, most Security Council members were not at all well informed. Rwanda, a small, land-locked country with few natural resources, had long been something of an orphan of the international community, with few countries even among Security Council members having resident embassies in Kigali and thus access to first-hand information about what was going on in the country. That was the situation of the UK, whose High Commissioner in Kampala was accredited to Kigali and paid at most a few short visits each year. So, when the peacekeeping mission's mandate came up for renewal at the beginning of April, the discussion was still focussed on that feeling of impatience and on the need to send a clear and strong message to President Habaryamana, who was in Arusha for further negotiations over the implementation of the peace agreement, that he needed to move ahead decisively. Security Council Resolution 909 of 5 April thus renewed the mandate for four months only and set in hand a review of the situation in Rwanda in light of the political problems that had arisen over the implementation of the Arusha agreement.

Within hours of the adoption of that resolution the situation had changed dramatically and for the worse. The next day news came through of the shooting down on its final approach to Kigali Airport of the Rwandese presidential plane and the consequent deaths of the presidents of both Rwanda and Burundi, who had been returning from Arusha where a decision to move ahead with the formation of a government of national unity had finally been taken. This news was rapidly followed by the first reports of mayhem having broken out in Kigali, with the massacre beginning of its Tutsi citizens and also of Hutu moderates, both by elements in the armed forces and by the ruling party's paramilitary militia known as the Interahamwe. Incitement to further killing was pouring forth from local radio stations, in particular one under government control – Radio Mille Collines. Among the first victims of the massacre was the (Tutsi) prime minister-designate in the proposed government of national unity and her bodyguard of Belgian UN peacekeeping troops. The Security Council met the next day (7 April) and immediately issued a presidential statement appealing to all Rwandese to desist from further acts of violence. It was an inadequate response to a situation whose full horror had yet to dawn on the members of the Council. In the margins of that first consultation I was approached by a troubled Madeleine Albright. She said that her instructions from Washington were to propose the immediate withdrawal of the peacekeeping force, its whole rationale and mandate having been invalidated by the events of the previous day. What did I think? I said I thought that would really not do. The peacekeeping force might not be able to carry on with its original mandate, but it might be able to perform some humanitarian tasks and to save lives. The UK would not be supporting any request for withdrawal. Could she not get her instructions changed? This she duly did, since she agreed with the analysis; and the proposal to withdraw was never put forward.

From that day onwards the Security Council met on an almost daily basis for informal consultations, attempting, unsuccessfully, to find an adequate response to the crisis. It was the most agonising and dispiriting process in which I have ever participated. The existing peacekeeping force soon began to collapse. The Belgian government, traumatised by the killing of their troops who had been guarding the prime minister-designate, withdrew their battalion without more ado. They too favoured withdrawal of the whole force to cover up their own embarrassment. The Secretary-General declined to follow that route, and he tried to persuade them at least to leave their equipment for any replacement troops he could find. This request was rejected. Then the

Bangladeshi battalion was also withdrawn, leaving only the stalwart Ghanaians and the Force Commander, General Roméo Dallaire, together with a group of unarmed military observers.

The Security Council and the Secretary-General were faced with two challenges: the first was to identify an effective and timely policy response to the unfolding disaster; the second to find troop contributors who would back such a response. To meet the first challenge without meeting the second would have been largely academic but, in truth, not even that was achieved. Some in the Council, and, at moments too, the Secretary-General favoured a full-blooded military enforcement operation under Chapter VII of the Charter. But the military arguments against that were quite compelling. The UN did not even control the one means of rapid access to the country, Kigali airport; and full-scale fighting between the government forces and the RPF had resumed as soon as the massacres began, with the RPF forces gradually establishing a stranglehold on Kigali, prior to capturing it, and controlling a steadily expanding amount of the country. In any case, in the aftermath of the debacle in Mogadishu six months before, there were simply no takers among potential troop contributors for an enforcement operation. No one seeking to understand the policy paralysis that overtook the Security Council, even when faced with what was clearly genocide, can afford to ignore the heavy shadow of Somalia which hung over the Council throughout its deliberations in the spring of 1994. The second US attempt to define a new mandate was not much better than the first. They favoured deploying a new force of peacekeepers, but exclusively outside Rwanda to protect the floods of refugees who were fleeing the fighting and the massacres into Tanzania, Burundi and Zaire. But the killing was going on inside Rwanda and it was evident that such a concept of operations would be largely irrelevant. There remained the option of strengthening the existing UN force in Kigali and hoping that this would enable it to expand its humanitarian efforts. But even that option, despite constant and desperate attempts at persuasion by the Secretary-General, speaking daily to many different heads of government, found no takers. That was the context within which the Security Council finally, as a stopgap measure until new troop contributors could be found, adopted Resolution 912 of 21 April. This resolution consolidated the small remaining UN peacekeeping force in Kigali and adjusted its mandate to the appalling circumstances in which it found itself. It has subsequently been castigated as a pusillanimous decision to withdraw two-thirds of the original force. In reality it was nothing of the sort; two-thirds of the force had already been withdrawn by the action of the troop-contributing governments.

By the middle of May, thanks largely to the activities of the international media, the full extent of the massacres that had been going on in Rwanda was apparent and was beginning to shift opinion in a number of capitals, which brought forward tentative offers of troops for a strengthened peacekeeping force. Security Council Resolution 918 of 17 May expanded the force to 5,500 troops, and extended its mandate to 'contribute to the security and protection of displaced persons, refugees and civilians at risk in Rwanda' and to 'provide security and support for the distribution of relief supplies and humanitarian relief operations'. It also recognised that 'the mission may be required to take action in self-defence against persons or groups who threaten protected sites and populations'. This looked good on paper, but on the ground the reinforcements were slow in arriving and the expanded force was not fully operational until early July, by which time Kigali and much of the country was in the hands of the RPF, the previous government of Rwanda had collapsed and hundreds of thousands of Hutu refugees were streaming towards and across the border with Zaire. In the same resolution the Council imposed an arms embargo on Rwanda which, apart from being an unprecedented step under which the Council took action under Chapter VII of the Charter against one of its own members (Rwanda, alone, voting against the imposition of an arms embargo), was very much a case of locking the stable door a long time after the horse had bolted.

This same resolution (918 of 17 May) also opened up the issue of bringing the perpetrators of the genocide to justice. The Secretary-General was requested to submit a report as soon as possible 'on the investigation of serious violations of international humanitarian law committed in Rwanda during the conflict'. Thereafter this process followed the same course as in the former Yugoslavia: the Secretary-General's report was submitted on 31 May, and Security Council Resolution 935 of 1 July requested the Secretary-General to establish an impartial Commission of Experts 'to examine and analyse information ... including evidence of possible acts of genocide'; then Security Council Resolution 955 of 8 November established an International Tribunal for Rwanda and, telescoping the earlier processes in respect of the former Yugoslavia, at the same time adopted the statute of the tribunal. This last resolution provoked a negative vote from Rwanda, now represented on the Council by the RPF-led government, which wanted to handle the whole process of retribution itself and which objected to the invariable UN practice of precluding the death penalty.

The collapse of the Hutu-led government of Rwanda and the massive exodus of Hutu refugees towards and into Zaire raised the spectre of another humanitarian disaster. It was clear that the reinforced UN peacekeeping force was not going to be deployed in time to do anything effective to manage the situation and to protect civilians. At this point the French government, which had so far lain low since the crisis broke with the death of their main Rwandese protégé, the previous president, and the involvement of the regime they had supported for so long in the massacres which followed, launched an initiative to deploy an interposition force between the retreating Hutu and the advancing RPF troops to allow the exodus of refugees to take place in reasonably orderly conditions. This initiative was far from welcome to a number of members of the Security Council. Not only were the French deeply suspect, to the RPF in particular, as having propped up for years the Hutu-led regime which was in the process of being overthrown; but it was also clear that, while an interposition force might save the lives of many fleeing Hutu civilians, it was also likely to provide an opportunity for members of the Rwandese armed forces and their paramilitary allies, the Interahamwe, to escape across the border and live to fight another day. The majority in the Council, including Britain, Spain and the USA, took the view that, however difficult the decision was, it would be quite irresponsible to reject any initiative which might reduce the number of innocent civilians losing their lives. But it was a very bare majority, with Brazil, China, New Zealand, Nigeria and Pakistan abstaining and only ten votes in favour. Security Council Resolution 929 of 22 June thus authorised what was called by the French 'Operation Turquoise'; the deployment went ahead rapidly; and the exodus of refugees, with the mixed consequences already foreseen but without any major new killings, was completed as the RPF forces assumed control of the whole of Rwanda.

As has already been apparent, a minor, purely New York subplot to these horrendous events was the presence of Rwanda on the Security Council. A country which was on the receiving end of a UN peacekeeping mission should never have been appointed to the Council in the first place. But the African system of rotating their three representatives on the Council did not permit any fine tuning of that sort; since the African group at the UN only put forward three names for three places, the rest of the membership did not have any say in the matter. Once disaster struck at the beginning of April, the Rwandese ambassador became a sullen but largely silent spectator at the Council discussions. Attempts were made by the rest of the Council to use him as a channel to bring pressure to bear on his government to stop the killings and to close down the incitements to further violence flowing out of Radio Mille Collines. But it rapidly became clear that the ambassador's influence in, indeed his capacity to communicate at all with, Kigali was close to zero. As things on the ground went from bad to worse, some desultory consideration was given to the possibility of suspending Rwanda from membership of the Council. But there were neither provisions or precedents for this; and many members of the Council, including some of the permanent members, were hesitant about going down that road. Eventually our hand was forced by the imminence of Rwanda assuming the monthly rotating presidency of the Council, which was due in September. A procedural decision was taken on 25 August to remove Rwanda temporarily from the presidency, it being reinstated in December, by which time its Ambassador in New York represented the new RPF-led government in Kigali.

Anyone who has lived through the period of these events in Rwanda and occupied a position of responsibility with respect to them, as I did, is bound to have to try to answer the question of whether the UN could have done any better than it did, whether the genocide could have been prevented or cut short. It certainly could not have done much worse than it did. Pretty well every aspect of the response was ineffective and inadequate. Even the Security Council's frequently reiterated calls for a ceasefire, totally unheeded by both sides, were really beside the point because the majority of the loss of life was not being caused by the fighting between the armed forces of the two sides but by the massacre of unarmed civilians in the parts of Rwanda controlled by the Hutu-led government. Does the finger of blame point at any particular actor or institution? Much of this was covered by the subsequent Commission of Enquiry set up by the UN and I would not wish to trespass onto the ground of its findings or to seek to vary them. But it does seem to me that what occurred was in fact a massive collective act of failure by the international community and by the policies and institutions which it had established under the Charter of the UN and the Genocide

Convention of 1948. Could it have been otherwise? Given the careful planning which we now know went into the advance planning of the genocide and given the speed with which a huge amount of the killing actually took place, I would be very cautious about any assertion that, once the sequence had begun, a disaster of major proportions could have been avoided, although its scale and duration could have been reduced. So it is on the prevention of such catastrophes in the first place rather than on their handling once they occur that the international community needs to concentrate its efforts. But that is a story for a later chapter in this book.

Haiti: Aristide restored

In the early months of the year the deadlock over Haiti showed no signs of shifting. The military regime of General Cedras remained in power, with many reports of serious human rights abuses emerging. The UN sanctions, not very effectively observed or enforced, in so far as they had an effect, further crippled the poorest economy in Latin America and seemed to be exerting no pressure on the governing elite, who found ways of evading them; and the flow of asylum seekers across the Caribbean to the USA continued unchecked, indeed was reinforced by economic migrants fleeing the impoverishment resulting from sanctions. Pressure mounted, particularly in the USA, for more drastic action to be taken. But this was far from straightforward. For one thing the United States had been traumatised by its experience in Somalia, which contributed, as we have seen in the previous chapter, to the fiasco in Haiti over the failure to deploy in October 1993 a UN peacekeeping force to implement the Governors Island agreement; there was little appetite for mounting a multi-national enforcement operation, not least at a time when proposals for mounting a similar sort of operation in Rwanda were falling on sterile ground. Moreover, Haiti only fitted awkwardly, if indeed it fitted at all, into the framework laid down in Chapter VII of the UN Charter. It was not easy to see how the events in Haiti – the overthrow of Aristide after a democratic election supervised by the UN and the unilateral rejection of the Governors Island agreement by the military regime – deplorable though they were, could be deemed to constitute a threat to international peace and security. This hurdle had initially been overcome, when economic sanctions had been

imposed, by the legerdemain of treating the refugee exodus as constituting such a threat. But would it stretch to authorising a military intervention, given in particular the visceral dislike in Latin America for US
military interventions in their region? These difficult policy issues were
debated extensively, not so much in the Security Council itself as in an
informal group known as 'the friends of Haiti', whose leading lights
were the USA, France, Canada and the two Latin American members
of the Council – Argentina and Brazil. Britain, which had virtually no
interests in or knowledge of Haiti, stayed on the sidelines; but we kept
abreast of what was going on.

The first upshot of the debate and of the response to the calls for
more robust action was contained in Security Council Resolution 917
of 6 May. This resolution considerably strengthened the sanctions
regime and sought to do so in particular in ways which would impact
directly on the coup leaders and the military. A civil air embargo on all
flights other than scheduled commercial passenger flights was imposed;
an international travel ban was placed on the Haitian military and
police and their families and all participants in the 1991 coup; states
were urged to freeze the assets of all those categories of people covered
by the travel ban; and measures to enforce the economic sanctions were
authorised. The same resolution also set out clearly and fully what
would need to be done if the measures were to be suspended, including the retirement of Cedras and his police chief, other changes in the
upper ranks of the military and the police, full implementation of the
Governors Island agreement, including the return of President Aristide,
and the deployment of a UN mission. This extremely tough resolution
was adopted by unanimity; but it did not have the desired effect, and
the deadlock on the ground persisted.

The Security Council's next move, Security Council Resolution 940
of 31 July, carried it right across the Rubicon of authorising the use of
force. The somewhat shaky legal framework was buttressed by recognising 'the unique character of the present situation in Haiti and its
deteriorating, complex and extraordinary nature, requiring an exceptional response'. The support of the Secretary-General for action under
Chapter VII was prayed in aid. And the formation of a multi-national
force 'to use all necessary means to facilitate the departure from Haiti
of the military leadership . . . the prompt return of the democratically
elected president . . . and to establish and maintain a secure and stable
environment that will permit the implementation of the Governors

Island Agreement' was authorised. This resolution, unlike its predecessors, was not passed by unanimity, there being abstentions by Brazil and China. For the Brazilians, obnoxious though they undoubtedly found the Cedras regime, voting in favour of a US-led military enforcement operation was simply a bridge too far. Their abstention was, however, explained in muted and non-confrontational terms by their dour but highly professional ambassador Ronaldo Sardenberg; and the vote in favour of the resolution by Argentina, the other Latin American country currently on the Council, meant that the regional attitude was split rather than negative. The Chinese abstention reflected rather more than their customary distaste for what they regarded as excessively interventionist policies. There was a Taiwan twist to the tale. Haiti was one of the small group of Caribbean and Central American countries which still recognised Taiwan; and Aristide had unwisely made some approving public reference to Taiwan. This provoked the threat of a Chinese veto which was only lifted after receipt of a suitably grovelling apology, the suitability of the first effort by the Haitians having been judged insufficient by the Chinese and a second even more comprehensive retraction having been dictated by them. This strange episode threw some light on the limits of Chinese efforts to present a smiling and positive face at the UN (limits which were even more sharply underlined, some years later, by their veto on the prolongation of the UN peacekeeping operation in Macedonia on similar grounds); it was not behaviour that any of the so-called 'imperialist' powers could ever have got away with.

The USA was in no rush to launch the enforcement operation that had now been authorised. On the contrary, very wisely, they did all they could to use the authorisation contained in Security Council Resolution 940 to preclude the need for any actual use of force. They brought into play the good offices of a group which included former President Carter and the former Chairman of the Joint Chiefs of Staff, Colin Powell, to try to persuade Cedras and his associates to give in without a fight. At first these efforts too seemed to have failed, but then, when the troops of the intervention force were actually emplaning, Cedras blinked and was flown into exile. The multi-national force was deployed to Haiti on 19 September; and shortly afterwards President Aristide was restored. Security Council Resolution 944 of 29 September terminated all the sanctions imposed on Haiti; and Security Council Resolution 964 of 29 November authorised the deployment of a UN force to take over from the multi-national force. The story of the UN's subsequent all-too-brief and inadequate involvement in Haiti lies outside the period covered by this account. Suffice it to say that it was a copybook example of the inadequacy of the instruments and policies available to the UN for post-conflict peacebuilding and for handling the case of a state after it had failed.

Iraq: a border scare and a border settled

1994 was not quite such a trouble-free year in the Security Council's handling of the post-war settlement in Iraq as 1993 had been. In particular Iraq's refusal to accept the demarcation of the Iraq–Kuwait border by the UN Commission remained a cause of concern, and the friction over the work of UNSCOM in ridding Iraq of its weapons of mass destruction was endemic. In early October the Iraqi Revolutionary Command Council issued a statement threatening to withdraw its cooperation with UNSCOM and Iraqi troop movements took place towards the border with Kuwait; both developments sharply raised the tension. Following a presidential statement by the Security Council on 8 October in response to these developments, the Council on 15 October adopted Resolution 949, which condemned the recent Iraqi military deployments in the direction of the border with Kuwait, and demanded that Iraq complete the withdrawal of all military units recently deployed to the south and that it should not again use its military forces in a hostile or provocative manner.

This resolution, which was adopted by unanimity, demonstrated yet again how effective firm Security Council action could be. Indeed the mere process of negotiating this resolution had precipitated a reversal of Iraq's original deployment to the south which was recognised in the text of the resolution itself when it spoke of 'completing the withdrawal' of Iraq's units. But the negotiation of the resolution also marked a further stage in the widening of the gap between the USA and the UK on the one hand and France and Russia on the other. The original draft of the resolution favoured by the USA and the UK would have imposed on Iraq a mandatory obligation to notify to the UN any troop movements in an area contiguous to the Kuwaiti and Saudi frontiers, but this provision had to be dropped due to French opposition. And a last minute Russian attempt to abort the resolution entirely on the grounds that the Russian foreign minister Andrei Kozyrev had been to Baghdad and had secured Saddam Hussein's agreement to reverse his troop deployments also had to be fended off. In any event in the short term the outcome of the whole episode was entirely satisfactory in that not only were the Iraqi troop deployments reversed but a month later Iraq, in the form of a Revolutionary Command Council decision of 10 November, signed by Saddam Hussein, and coupled with a similar resolution from the Iraqi National Assembly, confirmed its irrevocable and unqualified recognition of the international boundary as demarcated by the UN Commission. This development brought a rare signal of approval from the Security Council which described it as 'a significant step in the direction towards implementing the relevant Council resolutions'.

Other African trouble spots (Mozambique, South Africa, Angola, Somalia): a patchy record

The events in Rwanda, described earlier in this chapter, were by no means the only African problems which forced their way onto the Security Council's agenda in 1994; nor did the UN's abject failure in that country typify its performance in the continent as a whole. In Mozambique a complex peacekeeping operation was brought to a successful conclusion with free and fair elections whose outcome was accepted by the rebel movement which was defeated at the polls. In South Africa a process, driven admittedly more by internal dynamics than by the intervention of the UN, which was, in the later stages, a marginal player, resulted in a multi-racial, democratically elected government replacing the previous apartheid regime and in the healing of a wound which had troubled the UN almost from the time of its establishment. In Angola, a peacekeeping operation which had remained on care and maintenance since it broke down in 1992 showed some, admittedly uncertain and in the end misleading, signs of revival. Only in Somalia was there failure almost as abject as that in Rwanda, although in the short term less costly in human lives.

The success of the Mozambique peacekeeping operation, both in terms of peace and security and of the subsequent revival of the Mozambican economy, and its relatively trouble-free history have resulted, as is so often the case, in its being virtually forgotten. But it certainly did not seem like a sure thing at the time, and there were plenty of alarms and excursions along the way. Security Council Resolution 898 of 23 February authorised rather grudgingly the deployment of a civilian police element as part of the peacekeeping force, an element which was becoming more and more standard in UN operations following a civil war but one which presented even more daunting problems over recruitment than did the military side of things. The feeling of overstretch was reflected in a request to the Secretary-General for a timetable for winding down the operation at a moment still many months before the all-important elections for a president and parliament were to be held. And the chief concern about the whole operation, the slowness of both government and rebel troops to move to their assembly points and to begin the process of demobilisation and the formation of a national army drawn from both groups, was heavily emphasised. The next Resolution, 916 of 5 May, with the agreement of all parties, firmly established the date for national elections as 27–28 October. Then in August a Security Council mission was sent to Maputo to bring the full weight of the international community's concerns to bear in the runup to the elections. This diplomatic tool of the despatch of a Security Council mission, which was to be increasingly used in the years to come, was at first greatly undervalued in London, and I would freely admit that I contributed to that undervaluation myself, failing to recognise how such missions could do something to remedy the otherwise excessively bureaucratic and other-worldly impression created by Security Council policy-making in New York.

The October elections passed off peacefully, an outcome which I watched with even greater trepidation than usual as I had a son, a fluent Portuguese speaker from his time at university in Brazil, working as part of the UN election team in the north of the country, at Nampula. As the results came in, and it became clear that the government party, Frelimo, had won relatively narrowly both the presidential and the parliamentary elections, the attitude and response of the former rebels (Renamo) and of their leader Dhlakama was clearly going to be crucial. The sequence of events in Angola in 1992 when Savimbi's UNITA rebels had challenged the election results and civil war had resumed was, of course, at the front of everyone's minds. For some hours Renamo's response remained in doubt. But concerted international pressure, including that from Renamo's former South African sponsors in Pretoria, finally brought about acceptance of the outcome. Security

Council Resolution 960 of 21 November endorsed the Secretary-General's judgement that the elections had been free and fair, the Council having already, even before that, in Resolution 957 of 15 November, chivvied him urgently to bring forward a schedule for the withdrawal of the peacekeeping troops. The whole operation in fact wound down with great rapidity; and on this occasion, although not in a number of others, it did so without any damage to the security, stability and reconstruction of the country.

The UN's involvement in South Africa was much less than in Mozambique even if its stake in a successful outcome to the first ever multi-racial elections there was much greater. This was no peacekeeping operation, merely assistance with an election process which was entirely in the hands of the South Africans themselves. Security Council Resolution 894 of 14 January encouraged the Secretary-General to help coordinate the various teams of election monitors who were flooding in from the Commonwealth, the EU, the USA and elsewhere. Then, following the election of Nelson Mandela as president, Security Council Resolution 919 of 25 May lifted the arms embargo and all other UN measures against South Africa and wound up the Security Council Committee tasked to oversee these. The resolution concluded without the usual, ritual reference to the Security Council 'remaining seized of the matter'; and in my own statement at the Council meeting I expressed the hope that South Africa would never again figure on the Security Council's agenda. It was a moment of great elation.

Ever since the breakdown in 1992 of the earlier peace agreement in Angola (known as the Bicesse Accords), the UN had been trying to put the pieces together again and to persuade the two warring parties, the Government of Angola and the UNITA movement, to agree to a durable cessation of hostilities and to power-sharing arrangements. The obstacles in the way of reaching any such agreement were formidable, even if the external support for UNITA had sharply reduced over the intervening period as a result of developments in South Africa. The two parties each had no confidence in the good faith of the other in implementing any agreements reached; both parties had access to sufficient resources to continue the armed struggle – the government from increasing levels of production of offshore oil, UNITA from illicit diamond sales; and both believed in the possibility of and hankered after a military solution to the dispute. Despite all that, 1994 saw a major renewed effort to negotiate a peace deal, supported by most of Angola's neighbours who were adversely affected by the continued fighting and focussed around a series of negotiating sessions in the Zambian capital, Lusaka. The UN did all it could, both through the active involvement in the Lusaka negotiations themselves of a new special representative of the Secretary-General, Alioune Blondin Beye, and through the external pressure brought to bear by the Security Council, to bring matters to a successful conclusion.

A series of Security Council Resolutions, beginning with Resolution 903 of 16 March, fell into a familiar pattern. The parties were urged to redouble their efforts in the Lusaka negotiations; some modest strengthening of the UN's currently exiguous presence in Angola was promised as soon as an agreement was struck; and the threat of an increase in the mandatory economic sanctions against UNITA, first referred to in Security Council Resolution 864 of 1993, was brandished but suspended in view of the ongoing negotiations. When the mandate of the UN's force in Angola (UN Angola Verification Mission II; UNAVEM II) was renewed for a further two months (Security Council Resolution 922 of 31 May), a note of impatience was struck with reference to reconsidering the whole role of the UN in Angola if the Lusaka negotiations were not concluded by the end of that period. When the end of June arrived without the negotiations being concluded, a further three-month extension of UNAVEM II's mandate was agreed (Security Resolution 932 of 30 June); and a deadline of 31 July was set for imposing more sanctions against UNITA if the movement had not by then accepted the proposals for national reconciliation put forward by Blondin Beye (which had already been accepted by the government side). This end-of-July deadline for UNITA was subsequently extended to the end of August (Presidential Statement of 12 August). On 5 September a positive response to Blondin Beye's proposals from UNITA was considered to have opened the way for the conclusion of a full settlement (Presidential Statement of 9 September); and further short extensions to UNAVEM II's mandate were agreed in September and October (Security Council Resolutions 945 of 29 September and 952 of 27 October). Finally the text of a full settlement was initialled by the parties in Lusaka on 31 October and signed on 20 November, with a ceasefire to enter into effect on 22 November. These developments were warmly welcomed in Security Council Resolution 966 of 8 December, which authorised the Secretary-General to restore UNAVEM II to its previously mandated strength and encouraged him to come forward with new proposals for the sort of full UN peacekeeping force which would be needed to administer and help to implement the agreement reached in Lusaka. Any hopes, however, that the Angolan situation was about to take a decisive turn for the better were soon dashed. The cease-fire did not hold; the Lusaka agreements were never implemented; and several more years of civil war ensued until the death of Savimbi in a bombing raid on his headquarters in 2002 and the subsequent collapse of UNITA at last brought one of Africa's bloodiest conflicts to a conclusion. Diplomats and mediators like to say of every dispute that a military solution is either unrealistic or unsustainable, and they are often right. But Angola was an exception to that rule, even if many Angolans had to die to prove it.

With the benefit of hindsight it is clear that the UN's operation in Somalia was doomed to failure once the USA had announced the withdrawal of its troops, which was completed in the first quarter of 1994. At the time, however, it was still hoped that something useful could be saved by persevering with a more classic type of peacekeeping operation. This transformation was set out in Security Council Resolution 897 of 4 February. The mandate was redefined in much more consensual terms, emphasising the need to encourage and assist the Somalis to work together to achieve disarmament, to protect ports and airports vital to the provision of humanitarian assistance, to assist in the reorganisation of the police and the judicial system and, above all, to assist what was described as 'the ongoing political process in Somalia, which should culminate in the installation of a democratically elected government'. The problem was that no such process was in fact ongoing; rather it was going round in circles and getting nowhere while fighting continued on the ground and UN troops continued from time to time to be targeted by one or other of the factions. The UN would assemble as many Somali faction leaders as possible in some foreign capital – Addis Ababa or Nairobi – and would try to get them, with mixed success, to agree on the way ahead and the need to cooperate and would then watch the whole process disintegrate as soon as the participants had returned to their home ground. The UN's efforts at humanitarian relief and at post-conflict reconstruction were stymied by the fact that security conditions hampered any meaningful development activity. Security Council Resolution 923 of 31 May renewed the mandate of what was called UNOSOM II (United Nations Operation in Somalia II), but only for a period of four months rather than the traditional six,

demonstrating waning confidence that the operation could be successfully completed.

By the early autumn the will to continue with what was a large, elaborate and costly peacekeeping operation, which was getting nowhere,
was rapidly ebbing away. On 22 August, in a particularly serious incident, seven Indian peacekeepers were ambushed and killed, thus
reminding troop contributors that their soldiers were at serious risk to
no good purpose. When the mandate came up for renewal at the end
of September (Security Council Resolution 946 of 30 September), it
was prolonged for a single month only. And the Security Council began
contemplating the sending of a mission of its members to see the situation on the ground. At this point, as I took over the presidency of the
Security Council for the month of October, I had a private conversation with the Secretary-General. I said it seemed to me that a decision
to wind down and withdraw the UN operation was unavoidable.
Boutros-Ghali did not disagree. In that case, I said, it was surely important for all the UN institutions to act in concert and to share the responsibility for a painful and humiliating decision. If he would come and
brief the Council frankly on the prospects and the options, I believed
we would get a consensus on the need for withdrawal. Boutros-Ghali,
unwisely in my view, declined to do that, arguing that any decision to
withdraw was a matter for the Council alone, for which it should
assume full responsibility. On 20 October the Security Council decided
to send a mission to Somalia and agreed guidelines for its despatch
which leaned heavily towards withdrawal. And on 4 November, following the return of the mission, the Council unanimously adopted
Security Council Resolution 954, setting 31 March 1995 as the end date
for the operation. It was a sorry end to a massive, and at first successful, humanitarian operation which had begun with such promise.

*   *   *   *

So much for what were the main components for the UN's activity in
another hectically busy period. But much more than that, which there
is not space to describe here in detail, was crowding the agenda. In
Guatemala, UN human rights monitors were deployed in an attempt to
control paramilitary killings and abuses by the armed forces.

A mini-crisis in the Yemen, when the formerly separate South Yemen
tried to break away again with some relatively low-key sympathy from

Saudi Arabia, Oman and the UK, was brought to a peaceful conclusion largely thanks to the skilful diplomacy of Lakhdar Brahimi, the UN Secretary-General's special envoy and a former Algerian foreign minister, making the first of his many appearances as a UN peace facilitator, mediator or special representative (he was subsequently to play one or other of these roles in Haiti, in Afghanistan, in Iraq and in the Sudan).

A renewed effort to move towards a settlement in Cyprus, this time through the negotiation of confidence-building measures, which would have returned a small amount of territory to the Greek Cypriots and would have reopened Nicosia Airport to use by both sides, foundered after lengthy and complex negotiations on what I described at the time as 'a new variant of the Cyprus two-step, when one steps forward, the other steps back'.

Voter registration for a referendum on the territory's future finally got under way in the Western Sahara, although expectations of that ever taking place were not high: 'The possibility of a referendum being held in 1995 shimmers like a mirage. It may well prove just that'. It did.

A UN Summit Conference on Population was held in Cairo and despite public clashes over abortion and family planning, and the bizarre spectacle of an unholy alliance against birth control between the Vatican and Islamic fundamentalists led by Iran, reached some useful conclusions, including increased funding for the UN's family planning agency.

Moreover, alongside the frustratingly sterile discussions over the possible enlargement of the Security Council, which ran on throughout the year without making any progress, tentative moves got under way to address some of the more glaring systemic weaknesses of the UN system. The Security Council itself, tiring of waiting for the outcome of the enlargement debate, introduced a number of changes designed to increase the transparency of its proceedings (advance publication of agendas, better briefing for the wider membership on the outcome of meetings). It also addressed a major and legitimate grievance of troop contributors to UN peacekeeping operations who were not members of the Council that they were not properly briefed or given a sufficient opportunity to comment on changes in the mandate which could be of crucial importance to the troops they had put at the UN's disposal. A system of consultation meetings in advance of mandate renewals between the senior Secretariat officials responsible for peacekeeping, the members of the Council and the representatives of the troop contributors was instituted on an initiative by New Zealand. Negotiations also began on the hugely sensitive issue of the calculation and assessment of contributions to the UN budget. While the regular budget, which covered everything but peacekeeping, had been broadly stable in real terms and gave rise to relatively little controversy, the peacekeeping budget had grown exponentially with the burgeoning worldwide of peacekeeping operations. The slowness with which the method of calculation took account of shifts in relative prosperity between member states was a particular source of complaint. Changes which would result in some reduction of the US share, a major object of Congressional criticism, and an increase, among others, in the Japanese share began to be discussed. And, for the first time, attention began to be given to ways in which regional organisations with responsibilities for peace and security (bodies such as the EU, the CSCE, the OAS, the OAU) could work more closely with the UN and could strengthen and be strengthened by its work in those fields. The UN Secretariat held a first conference to discuss these issues with the organisations in question and, although little came out of it immediately, a seed had been planted. The UK and Nigerian governments launched a joint initiative at the UN to consider ways in which African peacekeeping efforts could be reinforced by support from the developed countries for training and equipment of African peacekeeping troops and their speedier deployment. A series of proposals to this effect were passed to the Secretary-General and formed the basis for much future work in this field, particularly once the OAU had in July 2002 metamorphosed into the more effective and better organised African Union (AU).

But, when all was said and done, my contemporary judgement on 1994 that it had been another tough year for the UN must be right: 'More things went wrong than went right. Public support for the UN weakened, most notably in the USA. The organisation approaches its 50th jubilee year in 1995 more in a state of mid-life crisis than of triumph and assurance'. The triple failures in Bosnia, in Rwanda and in Somalia weighed heavily in the balance: 'The Bosnian poison continues to circulate in the veins and to debilitate every international organisation involved, the UN, NATO, the EU and the CSCE'. Not only would finding a way forward on Bosnia be a key priority for 1995, but it was also clear that some adjustment to policy on Iraq would be needed if splits between the P5 of the Security Council were not to widen even further. 'A controlled shift of policy that leaves Saddam Hussein on a short, tight leash is probably achievable' was the best guess at the time, which proved, at least partially, correct.

By the end of 1994, Boutros-Ghali was more than half way through what it was already clear he wanted to be only his first term of office. Although the campaign for a second term was not yet fully under way, it was beginning to dominate his personal agenda. I remarked at the time on his formidable resilience; but also that his position had weakened quite a bit in the last year and that he had begun to travel too much, losing some grip on the decision-making process: 'Re-election will not be a shoo-in'. One major weakness had by that time become clear and that was in his relationship with the Security Council. Boutros-Ghali had, of course, never served as a member of the Council, and I felt that he never really understood how it worked and how its collective thinking evolved and could be influenced by the Secretary-General. His predecessor, Perez de Cuellar, who had served on the Council before he became Secretary-General, used to spend many hours simply listening to Council discussions, testing the way opinions were moving and talking quietly in the margins to its members; Boutros-Ghali had neither the time nor the patience for that. But nor was he prepared for any other senior member of his staff to fill the vacuum. Indeed he explicitly forbade his Under-Secretaries-General to attend informal consultations of the Council, which infuriated the members who, not unreasonably, expected to be able to conduct a dialogue with the Secretariat on the many issues on the agenda. Faced with growing complaints, Boutros-Ghali appointed one of his senior advisers (Chinmaya Gharekan) to attend consultations on a regular basis but, since Gharekan had no executive responsibility for peacekeeping or conflict prevention or humanitarian affairs and had to consult those who did when policy issues were raised, that was not much of an improvement.

Chapter IX

1995: Recessional

There was no doubting the down-beat mood at the UN as a new year began, following the setbacks of 1994. This mood was perhaps reasonably well captured in a note I wrote at that time: 'The triumph of the Gulf War and the success of several other UN missions stand in the deep shadow cast by Bosnia, Somalia and Rwanda. The pendulum which swung too far towards euphoria after the Gulf War has swung too far towards despair. From being an organisation which was wrongly thought capable of solving everything, the UN now tends, equally wrongly, to be regarded as incapable of solving anything'. The failed peacekeeping mission in Somalia was in the final stages of being wound down and the country left to its own anarchic devices. Bosnia festered. The possibility of a resumed peacekeeping operation in Angola remained just that, a possibility, throughout the year, before the country slid back yet again into resumed civil war. The Security Council tried to grapple with, but eventually flinched away from any direct involvement in, the worsening security situation on Rwanda's western border in the massive refugee camps established there, after the Hutu exodus from Rwanda. These refugee camps fell rapidly into the grip of the Interahamwe militia of Hutu extremists and thus represented a threat to the new government in Kigali. Attempts to organise an international response came up against a firm refusal by President Mobutu to give his consent for any UN peacekeeping presence in the camps, despite the increasingly destabilising effect they were having on the eastern regions of Zaire, and also against the continuing reluctance of the main potential troop contributors to take on such a messy and high-risk situation. The possibility of international intervention was much talked about at the beginning of the year but never materialised, perhaps the worst combination imaginable.

Iraq: oil for food

I had been arguing for some time towards the end of 1994 in favour of the need for some controlled shift in our sanctions policy towards Iraq, if we were not to be confronted fairly soon by an uncontrolled shift, as international support for the draconian sanctions regime currently in force ebbed away. The increasing sufferings of the Iraqi civilian population, carefully orchestrated by the regime but none-the-less real for all that, were undermining both wider public support and support in the Security Council. At the same time, the so far incomplete implementation of UNSCOM's mission to rid Iraq of all its weapons of mass destruction and Iraq's continuing policy of obfuscation and of playing cat and mouse with the UNSCOM inspectors pointed towards maintaining reasonably tough sanctions. This shift in policy came to be known as 'building a bigger cage for Saddam'. There was little trouble convincing London of the validity of this approach. Washington, where the usual tug of war between hawks and doves was endemic, was another matter. But by the early months of 1995 the USA too had been convinced, and Madeleine Albright and I received instructions to begin negotiating an oil-for-food scheme similar to the one that had been endorsed by the Security Council in 1991 in Security Council Resolutions 706 and 712, and which had subsequently run into the sands as a result of Iraq's refusal in their negotiations with the UN Secretariat to accept satisfactorily water-tight implementing provisions (a fuller account is given in Chapter V). On this occasion we were joined from the outset of the Security Council negotiations, as co-sponsors, by Argentina, whose able and hard-driving ambassador Emilio Cardenas proved an invaluable go-between with those members of the Council who were more favourable to Iraq's attempts to influence the outcome.

The negotiations were long and complex, because the basic subject matter was complicated, not because of policy problems in the Council. In fact the underlying political consensus there for the shift of policy proposed was clear from an early stage. The members of the Council who traditionally argued at each periodical 60-day review of sanctions for their impact on the civilian population to be eased (France, Russia, China and most of the non-permanent members) were pleased that the scheme proposed would, if implemented by the Iraqis, have that effect. No one suggested that Iraq's compliance with the WMD provisions of Resolution 687 was satisfactory or even near complete (and revelations a few months later when two of Saddam Hussein's sons-in-law fled to Jordan and revealed the full extent of the biological warfare programme, whose very existence had been contested by the Iraqis up to that point, strengthened that view); nor did any member of the Council contest that full compliance was essential and required the continued imposition of sanctions. Moreover, it was clear that the quantitative limits on sales of Iraqi oil set out in the resolution (1 billion dollars-worth every three months) could be varied if the Council so wished (in fact the whole concept of a quantitative limit was eventually scrapped at a much later date). So Security Council Resolution 986 of 14 April when it was finally agreed was adopted by unanimity.

The main technical problems which arose in the negotiations were two: the direction of Iraq's main oil exports; and the system for the distribution within Iraq of humanitarian supplies purchased with monies from the UN escrow account into which the proceeds of oil sales had to be paid. Both problems were replete with political aspects which resulted in much frantic lobbying by the Iraqis. The bulk of Iraq's oil exports, apart from crude oil and oil products exported by truck to neighbouring countries, were carried by two pipeline terminals, one at Mina Al-Bakr on the Gulf and the other at the end of the Kirkuk-Yumurtalik pipeline at the Turkish Mediterranean port of Ceyhan. The Turks were determined that the Iraqis should be required under the resolution to export more than half of the quantities covered by the scheme from Ceyhan. They were extremely keen to recoup the substantial losses they had incurred by closing the pipeline from Kirkuk as soon as Iraq invaded Kuwait in 1990 and a UN embargo on oil exports was imposed. They also suspected that, if the Iraqis had unfettered control over the choice of terminals, they would use negotiations over the amounts to go through the pipeline to Ceyhan as a means of leverage on the Turkish government to secure their acquiescence in the evasion of sanctions. The Iraqis were equally keen to have a free hand over the choice of terminals, not least because the Mina al-Bakr terminal, which was entirely under their control, would offer the greater scope for sanctions evasion. The co-sponsors of the resolution were firmly on the Turkish side of the argument and, despite some Iraqi success in their lobbying of other members of the Council, the text of the resolution required 'the larger share' of the exports to go through the pipeline from Kirkuk.

The second problem, over the distribution of humanitarian supplies, was equally sensitive, involving as it did both arrangements within those parts of Iraq where the regime's writ ran and the division of the total amount available between those parts of Iraq and the Kurdish-populated areas where their writ did not run. The USA and the UK in fact accepted without too many reservations that distribution within the parts of Iraq where the regime's writ ran would have to be handled through the Iraqi government's own rationing system, which had been in operation since the time of the Iran–Iraq war and which worked reasonably satisfactorily. The UN would monitor the operation of that distribution system but would not be asked to take on the mammoth task of setting up a separate system. It was well understood that any attempt to impose a UN distribution system was likely to result in Iraq's refusal to accept the oil-for-food scheme at all. As to the division between the Kurdish-populated areas of Iraq and the rest, it was decided that between 130 and 150 million dollars out of the 1 billion total in every three-month period would be made available to the UN Humanitarian Programme in Northern Iraq for them to distribute. This latter system worked well throughout the duration of the oil-for-food scheme and did much to help restore life to normal in the Kurdish areas.

The subsequent negotiations, following adoption of the resolution, between the Iraqi government and the UN Secretariat were lengthy and tortuous but eventually successful. Saddam Hussein's unwillingness to accept the detailed terms required, and thereby to reduce his ability to use the plight of his own people as a lever in his diplomatic campaign to get sanctions lifted, was finally overcome by Tariq Aziz, who oversaw the negotiations throughout. The scheme thus did not come into effect while I was in New York. But, in view of the notoriety of the whole oil-for-food programme following the revelations of maladministration and impropriety in the later years of the scheme's operation, it is worth noting that it operated in a reasonably effective way for several years before the Iraqis were able to subvert it in any substantial way.

Nuclear non-proliferation

Nuclear proliferation did not often figure on the Security Council's agenda. But, ever since the NPT was signed in 1968, it had been a cornerstone of the international security system. That had been demonstrated clearly when the Security Council Summit meeting in January 1992 had stated flatly that nuclear proliferation was a threat to international peace and security. The policy of international safeguards against civil nuclear programmes becoming a route to a nuclear weapons capability was in the hands of an agency of the UN, the IAEA; and the ultimate backstop to the safeguards system was referral by the IAEA Governing Board to the Security Council if the IAEA believed that such leakage was taking place. That was what had brought North Korea's nuclear programme to the Security Council's attention in 1993; and Chapter VII of this book gives some account of the far from satisfactory handling of that issue by the Council and the subsequent, somewhat reluctant consensus that in future it should be dealt with bilaterally in direct negotiations between the USA and North Korea.

However, North Korea apart, the immediate post-Cold War period was one in which the NPT regime appeared to be going from strength to strength. South Africa, whose clandestine nuclear weapons ambitions had long been suspected, abandoned its programme and was given a clean bill of health by the international inspectorate. Iraq, whose clandestine programme had also been suspected, had had its nuclear installations largely destroyed during the war that followed its seizure of Kuwait in 1990, and the rest systematically dismantled by IAEA inspectors in the years that followed. Moreover the unexpected extent and advanced state of Iraq's clandestine programme had alerted the IAEA to weaknesses in the safeguard system which were starting to be plugged by an Additional Protocol to safeguards agreements, giving the IAEA a much greater capability for intrusive and snap inspections. Two recognised nuclear-weapon states (NWS), China and France, which had hitherto stood outside the NPT system, now signed the Treaty. And the other recognised NWS, Russia, the UK and the USA, all began to make significant reductions in their number of warheads and in their delivery systems, thus providing some credibility to the vague commitments they had entered into to move towards nuclear disarmament.

This was the background against which, in the spring of 1995, the NPT signatories held the latest of the quinquennial reviews provided for under the Treaty. At each previous review a decision had been taken to roll the Treaty forward for another period. But this system of periodic decisions to prolong the NPT was inherently unstable and, in the improved international climate following the end of the Cold War, it was decided in 1995 to remove the requirement for a periodic roll over and to renew the NPT *sine die*; that is to say, in perpetuity. As always with NPT deliberations the consensus around this major strengthening of the regime was a fragile one, resting as it did on the basically discriminatory provisions of the Treaty itself, which treated five countries (the nuclear-weapon states, NWS) quite differently from the rest. At this particular point in time one of the other main causes of fragility, the existence of three other countries, India, Israel and Pakistan, which had never signed the NPT and all of which were suspected (correctly) of having nuclear weapons programmes, was not as major a factor as it was later to become, partly because the Oslo agreement between Israel and the PLO had held out hope that the Palestinian dispute might be moving towards a negotiated solution.

At the time of previous NPT reviews, concerns over the discriminatory nature of the Treaty had partly been addressed by unilateral statements from the NWS, known as 'negative security assurances'. In 1995, as a counterpart to the decision to renew the NPT in perpetuity, it was decided to multilateralise these assurances by incorporating them in a Security Council Resolution. Resolution 984 of 11 April therefore noted the five unilateral security assurances against the use of nuclear weapons given by the NWS to the non-nuclear-weapon states (NNWS) which were party to the NPT; recognised the legitimate interest of the NNWS to receive assurances that the Security Council would act in the event of such states being the victim of an act, or the object of a threat of aggression, in which nuclear weapons were used; and recognised that the NWS would bring such a matter immediately to the attention of the Security Council and would seek Council action to provide the necessary assistance to the state victim.

On this occasion, as also at the next quinquennial review in 2000, it proved possible to overcome the basic inequity enshrined in the NPT and to move ahead on an agreed basis. Such was not to be the case in 2005 (see Chapter XIII).

Debacle in the former Yugoslavia

The year began reasonably quietly in the former Yugoslavia. In Bosnia a temporary ceasefire agreement brokered by former US President Jimmy Carter more or less held for the first four months. There were changes in the UN's military commanders, both in Bosnia, where another British general, Rupert Smith, took over from Michael Rose, and in the overall peacekeeping operations in the former Yugoslavia, where another French general, Janvier, took over from de la Presle. These changes were to assume considerable significance when the ceasefire broke down and fighting resumed in both Bosnia and Croatia. Smith soon came to the conclusion that the UN's present strategy and tactics in Bosnia were unsustainable and he was more prepared to contemplate the strategic, and not just the tactical, use of NATO air power than his predecessor had been. Janvier, on the other hand, became a serial rejecter of almost any request for the use of air power to back up his beleaguered forces on the ground and thus heavily reinforced the tendency of both Akashi, the Secretary-General's special representative in the former Yugoslavia, and of the Secretary-General himself, to back away from any use of force.

The first crisis of the year occurred not in Bosnia but in Croatia. In May the Croatian armed forces, without any warning or attempt at negotiation, forcibly took control of Western Slavonia, one of the three mainly Serb-inhabited, UN-protected areas in Croatia (Eastern Slavonia, Western Slavonia and the Krajina), in the process simply brushing aside the lightly armed and sparse UN military presence in the area. This action provoked some irritation in the Security Council but no effective response; the Russians were indignant, spotting as usual an anti-Serb bias in everyone else, while the Americans went through the motions of condemning the Croatian move but were clearly not prepared to agree to any action which would give the Croatian government pause for thought. Security Council Presidential Statements of 1 and 4 May were followed by a fairly limp Security Council Resolution 994 of 17 May, all of which called for the restoration of the status quo before the Croatian military action and to none of which the Croatians paid any attention. No consequences, serious or otherwise, were threatened. The government of Croatia could have been forgiven for concluding that the use of force to seize control of what they anyway considered to be part of their own territory was not likely to incur any really damaging penalties. One other telling feature of this episode was the complete absence of any response from the other Serb-inhabited enclaves in Croatia, or the Bosnian Serbs or Milosevic in Belgrade. None of them lifted a finger to help their embattled ethnic compatriots in Western Slavonia.

In Bosnia, too, fighting resumed in the spring – the ceasefire, which had in any case by then broken down, expiring on 1 May. What was effectively a siege of Sarajevo resumed with increased intensity, and strains within the UN chain of command soon became apparent. A particularly vicious shelling of the airport area led Rupert Smith to request NATO air strikes, a request which was turned down by his superiors, both military and civilian. Then, following some pin-prick air strikes by NATO a little later, the Bosnian Serbs resorted to their favourite tactic of taking hostage a large number of unarmed UN military observers deployed across the parts of the country they controlled. On this occasion they added insult to injury by chaining their hostages to a number of potential targets for further NATO air strikes. This provoked an angry response from the Security Council in the form of Security Council Resolution 998 of 16 June demanding the release of the hostages, which was, with many delays and much aggressive rhetoric from the Bosnian Serbs, finally conceded. This episode led some in the UN command (Smith) to conclude that UN personnel should not be spread out across the country in positions which were indefensible against the Bosnian Serbs, and others (Janvier, Akashi and Boutros-Ghali) to conclude that NATO air strikes were counterproductive and needed to be avoided if at all possible.

The steadily deteriorating situation in Bosnia was by now gradually driving the three main protagonists on the UN side of the equation, the USA, France and the UK, who had hitherto more often than not been at cross-purposes, closer together. The process was, however, agonisingly slow. French policy had become noticeably more robust towards the Serbs with the succession of President Mitterrand by President Chirac. Even the British, up to now the backmarkers on the use of force, had begun to show signs of irritation at the supine response of the UN chain of command to Bosnian Serb provocations. I had been instructed to protest strongly to Boutros-Ghali at the rejection of Rupert Smith's request for NATO air support over the shelling of the airport and did so. I had also been instructed to press for delegation of the UN authority to turn over the 'dual key' for air strikes to the military commander in Bosnia (Smith) or at least to the overall UN military commander in Zagreb (Janvier). Again I did so; but the point was not conceded, although later in the summer, after Srebrenica, it was to be so. In a key provision of Security Council Resolution 998, the deployment of a new, 12,500-strong rapid reaction force to Bosnia was authorised. This force, which was largely made up of French and British troops, was a very different animal from the rest of UNPROFOR. It was not blue-helmeted, it had artillery support, and it was clearly configured to be able to take on the Bosnian Serbs if that was required. At the same time as this major reinforcement was authorised, the two governments were also being forced to contemplate the eventuality that they might have to extract the whole UN peace operation from Bosnia under hostile conditions. This last possibility was one element forcefully concentrating the minds of the USA, who had given private assurances to help such an operation if it was required.

In reality US policy had been changing subtly for some time, ever since Richard Holbrooke had come back from the post of US Ambassador to Germany in 1994 to take over as Assistant Secretary for Europe at the State Department. Holbrooke, who was a hard-driving, proactive diplomatic operator of great skill, immediately began to breathe new life, and a much higher degree of US involvement, into the peace process. He had been the architect of the policy which had in the autumn of 1994 traded off some alleviation of the severity of UN economic sanctions on Serbia against Serbia's willingness to close its frontier with the Bosnian Serbs. He understood very well that if a peace settlement was to be concluded, pressure would have to be brought on all the parties and the USA would have to talk to all the parties; the simplistic view that the Bosnian Muslims were the victims and the Serbs were the aggressors would not hold up through such negotiations. But as yet he had no authority to commit any US ground troops to operations in Bosnia, whether as part of the ongoing UN peace operation or following a negotiated settlement.

By the summer of 1995 another factor was coming into play. The next US presidential election was due in November 1996; President Clinton was expected to stand for re-election; and his Republican opponent was expected to be Senator Robert Dole, who was a vociferous critic of the weakness of US policy towards Bosnia. This new dimension was brought home to me at a rather unusual occasion outside San Francisco at the end of June. UN ambassadors from New York had gathered in

San Francisco to celebrate the 50th anniversary of the signature of the UN Charter there in 1945. After the ceremony we were all bidden to a grand dinner being given by one of the president's Democrat supporters. I found myself seated next to Leon Panetta, President Clinton's Chief of Staff, and the conversation turned to Bosnia. It lasted a long time as the president decided to play a second round of golf and we all had to wait for his arrival before getting anything to eat. What, Panetta asked me from a number of different angles, was likely to be the situation in Bosnia in a year's time when the presidential election campaign would be getting into full swing? Much the same as now, only worse, was the gist of my reply. I said I could not see how, under present policies, a negotiated settlement could be achieved in that time frame, and, if that had not happened, bitter experience in Bosnia had led us to expect that many unpleasant developments would have occurred. In those circumstances the president was likely to come under a lot of pressure from Dole, was the Panetta reaction.

Anyway the unpleasant developments were not long in coming. Two weeks later General Ratko Mladic's Bosnian Serb forces overran the UN safe area of Srebrenica, brushing aside the presence of a battalion of Dutch peacekeepers. Soon afterwards the massacre of most of the male inhabitants of the enclave got under way, although it was some weeks before the full extent of the atrocities committed became evident. The Security Council, which had not been kept very well informed of what was happening in and around Srebrenica, was able to do little more than wring its hands. But, following Srebrenica, a concerted French, USA and UK response gathered pace. No further Security Council authorisation was sought or needed since that given in the original safe area resolution (836) was considered sufficient, as it had been when the first NATO ultimatum had been given in January 1994. The deployment of the UK/French rapid-reaction force around Sarajevo was completed. And when, in August, a repetition of the market place shelling of 1994 occurred, the rapid-reaction force went into action and a major NATO strategic bombing campaign of Bosnian Serb targets began.

Meanwhile, Croatian government troops had overrun the Serb-inhabited enclave of the Krajina and continued to push forward rapidly into Bosnia. By the time Milosevic compelled the Bosnian Serbs to accept a ceasefire, the proportion of Bosnia in Bosnian Muslim/Croatian hands fairly closely approximated to the 49 per cent/51 per cent split between them and the Bosnian Serbs which had been prescribed in the last UN-brokered peace negotiations the year before. The ceasefire was followed two months later by the Dayton peace settlement, which was brokered almost exclusively by the USA, nominally also by the other members of the Contact Group and not at all by the UN. This provided for peacekeeping to be handed over to a large NATO force, including a substantial US contingent. The humiliation of the UN was complete, it being considered necessary, for the purposes of getting US Congressional approval of the troop deployment, that the UN should have, and should be seen to have, no involvement in the ongoing peace operation. For the UN it was a miserable end to a long and tangled story.

*   *   *   *

My own involvement in the events described in this chapter concluded with my departure from New York on retirement from my post there and from the British Diplomatic Service at the end of July. Thereafter I followed the dramatic events of August and September by listening to the BBC's World Service as I travelled for two months through China, Pakistan and Uzbekistan. My reflections at the time, looking back on the previous five years' hard labour in New York, were naturally tinged with the impact of the debacle in Bosnia but they were not exclusively negative:

> New world disorder does not look like abating very quickly . . . .
> Since the United States will not and the rest of us cannot cope
> with new world disorder on our own, we will need a UN
> which is an effective instrument for handling and containing
> these problems if we are to avoid the risk of spreading
> regional instability and economic dislocation which is against
> our wider interests. We will need however to be a bit cautious
> and conservative about what we ask the UN to take on in
> future. It needs a higher success rate than it has recently
> achieved if it is not to be discredited. . . . so enforcement
> should be off limits, to be undertaken either by "coalitions of
> the willing", if possible with UN authorisation, or not at all.
> But we should not revert to pure, classical peacekeeping . . .
> nor should we rule all civil conflicts off limits. The UN has
> made great strides in developing a capacity to put a country

back on its feet and to take it down a path leading to elections,
a better respect for human rights and a return to normality.
We should continue to help it to equip itself for these tasks.

And, in a glance forward to 1996, which was an election year at the UN
as well as in the USA, with Boutros-Ghali already campaigning vigorously for re-election, my thoughts were:

> We do not want a nonentity because no international
> organisation we value is going to be run to our satisfaction by
> a nonentity. Boutros-Ghali's age will tell against him but there
> are few Third World politicians likely to be as responsive as he
> has been to European interests and attitudes. The Americans
> may hand him the black spot; but infirmity of purpose is
> endemic in this administration so, again, they may not.

And just in case this last comment, and others made earlier in the preceding chapters, may sound somewhat excessively critical of the USA,
my thoughts on that crucial relationship between the USA and the UN
were: 'We should continue to bring home to the Americans the value
we and other Europeans attach to an effective United Nations . . . where
possible we should try to find solutions and reforms which help the
American body politic feel more comfortable with the UN, but not to
the extent of damaging the organisation's structure and viability'.

Chapter X

The path to reform

The earlier chapters of this book have demonstrated rather clearly how little was done in the years immediately following the end of the Cold War to adapt and reform an organisation which had known no other context than the Cold War since its establishment in 1945. Such changes as were made, the breakthrough on environmental issues at the Rio Summit in 1992, the massive expansion in peacekeeping and the increasing involvement in the internal affairs of failed or failing states, and the challenge to impunity for gross breaches of international humanitarian law by setting up international tribunals, were undertaken in a piecemeal and purely reactive fashion. No systematic attempt was made to examine the policy implications of the new circumstances and the way in which the challenges facing the international community were now quite different in their nature and their scale and required quite different responses. The opportunity presented by the Security Council Summit meeting in January 1992 was frittered away. The attempt to enlarge the Security Council and to identify new permanent members of it became bogged down in the 'never-ending' working group, and fell prey to the rivalries between those who wanted permanent membership and those just behind them in the international pecking order. The UN's default option in those years became that most British of policy prescriptions, 'muddling through'.

And yet the changes facing the UN were pretty fundamental. A basically bi-polar world, kept relatively stable by a balance of terror expressed in the doctrine of mutually assured destruction, with large parts of every continent under the tutelage of one or other of the superpowers and thus essentially no-go areas for the involvement of international organisations, had disappeared virtually overnight. In its place there was a world with only one remaining superpower, the USA, militarily predominant but not wishing and not able to become the arbiter and policeman of every dispute, a world in which many policy options, particularly for the involvement of international organisations, were no longer off-limits, and one in which the forces of globalisation in full flood were throwing up opportunities but also plenty of problems. A new phenomenon, that of the failed or failing state, exacerbated by the sudden creation of a large number of new states in the former Soviet Union and the former Yugoslavia, was surfacing in every part of the world, demanding responses in the form both of conflict prevention and of post-conflict peacebuilding.

As time passed, this phenomenon gave rise not only to localised instability and suffering, but to regional mayhem, genocide, ethnic cleansing and, somewhat later, havens for terrorists. The developing countries of the Third World, which had previously devoted so much of their time and energy to playing off the two superpowers against each other and which had more losers than winners in the early stages of globalisation, were, quite justifiably, demanding more attention and more resources from the 'haves' of the world. A number of deep-rooted disputes – over Palestine, Kashmir and in the Korean peninsula – which had been partially frozen during the Cold War became more threatening and less easy to ignore or to keep away from the UN. Add to these the organisational and administrative problems arising from the major expansion in the UN's responsibilities which was thrust upon it as so many new crises were piled onto its plate, and the case for a systematic review of the whole UN machinery, for an in-depth, overall look at what its shareholders, the member-states, expected of the UN and how they wanted it to perform these new responsibilities would seem to have been unanswerable. But it was not answered.

Gradually, as the 1990s, the first post-Cold War decade, wore on, the failure to conduct any such systemic review weighed more heavily on the UN. The balance between successes and failures became more weighted towards the latter. And new problems began to surface. It became clear that the member states were a great deal readier to demand more of the UN than they were to provide it with the resources, human and material, that it required to carry out these tasks. When the going got rough, as it did in Somalia, Bosnia and Rwanda, they would leave the UN floundering and unsupported, quite ready to apportion blame to an organisation which, by its very nature, could not answer back on equal terms, and to do that even when, as was the case with the USA in Somalia, they were themselves in full charge when things went wrong. Fundamental differences also began to emerge over the use of economic sanctions and over the circumstances under which the use of force should be authorised by the UN.

The relative ease with which the decision was reached in November 1990 to authorise the use of force in the black-and-white case of Iraq's aggression against Kuwait was not repeated. In 1999, in the case of Kosovo, despite it being quite clear that Milosevic's Serbia was in breach of mandatory Security Council resolutions, the threat of a Russian veto resulted in force being used without any prior authorisation by the UN. In March 2003, over Iraq the policy paralysis in the Security Council was complete, and, once again, force was used without UN authorisation. The close working relationship between the P5 of the Security Council, which had characterised the early post-Cold War years, dissolved in friction and futile scholastic debates over uni-polarity and multi-polarity. None of the five, least of all the USA, made the effort necessary to keep the earlier cooperation in good working order.

The second half of the 1990s was indeed a dispiriting period for the UN. The failures of the early part of the decade weighed heavily in the scales of public opinion. So, while the ebbing in the earlier massive demand for peacekeepers to be deployed worldwide was something of a blessing, it occurred in circumstances which discredited the organisation and cast doubt on its ability to manage large-scale peace operations effectively. In 1996 a long drawn-out tussle over whether Boutros-Ghali was to be given a second five-year term of office culminated, immediately following President Clinton's own re-election, in a US veto, a throwback to an earlier age which the absence of vetoes or veto threats during the 1991 election process had suggested might have been left behind. It was not immediately apparent that Boutros-Ghali's successor, Kofi Annan, a hitherto low-key Under-Secretary-General for Peacekeeping, would be able to retrieve the ground that had been lost in the latter part of his predecessor's term of office. Some believed that he would be 'more of a secretary, less of a general', and resented both the way in which Boutros-Ghali's reappointment was blocked and the implication that Annan was in some way a candidate picked by the USA. It took some time before his quiet authority and his willingness to speak out eloquently on even the most sensitive subjects, together with his determination to push forward the process of reform, displaced the earlier impression of him.

Nor did the process of reform prosper much during this period. Full-scale, independent international enquiries were commissioned into the Rwandan genocide and the Srebrenica massacre. The subsequent reports of these two enquiries were a very necessary political assumption of responsibility by the UN for two lamentable and blameworthy episodes, but they were too narrowly focussed and too backward looking to provide a basis for major reforms. Then in 1997, the then president of the General Assembly, Razali Ismail of Malaysia, made a determined attempt to broker a deal on enlargement of the Security Council, which would have brought in some new permanent members and a substantially enlarged Council. At first this attempt showed promise and it looked as if the usual obstacles might be overcome. But in the end the initiative ran aground at a summit meeting of the Non-Aligned Movement; and the issue lay relatively dormant for a number of years after that. Nor was proper advantage taken of the two great commemorative gatherings of world leaders which took place during this period: the UN's own 50th anniversary in 1995; and the Millennium Summit in 2000. On the first occasion an almost entirely content-free declaration was produced, vapid even by the UN's not very high standards in such matters; the second had a more substantial outcome in that it set a number of numerical targets to be achieved by 2015 aimed at reducing world poverty, boosting education and health care and addressing environmental threats. But little was done at the time to underpin these targets with the earmarking of the resources necessary to achieve them, nor did the developing countries themselves accept binding policy commitments which would have ensured that resources that were made available were put to good use. So the MDGs soon became discredited, as the progress towards achieving them was seen to be so inadequate. Only on the conduct of peacekeeping operations were some much-needed reforms introduced following the recommendations of the Brahimi report in 2000, but even in this instance as many of the report's proposals languished unimplemented as were put into effect.

This, then, was the UN which was struck by the shock of the Iraqi crisis in 2003. The unilateralist tendencies of the US administration of President George W. Bush had been apparent since it took office. But they had not inflicted much damage on the UN in the first two years of his term of office. Indeed the rapid and decisive action taken at the UN immediately following the terrorist outrages of 11 September 2001 had established the UN as an integral part of the counter-terrorist strategy which was supported at the time by all member states. And the US-led action to overthrow the Taliban regime in Afghanistan and to hunt down Osama bin Laden and al-Qaeda was broadly recognised to be an exercise of the legitimate right of self-defence under the Charter. When the peacebuilding operation, which followed the end of hostilities in Afghanistan, was brought fully under the aegis of the UN, with the skilful assistance of Lakhdar Brahimi in shaping the rapid emergence of an interim administration under Afghan leadership, there continued to be broad support. But all this was torn to shreds by the move towards war in Iraq and the actual hostilities which began in March 2003. The paralysis in the Security Council in the winter of 2003, the noisy and ill-tempered debates there which pitted groups headed by permanent members of the Council against each other in ever more fundamental confrontation, and then the way the UN was simply brushed aside by the US-led coalition, all inflicted great damage. Some have argued that, by standing up to US and UK pressure and refusing to authorise the use of force, the Security Council gained credit and disproved the view that it was simply the creature of US policy; and there may be something in this. But, if it was a kind of victory, it was certainly a remarkably pyrrhic one.

The second Iraqi shock, the killing of the UN's head of mission in Baghdad, Sergio Vieira de Melo, and 20 of his colleagues, at the beginning of the insurgency in August 2003, had no such silver lining. It was an unmitigated disaster. It undermined the authority of the Secretary-General, who was criticised by many of his own officials for putting the mission in harms way; and it put paid to any hope, always a slender one given the US administration's unwillingness to follow the Afghan precedent and bring representative Iraqis back at an early stage into the peacebuilding phase, that the UN's divisions over the war could be gradually healed by working together in post-war Iraq.

It was against this sombre backdrop that Kofi Annan decided to blow the whistle and to try to stem the process of decline and discord. Speaking to the General Assembly at the annual 'state of the union'-style occasion on 23 September 2003, he said flatly that the organisation was at a fork in the road. It could either take the path of reform, designed to strengthen multilateral disciplines and make itself more effective, or it could slide towards a kind of Hobbesian world in which the law of the jungle prevailed. He announced that he was setting up a high-level panel to advise him on the threats and challenges the world now faced and to recommend the changes that would be needed if the UN was to overcome them. When he had the Panel's recommendations, he would return to the General Assembly in 2004 and call for action. This initiative did not at the time attract a great deal of attention. After all, UN panels came and went; and their reports were often simply left to gather dust in the UN's archives. But no one contested Annan's analysis that the UN was at an important turning point, and there was no criticism of his decision. In reality Annan's move was something of a gamble: the Panel might come up with impractical, overambitious or wrong-headed proposals; its proposals, however cogent, might simply be left to wither on the bough by a divided membership. So he was raising the stakes. If the initiative went wrong the UN's predicament would be even worse than if he had not made a serious attempt at achieving reform.

*   *   *   *

My own path to reform was a good deal less dramatic than Annan's. I had, of course, lived through the events of the first half of the 1990s at the heart of the UN's policy-making machinery. I had experienced at close range the triumphs and the disasters of that period. I was certainly aware of, and shared some of the blame for, the failure to adapt the UN and its structures to the new demands and challenges of the post-Cold War world. Following my retirement from the British Diplomatic Service in September 1995, I had not enjoyed a long respite from international diplomacy or indeed from working with the UN. In the spring of 1996 I accepted an invitation from the Foreign Secretary Malcolm Rifkind to take up a newly created, part-time appointment as the British Special Representative for Cyprus. My task was to revive the fairly moribund UN peace process, the most recent stages of which have been described in the earlier chapters of this book. Following the collapse of the negotiations for confidence-building measures in early 1995, the UN efforts had lapsed into stagnation. The urgent need to revive the process derived from the fact that the EU had by now pretty irreversibly committed itself to accepting Cyprus as a member, without posing any clear-cut condition that the dispute over the future of the island should first be settled. In my previous incarnation in New York I had argued strenuously against such a commitment, pointing out that it would greatly weaken the UN's hand in any revived negotiations for a comprehensive Cyprus settlement. For some time I managed to hold the line so far at least as British policy in the EU was concerned. But gradually all the other member states, with France and Germany in the lead, rallied to supporting a commitment to Cyprus, and the British position became untenable. It was perhaps poetic justice that I was now asked to go and pick up the pieces in circumstances which I had myself argued, reasonably cogently, would be unpromising.

For the next seven years I struggled with this most intractable of international problems (the full story of the negotiations is told in the book I wrote after standing down as special representative in May 2003, *Cyprus: The search for a solution*). The intractability of the problem was deeply rooted in many of its main characteristics. For one thing, whatever they might say, none of the main protagonists were at the outset under real pressure to move away from the status quo nor were they deeply dissatisfied with it: the Greek Cypriots were making progress with their EU application and were running an increasingly prosperous economy; the Turkish Cypriots had the comfort blanket of a 35,000-strong Turkish troop presence and a hefty annual subsidy from the Turkish exchequer.

Successive Turkish governments took the view that there was no problem which needed solving if only we would all grant recognition to the secessionist Turkish Republic of North Cyprus, and successive Greek governments often found it useful to have a Cyprus grievance to nurse and to add to their long list of disputes with Turkey. Many of these attitudes would change under the impact of developments in the relationships of Cyprus and of Turkey with the EU and of Greece and Turkey with each other; but those changes only influenced the main political actors with agonising slowness. Then, throughout the period I was involved in the problem, at least one of the two Cypriot leaders was determined to resist any negotiated settlement proposals on terms which could possibly have been accepted by the other side. For most of the period the Turkish Cypriot leader Rauf Denktash was the naysayer, and his grip on Turkish policy towards Cyprus as well as on his own people was very strong. Then, no sooner had a Turkish government which was genuinely committed to finding a way round the Denktash

roadblock taken office in Ankara (in November 2002) than the Greek
Cypriots elected a new leader, Tasos Papadopoulos, who was every bit
as negative from the opposite side as Denktash had ever been, to replace
Glafcos Clerides, who had worked hard and constructively for a negotiated outcome. The baton passed without a beat being missed. Beneath
these negative factors lay deep-rooted suspicion by each side of the
other, rooted in a poisoned historical legacy, and an absolute determination to approach any negotiation as a zero-sum game in which any
provision that benefited one side must by definition be of equal detri-
ment to the other.

But neither the UN, which had always been and continued to be
accepted by all concerned as the only conceivably acceptable facilitator
and manager of the peace process, nor the EU, which desperately
wanted the Cyprus it was committed in due course to admitting as a
member to come in reunited after a comprehensive settlement and not
divided, could afford to be discouraged by these negative factors.
Tension was rising as a result of the Greek Cypriot purchase of sophisticated missile technology from Russia, and Turkey's reaction both to
this and to Cyprus' progress towards EU membership was unremit-
tingly hostile; the implications of a still-divided Cyprus' accession to the
EU for Turkey's own increasingly pressing candidature were already a
large cloud on the horizon. The challenge was not so much to devise a
completely new peace plan, although important innovations were
required to previous proposals, particularly to take account of developments such as the increasingly prominent EU dimension, but to
reach a settlement in which flesh was put on the bones of the bi-zonal,
bi-communal federation that the two sides had agreed as a framework
as long ago as 1977. Given the proclivity of both sides to haggle over the
most minute details, such a settlement needed to be sufficiently comprehensive as to preclude the need for further negotiation once a deal
had been struck and approved by referendums in the Greek and Turkish
Cypriot communities. Four crucial issues had to be resolved: first, the
constitution and institutional structure of a new, federal Cyprus, quite
different from the unitary state established at the time of independence
in 1960, and ensuring substantial autonomy to the two component
federated states but also the viability of the federal government; secondly, a territorial transfer of a substantial kind from Turkish Cypriot
to Greek Cypriot control to remedy the disproportionate share of the
island which had fallen under Turkish control following the military

intervention in 1974; thirdly, security arrangements providing for with-drawal of the Turkish troops from the island, for the demilitarisation of Cypriot forces and for an international military presence; and fourthly, a property settlement based on a combination of limited returns of dispossessed property-owners in both directions and fair compensation for those who did not return. In addition to these four salient issues there were two wild cards: the treatment of the consider-able number of mainland Turks who had come to the island since 1974; and the 'here to there' problem of how to achieve continuity between the two existing states (one unrecognised) and the new Cyprus which would effectively, if not legally, take their place. This was the Rubik's cube which faced us.

It was no simple task even to get a negotiating process under way again at all, let alone to get it moving towards a settlement. Neither Cypriot party showed any enthusiasm for resuming the search for a solution. The Greek Cypriots preferred to play the blame game, at which they were adept, and Denktash was more interested in pursuing the will-of-the-wisp of recognition. Boutros-Ghali, bruised by his two previous lengthy and wearying brushes with the protagonists, was reluctant to have a third try. A first phase, in 1997, which never got beyond talks about talks fizzled out when Denktash, taking advantage of a furious row between Turkey and the EU over the handling of Turkey's EU candidature, declined to continue. Two years were then consumed averting a crisis between Cyprus and Turkey over the for-mer's plans to deploy a new and sophisticated surface-to-air missile sys-tem (the missiles were eventually diverted to Greece) and putting Turkey's relationship with the EU back on the rails. Then a formal, but indirect, negotiating process got under way at the end of 1999, with the UN shuttling between the two parties and little, if any, progress being made. After just under a year, in November 2000, Denktash, with the support of the Ecevit government in Ankara, walked out again, this time on the grounds that the UN was playing too active a role in facil-itating the negotiations. This second hiatus lasted another year, at the end of which Denktash unexpectedly returned to the negotiating table but showed no more intention of negotiating in a spirit of give and take than he had done before. Nevertheless, during the period from December 2001 until November 2002, the UN, helped by increasing signs of flexibility from the Greek Cypriot side and by intensive con-tacts in Ankara with the Turkish government, was able to piece together the complex component parts of a comprehensive settlement and to table what was called the Annan Plan in mid-November 2002. Annan's increasingly sure-footed handling of the negotiations and the skill of his Special Adviser for Cyprus, Alvaro de Soto, meant that there was now a real chance of a settlement. Cyprus' own EU accession negotiations were due to reach a climax in Copenhagen in December 2002; and Turkey's EU candidacy was set to take a decisive step forward towards opening accession negotiations on that same occasion. But Denktash, helped by a bout of ill-health, managed to filibuster his way past the Copenhagen meeting; and the new Turkish Erdogan/Gül government, which, unlike its predecessor, was genuinely committed to negotiating a Cyprus settlement, was too distracted by the handling of its own relationship with the EU and by the extremely tense runup to the Iraq war to bring effective pressure to bear on Denktash. In March 2003, Denktash walked out again, having rejected the third iteration of the Annan Plan, which had by then twice been revised to take account of points made by both sides. In April 2003, Cyprus' Accession Treaty with the EU was signed and all leverage from that quarter was lost. A year later, with Denktash by now having been marginalised by the Turkish government, intensive negotiations between Annan and the parties led to a fifth iteration of the Annan Plan. It was this text which was put to referendums on both sides of the island in April 2004, the Turkish Cypriots voting by a two-thirds majority in favour and the Greek Cypriots, egged on by President Papadopoulos, voting by a three-quarters majority against.

Those seven years of hard labour on the Cyprus problem had taught me a good deal about an aspect of the UN's activities, peace-making by negotiation, of which I had had little direct experience before. The first lesson I drew from it was that here, as in other fields such as peacekeeping, one was continually reminded of the organisation's indispensability. There was simply no question of the Cypriot parties on their own generating the flexibility and political will to negotiate a settlement; nor was any intermediary other than the UN acceptable to all concerned, particularly once the EU, with Greece as a member, became an active component of the negotiations. Reluctant though the UN might have been to return to the stony vineyard of Cyprus, it really had no choice once its most influential member states, quite justifiably, concluded that another effort to reach a settlement was required.

Secondly, while the UN Secretariat had formidable professional skills, from Kofi Annan downwards, which contributed towards a negotiated outcome that very nearly succeeded, it could not hope to pull off such a result entirely on its own. It depended crucially in this instance on the active support of a network of governments (the USA and the member states of the EU) and of organisations (the EU Commission) to stand any hope of success. This had been the case with a different regional constellation in the earlier negotiations for a peace settlement in El Salvador and it was certainly true of Cyprus.

Thirdly, the sequencing of external events and pressures, over many of which neither the UN nor its supporters had full control, could be of fundamental importance. Had Denktash not wasted, cumulatively, some three to four years of negotiating time while Cyprus was, in parallel, edging its way painfully towards EU accession, then I believe the outcome, particularly of the referendums, might have been quite different. Had the Iraq crisis not supervened and distracted several of the main players at the end of 2002 and in the early months of 2003, a similar speculation could be legitimate. And then, fourthly, if one of the key parties to a negotiation is absolutely determined to wreck it and to prevent a successful outcome, as Denktash was throughout and as Papadopoulos was once he came to power in early 2003, there is very little the UN or even its most influential and powerful supporters can do to avoid that. The UN has no magic wand. It cannot threaten the use of force or even meaningful sanctions in circumstances such as these. It has to depend on rational argument and ingenuity; and that is not always enough. One further consideration in this and perhaps in other such cases is important. The primary objective was to get a comprehensive settlement of the Cyprus problem. But the secondary objective was to use the negotiating process to avoid a dangerous increase in tension in the eastern Mediterranean; and that secondary objective was certainly achieved. A peace process can be an effective tool for conflict prevention.

*   *   *   *

My own involvement in the Cyprus negotiations ended in May 2003. With yet another veto by Denktash (at The Hague in March 2003); with the leadership on the Greek Cypriot side passing to Papadopoulos, with whom my dealings while he was still in opposition had convinced me he was an out-and-out rejectionist; and with the signature of a divided Cyprus' accession treaty to the EU in April 2003, I was convinced that the best chance of getting a settlement had passed, and I was more than a little doubtful whether a renewed effort, such was in fact undertaken in the first quarter of 2004, was likely to succeed. Moreover my personal role as part of the UN's back-up team was being more and more challenged from the Greek Cypriot side. The Greek Cypriots seldom pass up an opportunity to play the man and not the ball; and, when the person in question could be depicted as a scion of the old British colonial oppressor, the temptation was irresistible. It was being suggested (untruly) that I was the real author of the Annan Plan. From being a part of a possible solution, I was becoming part of the problem.

When, in September 2003, Annan told the UN General Assembly that the organisation was at a fork in the road and that he was setting up the High-Level Panel on Threats, Challenges and Change, I was, like many others, greatly encouraged and felt that it was indeed essential to try to plot a new course for the UN's future; but it never occurred to me that I might be a part of that effort. Then, a month later, I was telephoned from New York by Kieran Prendergast, the Under-Secretary-General for Political Affairs, whose task it was to get the Panel up and running, to ask me on behalf of the Secretary-General whether I would be prepared to serve on it. He explained the broad lines of the remit and the rough timetable for submitting the report; and sketched in the Panel's membership (one national from each of the P5 of the Security Council, with an appropriate regional and gender balance for the other 11 members). I discovered a good deal later that I had not in fact been the first Briton to be approached. Annan's first thought had been that there should be one member of the Panel from the International Court of Justice and he had made an approach to Dame Rosalyn Higgins, the British member of the Court (and subsequently its president). But the Court had taken the view that it should not get involved in policy matters which might well subsequently be at issue in cases brought before it, so that plan had fallen through.

I did not hesitate long before accepting. My experience over the previous 13 years, first as British permanent representative between 1990 and 1995 and then as Special Representative for Cyprus, was directly relevant to much of the subject matter to be covered by the Panel. I had long felt that the hand-to-mouth, muddling through approach to policy-making at the UN was subject to the law of diminishing returns.

Importantly also I felt that Annan, with his calm, consensual approach, his considerable moral authority and his capacity to keep his head through even the worst of crises, had the capacity to be an effective reforming Secretary-General before this second term of office, due to expire at the end of 2006, was up.

I had first met Annan in 1990, shortly after I had arrived in New York as permanent representative and when he was a middle-ranking secretariat official with the tricky task of extricating from Iraq and Kuwait a number of UN and other international civil servants who had been trapped by the outbreak of hostilities in August of that year. He performed that task admirably. Then, as he made his way up the promotion ladder, first to be Assistant-Secretary-General and then Under-Secretary-General for Peacekeeping, I had seen a lot of him, most intensively in the context of the Bosnia peacekeeping operation. I had invariably been impressed by his constructive, matter-of-fact, problem-solving approach and by his capacity to smooth off the rough edges of the conflicts of interest between member states which so often arose at the UN. He was someone with whom it was almost impossible to quarrel; and his sense of humour lightened up even the most demanding of policy discussions. We became good friends. When I left New York in 1995 he gave me a book on the Ashanti Wars in his native Ghana, whose dust-cover depicted a British cavalryman cutting down an African warrior; inside he noted 'one peacekeeping operation which went a bit wrong'. Since then we had hardly met. But, on a visit I made to New York on Cyprus business in the autumn of 1996, when the issue of whether or not Boutros-Ghali was to get a second term and who might succeed him was coming to a head, he had sought me out and asked for advice. I said I thought he should dig a deep trench and keep his head well down until all the shooting had stopped. If he started to campaign prematurely for the job, he risked being caught in the cross-fire. Then, once he became Secretary-General, we had again worked closely together over Cyprus, where I had marvelled at his ability to keep on good terms with both sides and to dodge every attempt that both invariably made, first to enlist him on their side and then, if that failed, to demonise their UN interlocutor. So not only did I accept his offer to join the Panel with alacrity; but I looked forward to working with him again.

Chapter XI

The High-Level Panel on Threats, Challenges and Change: the people and the process

The members of the Panel and their staff

Assembling a UN Panel is invariably a delicate matter of balancing different interests and geographical regions, achieving some gender balance, and of getting people whose experience is relevant to the task in hand but who are, at the same time, not so busy with their day jobs that they are unable or unwilling to devote sufficient time to meetings of the Panel and to make a genuine personal contribution to the preparation of its report. This particular panel had 16 members, not entirely fortuitously just one more than the membership of the Security Council, whose regional pattern of membership it more or less replicated. Thus five of its members were drawn, one each, from the countries which were permanent members of the Security Council; of the remaining 11, three were from Africa, two were from Latin America, two were from the 'Western European and Other Group' – which includes Australia – and four, including the chair, from Asia. The gender balance was 12 men to four women. As for experience, there was considerable overlapping, with different individuals having often occupied both senior national and multilateral positions, or served as diplomats but also occupied positions at the political level. Allowing for this overlap, the Panel had two military men, one of whom had commanded a major UN peacekeeping operation, four diplomats, nine members who had held senior ministerial posts in national governments (mostly either prime minister or foreign minister) and eight who had held senior posts in different international organisations. There was a certain amount of ribald comment in UN circles in New York about the high average age of the Panel members but, in reality, that was the price that had to be paid to get people able to devote a substantial part of their time for a year or more to the work of the Panel. By no means every member of the Panel knew all the others at the outset, but most knew most of them and many had worked together or negotiated with each other in the past. All were known personally to Kofi Annan, who took great care over the selection process.

The chair of the Panel, Anand Panyarachun, had been a Thai diplomat and also prime minister during a period of transition from a military to a democratic regime. His charm and emollient style made him an expert at smoothing over differences and tensions; he had no strong views on the policy issues before the Panel and was a champion of consensus at almost any price, which certainly irritated some of the stronger-minded members of the Panel, but also helped to move business along and to ensure that the final report was indeed agreed by all. Of the five members drawn from the P5, Brent Scowcroft was liked and respected by all; he made no secret of his disillusionment with the neoconservative, unilateralist trends in US foreign policy and of his belief that the Iraq venture was in his own words 'an aberration'. Yevgeny Primakov was a gregarious team player with a fund of not always printable jokes and a wealth of knowledge of the Middle East who, as time went on, distanced himself steadily more from his Russian diplomatic minders (who, contrary to the Panel rules, hovered around our meetings, sometimes not very well camouflaged as interpreters). Qian Qichen operated throughout on the basis of carefully typed up speaking notes provided for him by his substantial gaggle of Chinese diplomatic minders; this pretty flagrant breach of the rule that we were all operating as individuals without instructions from our governments was tolerated, if not much appreciated, as being partly justified by Qian's not very robust health and also because his contributions did not in fact cut across the main lines of the conclusions which began to emerge from the Panel's work. Robert Badinter had been French Justice Minister under President Francois Mitterrand and had been involved in the early stages of the international attempts to handle the break-up of the former Yugoslavia. A leading member of the French Jewish community, he brought great legal skills to the work of the Panel and showed a refreshing willingness to operate in English. As the only other member from an EU country, he and I worked closely together throughout and never had a disagreement on any point of substance.

The intellectual power-base of the Panel was undoubtedly Gareth Evans, formerly Australian Foreign Minister and by then running the International Crisis Group, an influential, non-governmental organisation specialising in conflict prevention; he threw off ideas like sparks from a circular saw cutting through stone and sometimes made people feel that that was what he was. But our work would have been the poorer and the outcome much thinner without his contribution. Gro Harlem Brundtland had been both a long-serving Norwegian prime minister and a powerful voice on environmental issues, as well as Director-General of the World Health Organisation; her common sense and incisive arguments made a major contribution to our debates. Enrique Iglesias, president of the Inter-American Development Bank, was the panellist with by far the most experience of economic issues and, although these were closer to the periphery than to the centre of the Panel's work, he provided an invaluable source of guidance on them. João Baena Soares had been Secretary-General of the OAS, whose anti-interventionist culture he personified. As such he tended to be a bit out of sympathy with the prevailing tendency on the Panel. Salim Salim, a former Secretary-General of the OAU, provided an impressive store of knowledge and experience about a continent whose problems were one of the main focuses of the Panel's deliberations; and he was able to make a major input on the role of regional and subregional organisations, amongst which the newly established AU was a central player. Mary Chinery Hesse supplemented that African experience on the economic side.

Of the panellists from Asia, Sadako Ogata, who had borne the brunt of so many of the worst crises of the 1990s when she had been the UN's High Commissioner for Refugees, made a major contribution right across the board. Satish Nambiar, who had commanded the UN forces in the former Yugoslavia in the earlier years of the crisis, provided invaluable first-hand experience of UN peacekeeping. Nafis Sadik, who had been an outstanding Executive Director of the World Population Fund, was an authentically Third World voice challenging the conventional wisdom of the Washington consensus and reminding us of the pressures building up in the Islamic world. And that latter role was played even more eloquently and effectively by Amre Moussa, whose organisation, the AL, straddled Africa and Asia, and who felt passionately the need to prevent the battle against international terrorism turning into a clash between Islam and Christianity.

So much for the cast of players on the Panel. But the Panel also had two small teams attached to it who played a crucial role in its work. The first, consisting of officials seconded from the UN Secretariat, looked after all the administrative side of the Panel's work, setting up the meetings, arranging travel, providing secretarial and translating back-up. The second team, who made up the Panel's research staff, played a role much closer to the substance of its work. Headed by Stephen Stedman, a US academic from Stanford University, and by his deputy Bruce Jones, a Canadian who straddled the disciplines of academe and the UN, and with three young researchers with different skills in the fields covered by the Panel's work, the research staff contributed much to the preparatory work and to the drafting of the report itself as it began to take shape. Stedman in particular became an increasingly influential asset to the Panel; overcoming an initial tendency to treat its members as if they were a gaggle of not very bright postgraduate students, he became adept at explaining even the most complex of issues in quiet, clear and persuasive terms and at overcoming tensions or disagreements within the Panel. After some initial friction, Stedman was able to establish a tight grip on the shaping up and drafting of the report and to avoid an all too common tendency for such reports under which various sections were farmed out to those members of the Panel most interested in them, and the outcome was a product which lacked any real coherence or overall balance. The research staff were notable too for being drawn from outside the UN Secretariat and thus not prone to peddling the pet nostrums that this or that part of the UN bureaucracy had been trying unsuccessfully to sell to the member states for many years. Those nostrums did flow in to the Panel as it proceeded with its work, but the research staff acted as an invaluable filter, sifting out the wheat from the chaff; and they were also able to test the Panel's thinking as it began to take shape on those departments of the Secretariat responsible for the issues in question.

The Panel's remit

The Panel's title, 'The UN Secretary-General's High-Level Panel on Threats, Challenges and Change', was a masterpiece of the sort of bureaucratic jargon for which the UN, like other international organisations, was so infamous. It epitomised one of the UN's greatest weaknesses: an inability to communicate with ordinary people in a language which they could understand. I did make one feeble attempt, when invited to serve on the Panel, to get the title changed for something a bit snappier and more comprehensible but was told sternly that it was now set in stone. It did have one merit in that it was incapable of being turned into one of those acronyms so beloved of UN officialdom.

The terms of reference given to the Panel by Kofi Annan were as crisp, concise and clear as its title was rambling and obscure. Stating flatly, 'The past year has shaken the foundations of collective security and undermined confidence in the possibility of collective responses to our common problems. It has brought to the fore deep divergences of opinion on the range and nature of the challenges we face and are likely to face in the future', they went on to lay down that 'The aim of [the Panel] is to recommend clear and practical measures for ensuring effective collective action, based upon a rigorous analysis of future threats to peace and security, an appraisal of the contribution collective action can make and a thorough assessment of existing approaches, instruments and mechanisms including the principal organs of the UN'. At the same time the panel was told what it was not to do. 'The Panel is not being asked to formulate policies on specific issues, nor on the role of the UN in specific places'. This was as clear an indication as could be wished for that it was not the Panel's job to rake over the ashes of the invasion of Iraq earlier in the year or to find some magic formula for solving disputes like those over Palestine, Kashmir or the Korean Peninsula. The terms of reference went on to suggest: 'while there may continue to exist a diversity of perception on the relative importance of the various threats facing particular member states on an individual basis, it is important to find an appropriate balance at the global level. It is also important to understand the connections between different threats'. Between these lines was clearly written a wise warning against focussing too exclusively on the Bush administration's 'war on terror'. One further useful definitional piece of guidance was given: 'The Panel's work is confined to peace and security, broadly interpreted. That is it should extend its analysis and recommendations to other issues and institutions, including economic and social ones, to the extent that they have a direct bearing on future threats to peace and security'. Interestingly the terms of reference made no mention of the phrase 'UN reform'. Annan made it clear to us when he saw us in New York on 5 December 2003 at the start of our work that this omission had been deliberate. He felt that the mantra of UN reform had become over-used and discredited, associated with institutional tinkering which failed to get to grips with the underlying issues of policy and substance. And he rubbed in that the leitmotif of all we recommended should be effectiveness.

It was a tribute to the skill with which the terms of reference had been drawn up that no member of the Panel sought to query or contest them. The same could not be said of the time-scale set for the Panel's work, which immediately gave rise to some controversy. When Annan had told the General Assembly of his decision to establish the Panel he had said that its report would be available in time for the opening of the following year's meeting of the Assembly, i.e. September 2004. At the Panel's first meeting with the Secretary-General, Scowcroft pointed out that this timing was hardly ideal given the fact that the US presidential election would take place in November 2004. If our report was published in the middle of the election campaign it would inevitably become a political football between the two contenders, with damaging consequences for whatever recommendations we might have made. Several other members of the Panel supported this reasoning. Annan was at first reluctant to set a new timetable, but, by the time of the Panel's second meeting (in February 2004), it was also clear that the September deadline was simply too tight to enable a proper job to be done. In those circumstances Annan wrote to the Panel adjusting the deadline for submission of its report to November/December 2004. One other consequence of that was not only to avoid the US election trap, but also to ensure that the report was not prematurely debated, without proper preparation, at the 2004 General Assembly but rather directed on a track leading to the 2005 General Assembly and the 60th anniversary of the UN's establishment.

The working of the Panel

From the outset the Panel settled into a pattern of holding three-day plenary meetings. There were six of these: at Princeton, New Jersey in December 2003; at Mont Pélérin in Switzerland in February 2004; at Addis Ababa in May 2004; at Baden, near Vienna, in July 2004; at Tarrytown, near New York, in September 2004; and lastly in New York City, near the southern tip of Manhattan, to adopt our report in November 2004. Attendance at the meetings was remarkably complete for a group involving members with many other responsibilities; a few members missed one session entirely but that was the limit; and most members attended the plenary sessions in full, avoiding the bad habits of so many international gatherings, with people turning up late and leaving early. By avoiding getting sidetracked into elaborate social programmes and into holding outreach meetings at the same time as plenary gatherings, and by meeting in all cases but one (Addis Ababa) in or near UN headquarters sites, it proved possible to keep virtually the whole of each three-day session for presentations on subjects under consideration and for in-depth discussion. As a result the members of the Panel got to know each other well and to engage in detail with each other's views. A group which had begun as a collection of individuals with very different backgrounds and starting points gradually forged a collective approach.

The first meeting was not entirely propitious. It began with a meeting in New York with the Secretary-General, after which we made our way painfully slowly through one of those blizzards in which New York specialises out to Princeton. However, it was not to the Ivy League Princeton University we might have anticipated, but to a gloomy company training establishment, cut off by mountainous snow-drifts and isolated in the midst of endless parking lots. There we spent a good deal of that first meeting having presentations by academic experts on issues such as the incidence and nature of state failure and of intra-state disputes, terrorism and the threat from biological weapons. Discussion other than through the questioning of the presenters did not get very far. But the Panel did agree from the beginning that it was going to focus its early meetings exclusively on policy issues and the substance of the threats and challenges facing the international community, and that it would only, much later, get to grips with the changes, including the institutional changes, needed to meet them. In this way it proved possible to avoid the traditional obsession with institutional tinkering and above all to avoid allowing the vexed issue of Security Council enlargement taking over the whole of our deliberations (in the event that issue only first came up for discussion at the meeting in July 2004).

The next meeting, at Mont Pélérin, went a lot better. Not only were the physical surroundings, a beautiful site in the hills at the far end of the Lake of Geneva, a great deal more agreeable, particularly for those who liked going for country walks and not sitting all day every day around a conference table, but serious discussion of policy issues really began to take off. In Addis Ababa in May, it was possible to go in considerable detail into the interface between the UN and regional organisations such as the AU and its subregional organisations. The Vienna meeting in July included not only a meeting with Kofi Annan, but also a presentation on the risks of nuclear proliferation by the Director-General of the IAEA; and there too we really got stuck into the issues of institutional change. The September and November sessions were entirely given over to shaping up and agreeing the Panel's report. The last meeting took place in the somewhat macabre setting of the downtown area of New York in a hotel directly overlooking the site of the twin towers of the World Trade Centre, demolished by the 9/11 attacks. The choice of venue was not deliberate, the main objective having been to keep out of reach of the swarms of UN ambassadors likely to be found in mid-town Manhattan; it rained almost constantly; the mood was rather sombre, not greatly helped by the re-election the day before of President George W. Bush; but there was too a sense of relief and of achievement that we had reached agreement on a serious document with a number of important recommendations.

The plenary sessions were, however, by no means the whole of the Panel's work programme. From the outset it had been clear that it needed to solicit the views of a much wider constituency than the diplomats and governments who so obsessively played institutional tiddley-winks in the buildings off First Avenue. So a major effort was put into inviting written contributions on UN reform from a wide range of civil society organisations; and many were submitted, circulated to the panel and considered by them. In addition a large number of regional consultations were put in hand. Some 40 of these officially sponsored seminars and colloquiums took place in the year the Panel was meeting. At pretty well every one, several members of the Panel were present as were members of its research staff. I myself managed to go to virtually all such meetings held in Europe and several of those outside it. They were extremely useful, enabling members of the Panel to hear a range of views and to test their own emerging views on a wider audience than that of their Panel colleagues. And beyond those officially sponsored meetings lay a whole penumbra of unofficial gatherings which each of us attended. I sometimes felt that the UN had taken over the whole of my life. Two seminars of particular importance were held in sites near New York and were restricted to attendance by UN ambassadors. No one ever doubted that the UN ambassadors were a key part of the

Panel's wider constituency; they, after all, would have to recommend to their governments how the proposals in the report should be handled and they would inevitably be part of any decision-making process on them. The trouble was that they were part of the problem as well as part of its solution. They had not been unduly impressed by Annan's decision to throw such a juicy morsel as UN reform to an outside panel; many would rather have kept it to themselves. They were also the source of much carping about the age and lack of up-to-date UN experience of the panellists.

But these two seminars showed that there was wide support for the Panel's work and a real expectation that it could open up the path towards meaningful reforms; they also showed there was a hard core of naysayers who would turn their thumbs down on pretty well anything the Panel put forward. It did not seem to me that the UN had changed a lot in that respect since I had worked there. In addition the Panel set aside two days in New York immediately before its session in September 2004 for meetings with any foreign minister or group of ministers who wished during the ministerial segment of the General Assembly to be briefed on our work or who wished to feed in views to the Panel. A good number took advantage of this invitation.

When Annan launched the Panel's work at our first meeting in December 2003, he had said that he wanted to work closely with us; and he had urged us to be bold in our recommendations. But how we were to interact with him was not suggested. Many UN panels such as ours had in the past seen little of the Secretary-General from the moment he launched their work until the time they submitted their report. 'Fire and forget' had sometimes seemed to be the watchword, but that would certainly not do for a panel which had been let loose on the most sensitive issues at the heart of UN policy-making. For one thing, if we put forward recommendations with which the Secretary-General was not in agreement, they would be dead on arrival. The first initiative came from the Secretary-General's side. When writing in February 2004 to extend the timetable for submitting the Panel's report, he suggested that we send him an interim report about the middle of the year. On reflection this did not seem to many of us a particularly good idea. Not only would we spend a lot of time putting together such an interim report, but the concept cut across the Panel's approach of dealing with the substance of the issues before getting into the institutional implications. And the inherent leakiness of the UN machinery would mean that any interim report would be sure to trigger an orgy of lobbying by the member states, directed both at what was in such a report and at what was not. So, as an alternative, we suggested we meet the Secretary-General at our July 2004 session near Vienna and have a thorough discussion with him. This was accepted and went extremely well. Thereafter we met him again, at the time of our September and November sessions. The upshot was that our report chimed closely with the Secretary-General's own thinking and he was able to endorse it without any reservations.

No member of the Panel said much about the contacts each had with his or her own government. That they took place, and needed to take place, was not in doubt. Scowcroft told me that he had the greatest difficulty extracting any views at all, either positive or negative, from the Bush administration, already heavily distracted by the deteriorating situation in Iraq. I did not have the same problem. I did the rounds of all the ministers in London most directly concerned in UN business. I saw the prime minister (several times), the foreign secretary and the secretaries of state for defence and for international development. All were extremely supportive of the Panel's work. All had been warned by the Foreign Office that I was in no sense the government's representative and could not be instructed to do this or that, and all respected that. Tony Blair was particularly interested in how the Panel would handle the ideas he had put forward in his speech in Chicago in 1999 on 'humanitarian intervention'. I explained that the phrase itself and his original ideas had provoked plenty of negative reactions. But the Panel was considering how to take forward these issues within the context of the doctrine of 'the responsibility to protect' which had emerged from a Canadian-sponsored international panel in the intervening period. It was important not to stir this issue up until the Panel was ready to put forward its conclusions. Blair took that on board. Through all my consultations in London the thread ran through of a deep desire to repair some of the damage that had been done to the UN (and to the Labour Party) by the disagreements over the war in Iraq. It was clear that the Panel's recommendations were likely to get strong UK support.

Both Robert Badinter and I, as the only members of the Panel from EU countries, were conscious from the outset that we needed to bring the EU as such within the ambit of our consultations. The Union had in fact, at the European Council meeting in December 2003, shortly after the Panel began its work, adopted what it called a European

Security Strategy, entitled 'A Secure Europe in a better world'. This document covered much of the ground the Panel was engaged in considering and set as an objective of the EU's policy the concept of 'effective multilateralism' which could well have been adopted as the Panel's own motto. A meeting was arranged in Dublin, right at the beginning of the Irish Presidency, in January 2004, where I (Badinter was prevented from attending for health reasons) briefed the Political Directors of the 15 member states and the ten applicant countries and heard their preliminary views on the Panel's work. I encouraged the Union to put in its own views in writing to the Panel and this eventually bore fruit in July. From the beginning it was clear that strengthening the UN and binding up some of the wounds caused by the war in Iraq was a cause which united the whole EU. The only subject of fundamental disagreement amongst them was enlargement of the Security Council, on which the German government was, with wide support including that of France and the UK, determined to get a permanent seat on the Security Council for itself, while the Italians, with somewhat fewer supporters in the EU, was as determined they should not. This barely concealed rock just beneath the otherwise smooth surface of EU unity was one around which most of the time it was possible to navigate; and it was greatly to the credit of all concerned that no attempt was made by those on either side of the argument to take the other reform proposals hostage against a successful outcome on Security Council enlargement. But it did remain a source of some distraction and disunity throughout the period of the Panel's deliberations and to an even greater extent during the follow-up period afterwards when decisions were being considered on the basis of its recommendations.

Chapter XII

The Panel's report

As the members of the Panel settled down to an intensive process of reading, briefing and discussion, together with the programme of outreach seminars described in the previous chapter, it soon became clear that the Panel faced two main challenges if its report was to have some hope of being genuinely influential and of making a difference, that is to say if it was to avoid the fate of so many previous UN reports of lying gathering dust on the shelves of the UN library with little to show for all the effort. These challenges could be crudely labelled as the macro and the micro challenges. The macro challenge was to fill the vacuum in strategic thinking about collective security which had existed for more than ten years since the end of the Cold War had given the global kaleidoscope a sharp shake and most of the pieces had ended up in different, not yet very well understood patterns. This required a better understanding of the threats, new and old, which the international community now and prospectively faced, how they interacted with each other and how in broad, conceptual terms they could best be confronted and overcome. The micro challenge was to analyse each individual threat and challenge and to devise specific policy responses which would have some chance of winning consensus or at least very broad support and which could be effectively implemented without undue delay. Both challenges would clearly require some rethinking of the role of UN institutions and perhaps some imaginative innovations, but, from the very outset, thePanel set out to define the threats and policy responses first and only thereafter to focus on institutional changes, in other words to fit the institutional changes to the policies and not the other way round as had so often been the case in previous attempts at UN reform.

The overall view: towards a new security consensus

Early discussions demonstrated that the Panel faced a choice between a broad and a narrower agenda of security threats and challenges. The arguments for a narrow, sharply focussed approach, giving absolute priority to countering terrorism and the spread of weapons of mass destruction, with the possibility of the latter finding their way into the hands of terrorists the ultimate doomsday scenario against which the world must concert all its efforts, emanated mainly from Washington and found no takers on the Panel. No one disputed the reality of those threats and the need to find policy responses to them, but to concentrate on them to the exclusion or marginalisation of others seemed both inadequate, given the much wider range and interconnection of other security threats, and also as unlikely to muster wide support around a world, in many regions of which – in Africa and Latin America for example – the narrow agenda was simply not seen as reflecting their priorities. Adding to the security agenda the problem of state failure, to which, as the previous narrative chapters of this book have shown, the UN had hitherto found no adequate remedies and to which it had fashioned no systemic response, was seen by all members of the Panel as essential. But beyond that lay wider problems arising from extremes of poverty, from infectious diseases and from environmental degradation, problems which had not hitherto been recognised as part of any classic security agenda at all, but which could no longer sensibly be treated in quite separate compartments, by entirely different parts of the UN system, with no recognition of the interconnections between them and the classic security agenda items. The deeper one delved, the more complex became these interconnections. State failure in Afghanistan had led to the harbouring of the most deadly terrorist network the world had yet seen, and in Rwanda and the former Yugoslavia to genocide and to regional chaos and hostilities. Pandemic diseases and poverty were sapping the ability of states to fulfil their responsibilities towards their citizens and to sustain their own existence. Transnational crime often undermined post-conflict peacebuilding, for example in the Balkans and in Haiti. Non-state actors were flourishing in the interstices of all these problems.

So, from quite an early stage in its deliberations, the Panel, following in the path identified by the 1992 Security Council Summit (see Chapter VI), opted for a widely defined security agenda, conscious that in doing so it could be criticised for having failed to prioritise between the different elements of it. The view taken was that prioritisation would indeed need to occur but that it should be within the policies for countering each individual security threat and not between the threats, with some being regarded as of lower urgency. The Panel's approach as set out in its report was summarised in the following introductory passage:

> Sixty years later [after the signature of the Charter in 1945], we know all too well that the biggest security threats we face now, and in the decades ahead, go far beyond states waging aggressive war. They extend to poverty, infectious disease and environmental degradation; war and violence within states; the spread and possible use of nuclear, radiological, chemical and biological weapons; terrorism; and trans-national organised crime. The threats are from non-state actors as well as states, and to human security as well as state security . . . . The central challenge for the twenty-first century is to fashion a new and broader understanding, bringing together all these strands, of what collective security means and of all the responsibilities, commitments, strategies and institutions that come with it if a collective security system is to be effective, efficient and equitable . . . . The case for collective security today rests on three basic pillars. Today's threats recognise no national boundaries, are connected, and must be addressed at the global and regional as well as the national levels. No state, no matter how powerful, can by its own efforts alone make itself invulnerable to today's threats. And it cannot be assumed that every state will always be able, or willing, to meet its responsibility to protect its own peoples and not to harm its neighbours.

This approach, based on a broad security agenda, also challenged one of the most prevalent and seductive temptations to those negotiating at the UN: the belief that there was somehow a direct trade-off to be achieved between the items on the development agenda, of principal interest to the developing countries, and the items on the classic security agenda, of principal interest to the developed countries. The trade-off was often referred to as a 'grand bargain'. The developed countries would come forward with increased sums of development aid and, in return, the developing countries would accept more rigorous and intrusive international disciplines for dealing with terrorism and the proliferation of weapons of mass destruction. There were two main defects to this kind of reasoning. The first was that it was simply not the case that the items on the classic security agenda posed no threat to the developing countries – for example, a major terrorist attack on one of the world's big financial centres was likely to cause massive economic dislocation which would probably impact most severely on the economically weaker members of the international community. Nor was it the case that the incidence of poverty or infectious diseases in the developing countries was without negative security consequences for the developed countries – the cases of state failure demonstrated that all too clearly. The second defect was more political than functional. It was hardly persuasive to the electorates of the developed countries to be told that an increase in their resource transfers to developing countries was needed in order to purchase the latter's acquiescence in measures to defeat terrorism or weapons proliferation. The Panel's analysis argued that there was a common interest for all countries, on whichever side they were of the, anyway by now rather artificial, line between developed and developing countries, to work together to counter all the threats on that broad agenda. It cannot be said that this reasoning entirely overcame the attachment of many of the players to the grand bargain theory, whose ghost continued to stalk the corridors of the UN throughout the decision-making phase following publication of the Panel's report and recommendations; but it did at least bring forward an alternative and coherent conceptual approach.

Economic, social and environmental threats

The Panel found itself in something of a quandary over the handling of the main economic, social and environmental threats. Its analysis showed that these were indeed security threats and its report firmly reflected that view. But it was precluded from going in any detail into prescribing the detailed policies required in response by the fact that another group, chaired by Professor Jeffrey Sachs, was working in parallel on analysing the progress, or in many cases the lack of it, towards achieving the MDGs which had been set in 2000 to be reached by 2015; and that group was not due to submit its report to the Secretary-General until a couple of months after the Panel's own deadline. The Sachs group report clearly was going to need to go in detail into all these economic, social and environmental issues. So the Panel confined itself to some fairly broadbrush conclusions and recommendations in those fields, the most significant of which were the following:

(i)   Developed countries falling short of the 0.7 per cent gross national income (GNI) target for official development assistance should establish a timetable for reaching it.

(ii)   WTO members should strive to conclude the Doha Development Round of multilateral trade negotiations in 2006.

(iii)   There should be greater debt relief from lender governments and the International Financial Institutions.

(iv)   A major increase in resources to meeting the challenge of HIV/AIDS should be committed.

(v)   A new initiative should be undertaken to build local and national health systems throughout the developing world.

(vi)   There should be incentives to develop renewable energy sources and environmentally harmful subsidies should be phased out.

(vii)   The international community should re-engage on the problem of global warming and begin new negotiations on measures to reduce emissions for the period beyond that covered by the Kyoto Protocol up to 2012.

These recommendations meshed well with those in the Sachs report and were thereafter drawn together in the Secretary-General's own March 2005 synthesis, called 'In Larger Freedom', which will be dealt with in Chapter XIII.

Conflict between and within states: the challenge of prevention

Like many others before us who had considered the problem of conflict both between and within states, the Panel had no hesitation about identifying prevention as the preferred option. In purely material terms the costs of preventive action were minimal compared with the costs of actual conflict and of external intervention should that become necessary, and of post-conflict peacebuilding. Beyond those utilitarian considerations lay humanitarian ones and there too the arguments in favour of proactive prevention were overwhelming. The main problem was not just a shortage of resources for the UN to operate effectively in a preventive role, although that was a real constraint, but the fundamental unwillingness of member states to turn to the UN for help as they began to slide towards quarrels with their neighbours or, more frequently in recent times, towards disintegration or the failure of their state institutions. The reluctance amounting to resistance of the Federal Government in the former Yugoslavia in 1991 to turn to the UN was one case in point; another was the rather few occasions when boundary disputes were referred by the parties to the International Court of Justice, even though the Court's record of adjudicating and resolving such disputes peacefully was a good one; and it was rather shocking that the preventive deployment of UN peacekeepers, which had worked so successfully in Macedonia, remained some years later the sole example of the use of that tool. So the Panel was under no illusion that either material or institutional recommendations would quickly remedy all the weaknesses of the UN system in the field of prevention. The key lay as much with the political will of its member governments, both those in trouble and those who could exercise influence over the former category. Nor did the Panel consider that the UN either had or should have a monopoly in the field of preventive action. In many cases individual neighbouring countries or groups of countries could best provide mediators or facilitators to prevent conflict; in others, regional or subregional organisations could be the preventive agents of choice (and that aspect will be covered later in this chapter).

The Panel's main recommendations were:

(i)   The Security Council should stand ready to use its authority to refer cases of suspected war crimes and crimes against humanity to the International Criminal Court.
(ii)   The UN should work to develop norms governing the management of natural resources for countries at risk of or emerging from conflict.
(iii)   The UN should build on the experience of regional organisations in developing frameworks for minority rights and the protection

of democratically elected governments from unconstitutional overthrow.

(iv)   Member states should expedite and conclude negotiations on legally binding agreements on the marking and tracing, as well as the brokering and transfer, of small arms and light weapons.

(v)   The Department of Political Affairs in the UN Secretariat should be given additional resources and restructured to provide more consistent and professional mediation support, including a field-orientated, dedicated mediation support capacity and competence in thematic issues which recur in peace negotiations.

(vi)   National leaders and parties to conflict should make constructive use of the option of the preventive deployment of peacekeepers.

In addition the Panel foresaw an important role in conflict prevention for the proposed Peacebuilding Commission, which will be considered in more detail at a later point in this chapter: 'The core functions of the Peacebuilding Commission should be to identify countries that are under stress and risk sliding towards state collapse and to organise, in partnership with the national governments, proactive assistance in preventing that process from developing further.' Given the firestorm of protest that this preventive role for the Peacebuilding Commission was to raise as soon as the Panel's report was published, it is interesting to note that its consideration within the Panel gave rise to no great controversy.

Nuclear, radiological, chemical and biological weapons

There was never any doubt that the Panel would need to address in a detailed and systematic way the threats and challenges arising from the possession and proliferation of what are somewhat loosely called WMD. As long ago as January 1992, the Security Council summit meeting had stated that 'the proliferation of all weapons of mass destruction constitutes a threat to international peace and security', thus employing the key words from the UN Charter which trigger the possible use of measures under Chapter VII of that charter. That statement came during a brief period which represented the high-water mark of efforts to stem the proliferation of such weapons. The two Cold War super-powers had considerably reduced their holding of nuclear weapons and had ensured that the successor states of the Soviet Union (Ukraine, Belarus and Kazakhstan) did not become NWS; the new, post-apartheid government in South Africa had abandoned what had been a fairly advanced programme for the development of nuclear weapons and had subsequently been given a clean bill of health by the IAEA; Saddam Hussein's Iraq had been revealed by the 1991 war to reverse his aggression against Kuwait to have had a series of massive programmes for the development of nuclear, chemical and biological weapons and for the means of their delivery by a sophisticated range of missiles, and was now in the process of being disarmed and placed under a contin-uing regime of international inspection; the Chemical Weapons Convention (CWC) had been signed in January 1993 and ratified by most countries in the world and provided for international challenge inspections in cases of doubt; and in 1995 one of the regular, quin-quennial review conferences of the NPT had decided that the Treaty would no longer be subject to any time limit but would remain in force *sine die.*

But, since then, a number of less-positive developments had occurred, which indicated that the international disciplines underpin-ning the policies of non-proliferation were coming under increasing stress. North Korea had withdrawn from the NPT and, despite under-takings to the contrary given to the USA in the context of a bilateral agreement in October 1994, was almost certainly continuing its nuclear weapons programme; Iran had been compelled by a leak of informa-tion to admit that it had been conducting for a number of years a clan-destine uranium enrichment research programme which, although the Iranian government insisted it was for peaceful purposes, was capable of eventually providing a shortcut to the production of weapons-grade fissile material; the head of the Pakistan nuclear weapons programme Dr Abdul Qader Khan was revealed to have been operating on the side what can best be described as a kind of nuclear weapons super-market, supplying, amongst others, Iran and Libya with material which could have nuclear weapons applications; and the terrorist attacks against New York and Washington in 2001 had raised the spectre of WMD falling into the hands of non-state actors who lay outside the reach of normal policies of interstate deterrence and who might not hesitate to use them in some form of suicide attack.

During that same timeframe the George W. Bush administration, which came to office in January 2000, had made its own contribution to undermining non-proliferation efforts. There had been much loose talk in Washington about the possible development of new generations of nuclear weapons, which was difficult to reconcile with the NPT obligation to move towards disarmament; the Anti-Ballistic Missile Treaty between the USA and the Soviet Union had been set aside; and the USA had abruptly blocked an attempt to negotiate verification provisions for the Biological and Toxic Weapons Convention (BTWC).

There were a number of reasons why these WMD issues were among the most tricky, sensitive and contentious ones which the Panel had to handle. First there were a number of technical issues which complicated matters. While it was normal to lump all these weapons together under the blanket title of WMD, each category of weapon in fact had quite different characteristics, was governed by quite different international obligations and required quite separate treatment. Moreover, while a number of members of the Panel had some familiarity with and experience of the broad issues raised by WMD, none had actually worked in the highly specialised field of disarmament and arms control negotiations; and quite a few Panel members had only the slightest acquaintance with the subject matter. So we were bound to be heavily dependent on the briefings we received from various specialists and from our own research staff.

But these technical problems were far from being the most significant ones which complicated the Panel's work. The biggest political problem arose from the differentiated nature of the provisions of the NPT and from the fact that three countries which were known to possess nuclear weapons (India, Pakistan and Israel) were not signatories of the treaty and thus not bound by its disciplines. While the CWC and the BTWC were universal in their provisions, banned all possession of such weapons and applied fully and equally to all member states, the same was not the case with the NPT, which recognised the legitimacy of the possession of nuclear weapons by five countries (who happened also to be the P5 of the Security Council). Both these elements of differentiation were the cause of considerable tensions within the Panel and dominated its deliberations on WMD. Amre Moussa was an eloquent and forceful advocate of the dangers represented in the Middle East by Israel's possession of nuclear weapons and of the need to work towards a nuclear weapons-free zone in that region; while Satish

Nambiar was a low-key, and Nafis Sadiq a much more strenuous, spokesman for the Indian and Pakistani points of view. The members of the Panel from the P5, and in particular Brent Scowcroft, had to weigh up carefully how far it was realistic to try to push the five recognised NWS; while other members of the Panel were anxious to avoid any recommendation by the Panel inhibiting the development of civil nuclear programmes in the NNWS. In the light of all these crosscurrents, it was quite surprising that the Panel managed to agree on 17 wide-ranging recommendations, and consensus on these hung in the balance right up until its final meeting.

The Panel's terms of reference had made it very clear that it was not its task to come up with a detailed response to the problems being caused by North Korea's and Iran's nuclear programmes. But we were well aware that the general proposals we made could, if followed up and implemented, strengthen the hand of those who were grappling directly with these two problems. The Panel's main recommendations were as follows:

Nuclear
(i)   The NWS (the P5) must take steps to restart disarmament, undertaking specific measures in fulfilment of their NPT commitments and reaffirming their previous commitments not to use nuclear weapons against non-NNWS (negative security assurances).
(ii)   The USA, the Russian Federation, other NWS and states not party to the NPT should commit to practical measures to reduce the risk of accidental nuclear war, including a schedule for de-alerting their strategic nuclear weapons.
(iii)   The Security Council should explicitly pledge to take collective action in response to a nuclear attack or the threat of such attack on a NNWS.
(iv)   States not party to the NPT (India, Israel and Pakistan) should pledge a commitment to non-proliferation and disarmament, demonstrating their commitment by ratifying the Comprehensive Nuclear Test Ban Treaty (CTBT) and supporting negotiations for a fissile material cut-off treaty. Peace efforts in the Middle East and South Asia should launch nuclear disarmament talks that could lead to the establishment of nuclear weapons-free zones in those regions similar to those already established in Latin America and the Caribbean, in the South Pacific and in South-East Asia.

(v) The Board of Governors of the IAEA should recognise the Model Additional Protocol (a system for safeguard inspections considerably more proactive and intrusive than the earlier system which had failed to detect clandestine programmes in South Africa, Iraq and Iran) as today's standard for IAEA safeguards, and the Security Council should be prepared to act in cases of serious concern over non-compliance with non-proliferation and safeguards standards (a highly camouflaged proposal that the Security Council should be prepared in certain circumstances to use its mandatory powers under Chapter VII of the Charter to impose an obligation to accept the Additional Protocol on a country which was dragging its feet about accepting it).

(vi) Negotiations should be engaged without delay and carried forward to an early conclusion on an arrangement, based on the existing provisions of Article II and IX of the IAEA statute, which would enable the IAEA to act as a guarantor for the supply of fissile material to civilian nuclear users.

(vii) While that arrangement was being negotiated, states should, without surrendering the right under the NPT to construct uranium enrichment and reprocessing facilities, voluntarily institute a time-limited moratorium on the construction of any further such facilities, with a commitment to the moratorium matched by a guarantee of the supply of fissile materials by the current suppliers at market rates.

(viii) All states should be encouraged to join the voluntary Proliferation Security Initiative (providing for concerted action by its members to intercept trade in WMD materials).

(ix) A state's notice of withdrawal from the NPT should prompt immediate verification of its compliance with the treaty, if necessary mandated by the Security Council (thus addressing the situation where a state sought to escape from its NPT obligations by withdrawing, even when it had been in breach of those obligations while still subject to the NPT – highly relevant to the case of North Korea).

(x) The proposed time-line for the Global Threat Reduction Initiative to convert highly enriched uranium (HEU) reactors and to reduce HEU stockpiles should be halved from ten to five years.

(xi) The Conference on Disarmament should move without further delay to negotiate a verifiable fissile material cut-off treaty that, on a designated schedule, should end the production of HEU for non-weapon as well as for weapons purposes.

(xii)   The Director-Generals of the IAEA and the Organisation for the Prohibition of Chemical Weapons should be invited by the Security Council to report to it twice-yearly on the status of safeguards and verification processes, as well as on any serious concerns they had which might fall short of an actual breach of the NPT and the CWC.

Chemical

(i)   All chemical weapons states should expedite the scheduled destruction of all existing chemical weapons stockpiles by the agreed target date of 2012.

(ii)   See (xii) above, which applies also to CWC.

Biological

(i)   States party to the BTWC should without delay return to negotiations for a credible verification protocol, inviting the active participation of the biotechnology industry.

(ii)   States party to the BTWC should negotiate a new bio-security protocol to classify dangerous biological agents and establish binding international standards for the export of such agents.

(iii)   The Security Council should consult with the Director-General of the World Health Organisation to establish the necessary procedures for working together in the event of a suspicious or overwhelming outbreak of infectious disease.

This complex and wide-ranging set of recommendations was certainly ambitious. It aimed to address in a coherent and reasonably comprehensive way most of the different weaknesses in the current non-proliferation regimes and to strengthen the regimes where they had been found wanting or where they did not cover emerging problems and threats to international security. Above all the object was to reinforce multilateral frameworks and disciplines in a way which would enable the international community to deal effectively and in a non-discriminatory fashion with individual country cases when they arose, as inevitably they would do. Of all the proposals, those that caused the most problems for the Panel were the linked recommendations ((vi) and (vii) above) for the establishment of an IAEA guarantee of the supply of enrichment and reprocessing services to *bona fide* civil nuclear users and the voluntary moratorium on the construction of new enrichment and reprocessing plants. These proposals were of critical importance, because such plants offered a shortcut to the production of weapons-grade fissile material and because there was nothing in the NPT itself to inhibit their proliferation. The Brazilian government was particularly nervous about the proposals in the light of their own plans for the construction of an enrichment facility which were at an advanced stage and the implications for the international safeguards on which they were currently negotiating with the IAEA; and this was reflected through the Panel's discussion by João Baena Soares.

I discussed the whole issue at some length with the Brazilian foreign minister Celso Amorim, an old friend from the time we had been ambassadors together in New York and when he had subsequently been ambassador in London. I argued that Brazil had really nothing to fear from the Panel's proposals which were, after all, no more than that and which would certainly take some months or even years of work before they emerged as actual policy decisions. They were unlikely therefore to have any direct impact on Brazil's plans. But it was surely not in Brazil's wider interest to prevent a yawning gap in the international community's defences against nuclear proliferation from being plugged. I had the impression that these arguments had some effect, and the Panel was in the end able to make its proposals without any formal dissenting voices.

Terrorism

The Panel met under the shadow of the Iraq war; but it also met under the shadow of the terrorist attacks on New York and Washington on 11 September 2001. And, while it was deliberating, the bombing of the Madrid commuter rail network in March 2004 and the Beslan school atrocity in September 2004 served as reminders, if such were needed, of the scale and immediacy of the threat the international community faced from international terrorism. From the outset of its work, therefore, the Panel faced an imperative need to bring forward proposals in this field. This was not to prove either straightforward or uncontentious for a number of reasons. Firstly, in purely technical terms, no one even in their wildest dreams supposed that the UN could or should provide the operational focus for action against terrorism. The organisation was simply too big, too leaky and too cumbersome to be able to do that. Operational cooperation was going to need to take place in smaller, regional groupings or, more often, in direct, un-institutionalised cooperation between national governments and their law enforcement agencies. What the UN could do was to provide a robust and universal normative framework within which such cooperation could take place. But a good deal of this framework had already been put in place, immediately after the 9/11 attacks, by Security Council Resolution 1373 and by the work of the Counter-Terrorism Committee set up by that resolution. And, before it reported, Security Council Resolution 1540 had strengthened that normative framework with respect to preventing nuclear materials falling into the hands of terrorists.

A second problem of a much more political nature was one which had bedevilled all previous attempts to agree a definition of terrorism and thus to plug the last remaining gap in the large corpus of international law outlawing such actions as hijacking, piracy, the taking of hostages and the financing of terrorism. This problem could loosely be summed up in the phrase 'one man's terrorist is another man's freedom fighter'. The occupation of Iraq by the US/UK-led coalition forces gave added point to those who used this paradox to prevent agreement. Many lawyers argued that the gap left by the failure to define terrorism was now so small and the body of law dealing with most terrorist acts so wide-ranging that there was no pressing need to plug that gap, that to try and fail again might be worse than not to try at all. But this was above all a political question; and there was no doubt the UN was damaged by its inability to agree on a definition of terrorism.

The Panel's debates covered all this ground exhaustively and sometimes quite heatedly. Amre Moussa argued forcefully that it was essential to avoid equating terrorism with Islamic terrorism; there were plenty of terrorists of other religious persuasions. And he was adamant that no definition of terrorism could be agreed which covered acts against uniformed occupying forces in Iraq or in the West Bank and Gaza in Palestine or which ignored crimes that might be committed by those forces. Many others on the Panel, with Robert Badinter and myself prominent among them, were equally insistent that we really must at least try to enable what was called the Comprehensive Convention on Terrorism, stuck somewhere in the UN's legal committee structure, to be agreed. In the end we did reach a consensus, which consisted of making it clear that the already existing Geneva Convention regulated the conduct of occupying forces vis-à-vis civilians and vice-versa, and of proposing as a definition of terrorism for inclusion in the comprehensive convention the following:

> any action, in addition to actions already specified by the existing conventions on aspects of terrorism, the Geneva Conventions and Security Council Resolution 1566 [the resolution adopted after the Beslan school massacre] that is intended to cause death or serious bodily harm to civilians or non-combatants, when the purpose of such act, by its nature or context, is to intimidate a population, or to compel a government or an international organisation to do or to abstain from doing any act.

This formulation clearly did not cover actions against uniformed occupying forces.

In addition to this central element of the Panel's proposals on terrorism the following principal recommendations were made:

(i)   The UN Secretary-General should take a leading role in promoting a comprehensive strategy against terrorism which should include:
  (a) dissuasion, working to reverse the causes or facilitators of terrorism, including through promoting social and political rights, the rule of law and democratic reform; working to end occupations and address major political grievances; combating organised crime; reducing poverty and unemployment; and stopping state collapse;
  (b) efforts to counter extremism and intolerance, including through education and fostering public debate;
  (c) development of better instruments for global counter-terrorism cooperation, all within a legal framework that is respectful of civil liberties and human rights, including in the areas of law enforcement; intelligence sharing, where possible; denial and interdiction when required; and financial controls;
  (d) building state capacity to prevent terrorist recruitment and operations;
  (e) control of dangerous materials and public health defence.

(ii)   The Security Council should extend the authority of the Counter-Terrorism Executive Directorate to act as a clearing house for state-to-state provision of military, police and border control assistance for the development of domestic counter-terrorism capabilities.

(iii)   The UN should establish a capacity-building trust fund under the Counter-Terrorism Executive Directorate.

The role of economic sanctions

The UN Charter of 1945 had explicitly envisaged the possibility of the Security Council using mandatory economic sanctions against a trans-gressor as one of the policy options for achieving international peace and security. Article 41 of the Charter states:

> The Security Council may decide what measures, not involving the use of armed force, are to be employed to give effect to its decisions, and it may call upon members of the United Nations to apply such measures. These may include complete or partial interruption of economic relations and of rail, sea, air, postal, telegraphic, radio and other means of communication, and the severance of diplomatic relations.

During the period of the Cold War economic sanctions had hardly ever been employed, given the determination of one or other of the super-powers to protect their protégés against such measures, although a mandatory arms embargo was imposed on the apartheid regime in South Africa. But, once the dead hand of the Cold War had been removed, the Security Council began to make use of this instrument quite frequently. Twice during the first half of the 1990s (against Iraq and against Serbia) comprehensive economic sanctions, i.e. a ban on all trade except medicines and foodstuffs, and most means of communications, were imposed. In a number of other cases (Libya, Haiti, the UNITA rebels in Angola) more limited sanctions were imposed. And arms embargoes were put in place in an attempt to limit the scale and spread of hostilities (on the former Yugoslavia, Somalia, Rwanda, Sierra Leone).

The experience in applying these sanctions had provided much material from which lessons could be drawn by the time the Panel began its work. One thing was very clear: economic sanctions were not a silver bullet which could bring hostilities to a halt or compel a transgressor to change policy fundamentally. While sanctions did weaken Saddam Hussein's Iraq quite considerably and thus reduce both its capacity for further aggression and for resisting the use of force when Kuwait was liberated, and while the raging inflation in Serbia triggered by sanctions and its isolation were certainly among the factors which brought Milosevic to the negotiating table, in neither case had there been any realistic chance that sanctions on their own would have ensured compliance with the Security Council's resolutions. At the same time many unintended humanitarian consequences of comprehensive sanctions became apparent. In particular, in the case of totalitarian (Iraq) or authoritarian (Serbia, Haiti) regimes – and almost by definition it was such regimes which found themselves on the receiving end of sanctions – these regimes were able to ensure that their ruling elites were spared from the impact of sanctions and that this impact fell disproportionately on the main mass of the population, whose suffering could then be used to strengthen support for the regimes themselves and for propaganda purposes to argue for an easing of the sanctions. Other problems had beset the various arms embargoes which had been imposed. The difficulty of enforcement in lawless regions such as the Horn of Africa or where abundant natural resources existed to finance illegal arms traffic such as in Angola and Sierra Leone, or where there was a sophisticated supply network established to find a way through the embargo such as in Bosnia and Croatia, had resulted in such embargoes being more honoured in the breach than the observance.

Faced with this rather unpromising record there was some temptation for the Panel to take an entirely negative view on the future use of economic sanctions. But this it was not prepared to do. To have done so would have been to knock away almost the only rung in the Security Council's escalatory ladder of pressure between diplomatic exhortation and the actual use of force. That, it was generally realised, would have been a counsel of despair. But the Panel did take the view that comprehensive economic sanctions were a method to be avoided in future, if at all possible, given the painful collateral humanitarian consequences of such action. And it put its weight behind a better targeting of economic sanctions with measures designed to hurt the ruling elites of the transgressor rather than the mass of the population. Such targeted sanctions were in fact proving reasonably successful in the case of Libya. It was clear, however, that the approach to devising targeted sanctions hitherto employed had been hopelessly over-politicised and unscientific. It was also clear that, fully justified as arms embargoes were in dealing with either interstate or intra-state hostilities, something needed to be done to enforce them more effectively. The Panel's main recommendations were as follows:

(i)   When the Security Council imposed a sanctions regime – including arms embargoes – it should routinely establish monitoring mechanisms and provide them with the necessary authority and capacity to carry out high-quality, in-depth investigations. Adequate budgetary provisions must be made to implement these mechanisms.

(ii)   Security Council sanctions committees should be mandated to develop improved guidelines and reporting procedures to assist states in sanctions implementation, and to improve procedures for maintaining accurate lists of individuals and entities subject to targeted sanctions.

(iii)   The Secretary-General should appoint a senior official with sufficient supporting resources to enable the Secretary-General to supply the Security Council with analysis of the best way to target sanctions and to assist in coordinating their implementation. This official would also assist compliance efforts, identifying technical assistance needs and coordinating such assistance, and make recommendations on any adjustments necessary to advance the effectiveness of sanctions.

(iv)   Donors should donate more resources to strengthening the legal, administrative and policing and border-control capacity of member states to implement sanctions. Capacity-building measures should include efforts to improve air-traffic interdiction in zones of conflict.

(v)   The Security Council should, in instances of verified, chronic violations, impose secondary sanctions against those involved in sanctions busting.

(vi)   The Secretary-General, in consultation with the Security Council, should ensure that an appropriate auditing mechanism was in place to oversee sanctions administration.

(vii)   Sanctions committees should improve procedures for providing humanitarian exemptions and routinely conduct assessments of the humanitarian impact of sanctions.

During the latter stages of the Panel's work a rising tide of media and political denunciation of the UN's handling of the Iraq oil-for-food programme (whose origins are described in Chapters V and IX) made itself felt, as Iraqi documentation of the regime's efforts to undermine and find ways round the comprehensive sanctions imposed on them came to light in Baghdad. While the task of enquiring into what had gone wrong with the oil-for-food scheme was not for the Panel but rather for the specialised enquiry set up by Kofi Annan under the chairmanship of Paul Volcker, the former head of the US Federal Reserve Bank, which reported long after the Panel was due to do so, the Panel did take account of some of the broad, generic problems which had arisen; and a number of the proposals set out in the preceding list (in particular (vi)) were designed to address these problems.

The use of force

Every one of the Panel's recommendations described and analysed so far in this chapter was designed to avoid or prevent the need to use force. There was never any doubt in our minds that policies of prevention, whether intended to deal with the more direct and obvious threats to international peace and security such as state failure, the proliferation of weapons of mass destruction or terrorism, or the less direct threats from poverty, pandemic disease or environmental degradation, were preferable to the use of force; and that the use of force must in every circumstance be regarded as a last resort, only to be contemplated once non-military preventive measures had been tried and failed. But we could not simply duck the issue of the use of force. Twice in the last few years (over Kosovo in 1999 and much more seriously and conclusively over Iraq in 2003) the Security Council had been paralysed by disagreements over the authorisation of the use of force. Moreover the USA had promulgated a new security doctrine in 2002 which appeared to contemplate the unilateral preventive use of force in certain vague and ill-defined circumstances. And the catastrophes in Bosnia and Rwanda had brought into sharper focus the possible need for the international community to use force to protect populations whose own governments were themselves either unwilling or unable to protect them. It was clear from the outset that we would need to venture into the minefields of the pre-emptive and preventive use of force, of its possible authorisation by the international community in the form of the Security Council and of the emerging international norm which had come to be known as the responsibility to protect.

It is often not fully appreciated that for the first 45 years of the UN's history, during the period of the Cold War, consideration by the UN of the authorisation of the use of force had been the exception rather than the rule. Only in the quite exceptional circumstances of the Korean War, when the Soviet Union had been boycotting the Security Council and when the Chinese veto had been in the hands of the authorities in Taiwan, and in the case of the peacekeeping operation in the Congo had such authorisations been given. During that time there had been plenty of conflicts, both international and civil, but the member states involved and their great power backers had chosen, to the maximum degree possible, to keep away from the UN. Even in cases of what would now be called humanitarian intervention, for example India's invasion of East Pakistan, Vietnam's of Cambodia or Tanzania's of Uganda, no attempt was made to come to the UN for legitimisation of the action being taken. Since the end of the Cold War all that had changed. The 1991 Gulf War to expel Iraq from Kuwait had been explicitly authorised by the Security Council. A good number of peace operations had received authority under Chapter VII of the Charter to use force to carry out their mandates. But, like so much else at the UN, the approach had so far been entirely haphazard and ad hoc. The challenge the Panel faced was to attempt to systematise the consideration at the UN of the use of force, but, in doing so, to avoid going so far as to provoke fundamental objections from the member states. We never had any illusion that proposing new, binding international legal rules seeking to regulate the use of force would pass that test; and we did not therefore propose any such rules. We also had to steer around one major immediate obstacle, the circumstances of the war in Iraq. While the overwhelming majority of members of the Panel were sharply critical of the decision by the US-led coalition to invade Iraq in March 2003, it rapidly became clear to us that, if we took sides on the legality and legitimacy of that action, any proposals we made on the use of force in the future would be dead on arrival. So we opted for the less than glorious expedient of silence on that point.

The first area we had to look at was the issue of a pre-emptive response to an imminent threat. Article 51 of the UN Charter referred to the 'inherent right of individual or collective self-defence'. The use of the word 'inherent' certainly seemed to imply that the right was in no sense conferred by the Charter. Many of those who had criticised the US-led invasion of Iraq (which they regarded as an abuse of Article 51, even though none of the invading states actually invoked that article to justify their action) were pressing on the Panel the need to rewrite Article 51 in a more restrictive sense, designed to make it more difficult to invoke in the future. And some of those who had supported the invasion wanted Article 51 rewritten so as explicitly to broaden its scope to cover the sort of unilateral preventive action against threats which were not imminent envisaged in the recent US security doctrine. Discussion in the Panel was quite difficult, with doubts expressed as to whether the unilateral pre-emptive use of force could ever be regarded as legitimate. But memories of 9/11 and other terrorist outrages were fresh in the mind and the possible need to act instantly to counter any such attacks was hard to gainsay. In the end it was decided to reject the pressures to redefine Article 51 in either a more restrictive or a more expansive direction. But we made it very clear that, in the Panel's view, any preventive action designed to counter a non-imminent and non-proximate threat should be brought to the Security Council and not decided unilaterally: 'Allowing one to so act [in unilateral prevention] is to allow all'.

There was much less disagreement in the Panel over the handling by the Security Council of cases where authorising the use of force was brought to the Council:

> The Security Council is fully empowered under Chapter VII of the Charter to address the full range of security threats with which States are concerned. The task is not to find alternatives to the Security Council as a source of authority but to make the Council work better than it has.

This trenchant approach stopped short of saying flatly that any use of force not authorised by the Council would be illegitimate or perhaps even illegal; but it was a very clear challenge to the hankering after self-authorised 'coalitions of the willing' so much favoured by neo-conservative circles in Washington. The Panel also proposed what it described as a set of five guidelines or 'criteria of legitimacy', which it was suggested should always be considered by the Council when it was deciding whether or not to authorise or endorse the use of force. These were:

(a)   Seriousness of threat. Is the threatened harm to State or human security of a kind, and sufficiently clear and serious, to justify prima facie the use of military force? In the case of internal threats, does it involve genocide and other large-scale killing, ethnic cleansing or serious violations of international humanitarian law, actual or imminently apprehended?

(b)   Proper purpose. Is it clear that the primary purpose of the proposed military action is to halt or arrest the threat in question, whatever other purposes or motives may be involved?

(c)   Last resort. Has every non-military option for meeting the threat in question been explored, with reasonable grounds for believing that other measures will not succeed?

(d)   Proportional means. Are the scale, duration and intensity of the proposed military action the minimum necessary to meet the threat in question?

(e)   Balance of consequences. Is there a reasonable chance of the military action being successful in meeting the threat in question, with the consequences of action not likely to be worse than the consequences of inaction?

These five guidelines drew heavily on much which had been written over the centuries on the criteria for a 'just war', with some updating to achieve relevance in the sort of circumstances which were likely to face the Security Council in the period ahead. They thus did not break entirely new ground, although the use to which it was suggested they should be put would have done so. On that last point the Panel proposed that the guidelines should be embodied in declaratory resolutions of the Security Council and the General Assembly. It was also suggested that individual member states should state that that was the basis on which they would judge the case for the use of force. It was thus quite clear from the outset that the Panel was not setting out to create new binding provisions of international law. But it did believe that the guidelines, if endorsed, would increase the legitimacy and acceptability of any decisions taken by the Security Council on the use of force, and that they would also have some deterrent value against potential transgressors by making it clearer than was currently the case the circumstances under which the international community would be likely to authorise the use of force. However, every individual case would remain to be decided on its merits by the Council. There was no question of automaticity of application or of a kind of self-executing template for decision-taking.

Where the Panel did break entirely new ground, although it was ground that had been well prepared by the 2001 Canadian-sponsored Report of the International Commission on Intervention and State Sovereignty (ICISS), was in its championing of what it described as:

> ... the emerging norm that there is a collective international responsibility to protect, exercisable by the Security Council authorising military intervention as a last resort, in the event of genocide and other large-scale killing, ethnic cleansing or serious violations of international humanitarian law which sovereign governments have proved powerless or unwilling to prevent.

This doctrine, which had hitherto merely done the rounds of international seminars, symposia and commissions, was now placed fair and square in the centre of the negotiating arena, a matter no longer just for debate and discussion, but for decision. The Panel did not come easily to the decision to back a new doctrine which departed so radically from past UN practice, and, some would try to argue, even from the wording of the Charter, in particular of its Article 2(7), which stated that 'nothing contained in the present Charter shall authorise the United Nations to intervene in matters which are essentially within the domestic jurisdiction of any state'; but which fortunately also added: 'this principle shall not prejudice the application of enforcement measures under Chapter VII'. The principal advocate of the 'responsibility to protect' on the Panel was Gareth Evans, who had co-chaired the Canadian-sponsored ICISS report referred to above, and, from the outset, he was supported by a majority of members. Gradually hesitations were worn down, both those from members of the P5 (China in particular) and those from Latin America and Africa who had traditionally been most resistant to talk of 'humanitarian intervention'. In the end there was unanimity, as there was later to be, somewhat more surprisingly, among the whole of the UN membership.

Fitting the institutions to deliver the new policies

The Panel's determination to deal with policies first and only thereafter, when the picture on policies was clearer, to turn to reforms of the institutions which would be needed if those policies were to be effectively delivered, held up well through its deliberations in the early months of 2004. But of course it was not possible totally to exclude the consideration of institutional issues in this first phase. As always at the UN they kept intruding. And in some cases, such as our consideration of the gaps in the international community's armoury when it came to dealing with conflict prevention and post-conflict peacebuilding, it was an integral part of the analysis itself and of the options for remedial action we considered. So, by the time the discussion of institutional reform was fully engaged at the plenary session in July 2004, the Panel's thinking was already beginning to take shape. From then on those institutional changes were at the heart of our debates.

The General Assembly

While it was evident that the Panel could not just bypass the General Assembly when it came to proposing reforms, it was a great deal less evident what could usefully and realistically be proposed. For one thing the General Assembly was in a sense sovereign and, so long as it acted within the Charter, was master of its own procedures; and yet over recent years attempts by successive presidents of the General Assembly to introduce modest and sensible reforms had run into the sands of indifference and obfuscation. It was obvious that a shorter, more sharply focussed and more topical agenda would provide a better framework for debate; but that would mean culling from the agenda a number of issues which were of critical importance to a particular country or group of countries. It was equally obvious that the committees of the General Assembly, with a theoretical membership of 192, were ridiculously unwieldy. And then some of the solutions could well have proved worse than the disease. Kofi Annan himself had canvassed the idea of adopting more General Assembly resolutions by majority vote and less by consensus, the latter practice having led to much meaningless and contradictory verbiage. But the risk of the 'tyranny of the majority' was a real one, as experience over the 'Zionism is racism' resolution had shown. And majority voting, which was in any case used when absolutely necessary, only exacerbated the extraordinary imbalance between major powers and micro-states, each with one unweighted vote. One radical proposal, to endorse the procedure of 'uniting for peace', under which the General Assembly would take responsibility for a peace and security issue if the Security Council was prevented by a veto from reaching a decision, was considered by the Panel but did not gain sufficient support, those members from P5 countries and from putative permanent members of the Security Council in particular being unwilling to go down that road.

In the end, recognising in any case that the General Assembly did one part of its job, the provision of a deliberative, almost parliamentary, forum in which every member state could have its say on a wide variety of issues, reasonably well, we put forward some relatively modest proposals:

(i)   The opportunity provided by the Millennium Review Summit in 2005 should be used to forge a new consensus on broader and more effective collective security.
(ii)   There should be a shortening of the agenda, and smaller, more tightly focussed committees.
(iii) There should be a better mechanism for enabling systematic engagement with civil society organisations.

The Security Council

From the moment the Panel was set up it was clear that there would be no escape from another attempt to harpoon the Great White Whale of UN diplomacy, enlargement of the Security Council. Within a few weeks representatives of the main aspirants to permanent membership, who became known as the G4 (Brazil, Germany, India and Japan), began limbering up for the negotiation; and so, naturally enough, did those countries just below them in the world-power pecking order (Argentina, Canada, Indonesia, Italy, Mexico and Pakistan) who were as determined as ever to prevent their aspirations being realised. It became clear that one of the main challenges for the Panel was going to be to avoid this issue drowning out the discussion of all other reform proposals, and, even more important, to ensure that, if Security Council enlargement again defied solution, it did not carry all the other reform proposals to the bottom of the sea with it.

Looked at in basically procedural terms, the Panel had three main options. The first was to condemn the continuing deadlock in the negotiations over enlargement and exhort the member states to renewed efforts to resolve the issue, without, however, putting forward any specific formula for doing so. This somewhat cowardly approach was not as difficult to defend as might be thought. Any hard-headed analysis of changes in the international scene since the failure of the last serious attempt at enlargement in 1997 led to the realisation that the climate of opinion was, if anything, less propitious to enlargement than it had been then, not more so: Chinese–Japanese relations had deteriorated to a point at which it was hard to see China accepting a permanent seat for Japan; Russia's more assertive foreign policy was likely to resist any dilution of its permanent member status; the Bush administration was deeply unmotivated about any enlargement at all; and the African conundrum of how many, and which, African countries should be considered for a permanent seat remained as difficult to resolve as ever. For the Panel to make no specific proposals would somewhat reduce the risk of linkage with its other reforms. I myself rather favoured this course, but our Research Director warned me in advance of the July plenary session that I would find little if any support for it. The second option was to propose a single, specific formula. The trouble about that option was that it would inevitably split the Panel, with some insisting on new permanent members and some resisting that. The third option would be to offer two or more alternative formulas.

As has previously been noted, no systematic discussion of these options had taken place in the Panel before the July 2004 plenary session. In preparation for that session the research staff circulated an alternative formula to the existing, deadlocked one which had provided for a Council of 24 members with five or six new permanent members. This alternative formula, which was for consideration alongside the previous one, provided again for a Council of 24 members, but with no new permanent members; instead there would be created a new category of longer-term elected members (for four-year terms, which could be renewable) in addition to the five existing permanent members and a continuing cohort of two-year elected members. However, before we had had a chance to discuss this alternative, the terms of the game were changed by the Secretary-General himself. Speaking to us over dinner on the first evening of our session in Baden, Kofi Annan said firmly that he wanted us to make a specific proposal on Security Council enlargement and that he wanted one formula, not two. He did not reveal which of the two principal alternatives he favoured. The next day there was no inclination to gainsay the Secretary-General's expressed preference. Since everyone was only too familiar with the pros and cons of the deadlocked formula, discussion focussed almost exclusively on the new approach of longer-term, renewable members. Its protagonists on the Panel, who were numerous, extolled the benefits of this approach, while those who might have been expected to resist it (the members from Brazil, India and Japan) showed some interest in it and some willingness to see it as a possible stepping-stone to eventual permanent membership. When we parted from Baden it was agreed that no decisions had been taken and no balance of preferences between the two formulas established. We would revert to the matter in September.

Shortly thereafter the one and only major (and inaccurate) leak from the Panel's deliberations occurred. An article appeared in *The Economist* speculating that the Panel was on the point of discarding the old formula providing for new permanent members and opting instead for the new longer-term but not permanent member approach. Predictably this triggered off a firestorm of protest from the G4. The Secretary-General was besieged and cajoled. And by the time we met him again, just before our September session, Annan told us he would now like us to produce two alternative formulas, not one. Since this reversal of his earlier position was likely to avoid the difficulties of a split in the Panel and to encourage consensus over that section of our report, the members of the Panel embraced it with relief. Thereafter our work was concentrated on setting out the two alternatives in a clear and comprehensible fashion, without expressing any preference between them.

The Panel began by setting out certain principles which it suggested should govern any reform of the Security Council:

(i)   That it should increase the involvement in decision-making of those who contributed most to the UN financially, militarily and diplomatically – specifically in terms of contributions to the UN-assessed budgets, participation in mandated peace operations, contributions to the voluntary activities of the UN in the areas of security and development, and diplomatic activities in support of UN objectives and mandates. Among developed countries, achieving or making substantial progress towards the internationally agreed level of 0.7 per cent of GNI for official development assistance should be considered an important criterion.

(ii)   That it should bring into the decision-making process countries more representative of the broader membership, especially of the developing world.

(iii)   That it should not impair the effectiveness of the Security Council.

(iv)   That it should increase the democratic and accountable nature of the body.

Using these criteria the Panel argued that a choice in favour of either Formula A or Formula B was now a necessity. Both formulas involved some adjustment to the existing UN regional groupings for electoral purposes to provide four constituencies (Africa, Asia and Pacific, Europe and Americas) of roughly similar size; but the proposal would have left the existing, more complex and more uneven regional groupings for electoral purposes untouched for all elections other than those to the Security Council. The alternative formulas proposed were:

(i)   Formula A – A Council of 24. Six new permanent seats to be added to the existing five (two for Africa, two for Asia and the Pacific, and one each for Europe and the Americas). The new permanent members would not have a veto. Three new, two-year non-permanent seats (divided more equitably among the regions than at present).

(ii)   Formula B – A Council of 24. No new permanent seats. A new category of eight, four-year renewable-term seats (two for each of the four regions) plus one new two-year, non-permanent and non-renewable seat.

In either of the two formulas the Panel suggested that the choice of countries to fill the new seats, whether permanent or longer-term electable, should give preference to states among the top three financial contributors to the regular budget in their relevant regional area, or to the top three voluntary contributors from their regional area or to the top three troop contributors to UN peacekeeping from their regional area. Whichever formula was chosen the Panel proposed that there should be a review of the composition of the Security Council in 2020 which would include a review of the contribution of permanent and non-permanent members from the point of view of Council effectiveness in taking collective action to prevent or remove new and old threats to international peace and security (this heavily camouflaged review clause contained within it a concealed threat to the status of the existing permanent members should they not pull their weight at the UN in the meantime, but it was a fairly slight threat and one which was not enforceable).

There was some discussion by the Panel of other Security Council-related issues, the most important of which was the veto. Somewhat to my surprise, since members from the P5 countries were in a minority, there was no disposition to change or challenge the existing veto powers of the P5. While the distortions these introduced to the Council's decision-making were deplored, it was recognised that none of the existing permanent members would willingly surrender their veto and that, without that willingness, the Charter provided no possibility of change. It was therefore felt that it would be counter-productive to the chances for general Security Council reform if abolition or attenuation of the veto were to be put forward. But there was rapid and unanimous agreement that there should be no expansion of the veto to any new permanent members. This particular proposal helped to shift the subsequent debate in a way helpful to the G4 and also to draw some of the sting from the argument that a larger Council would be a less effective one. The Panel did, however, make a proposal designed to reduce the use of the veto, particularly in cases where non-mandatory resolutions were being voted (a large number of the US vetoes on resolutions criticising Israel fell into that category). We suggested that there could be a two-stage process of voting. The first stage would be purely indicative and a permanent member would be able to vote 'no' without stopping the whole process. In the second, operative stage the existing rules would apply, but the permanent member which had previously voted 'no' would have the option to abstain rather than to veto. This subtle approach was put forward by Robert Badinter and the Panel decided to endorse it, although without any excessive expectations that it would find favour among the P5. As a last point the Panel proposed that various changes designed to improve the transparency and accountability of Council proceedings which had been developed over recent years should be formalised in its rules of procedure (which, bizarrely, throughout the Cold War period and since, had never been formally promulgated).

A peacebuilding commission

The inadequacies of the UN's handling of the phenomenon of state failure was not a question of debate by the time the Panel set to work, it was a matter of public record. States had by then failed in every part of the world, with catastrophic consequences not only for their own citizens but also for those of whole regions. Genocide, international terrorism, ethnic cleansing and massive abuses of international humanitarian law had bred in the interstices of state failure. And development policies, the struggle against poverty, malnutrition and pandemic diseases had been totally frustrated wherever a state had failed. The international community's response, including that of the UN, had been feeble and badly coordinated. There had been few instances of the successful prevention of a state failing – Macedonia being one of those few success stories. And, once a state had failed, the resulting breakdown of order and hostilities, often drawing in neighbours, not only took a long time to bring under control but left behind a challenge in the form of post-conflict peacebuilding to which no effective set of sustained responses had been found. Several such failed states had drifted in and out of collapse several times – Haiti, Afghanistan, Burundi, Sierra Leone and Liberia were examples – with short periods of international peacekeeping being followed by a reversion to the failure of the state's inadequately re-established structures and institutions. Nor was the problem one of a lack of advance warning. By this time many international organisations, national governments, non-governmental organisations, research departments of universities and think-tanks had produced matrices setting out the main indicators of impending state failure. More often than not their predictions were proved right. But that had so far increased neither the capacity for prevention nor for post-conflict peace-building.

So far as prevention was concerned, the main obstacle was the unwillingness of the rulers of the failing state to enlist the involvement and support of the international community, matched by the unwillingness of the international community to intervene without the consent of the state in question. In some cases too, actions by the International Financial Institutions (the International Monetary Fund and the World Bank) actually made the plight of the state in question worse, with economic policies being imposed that it was in no position to support. When it came to post-conflict peacebuilding, the problems were different. Then it was a lack of sustained, properly coordinated support by all those involved over a period of time much longer than that normally envisaged for peace operations that was at fault. Often, too, there would be funding gaps which it proved difficult or impossible to fill. A peace settlement would contain detailed prescriptions of the disarming, demobilisation and resettlement of warring militias, or for de-mining of war zones; but the UN would not be allowed to meet the costs of these programmes on assessed contributions and voluntary donations would fall short of what was needed. Dovetailing the immediate requirement for emergency relief into longer-term development, two functions all too often in the hands of completely different international organisations or NGOs, was another major area of weakness.

One institutional prescription which was frequently canvassed as the problem of state failure loomed larger was to revive the now dormant powers of the UN's Trusteeship Council and apply them to the victims of state failure. The Trusteeship Council had been established in 1945 to handle the transition of UN trusteeship territories, some of them inherited from the League of Nations, to full independence. It had gradually worked itself out of a job, with the grant of independence to the last remaining US-administered trust territories in the Pacific in the 1990s. It was argued that the Trusteeship Council could provide a framework within which the problems of failed states could be effectively handled. But the more the Panel examined the problem, the less attractive this option seemed. There was the problem of the title of the Trusteeship Council which, in French at least – Le Conseil de Tutelle – was singularly unappealing. Nor did the powers of the Trusteeship Council fit the circumstance of failed states since they were designed to handle territories which had not hitherto been states at all. And the procedures of the Trusteeship Council were heavily dominated by the P5 of the Security Council, another extremely off-putting feature. The conclusion was that to fit the Trusteeship Council to handle failed states you would need to rewrite that whole section of the Charter, a time-consuming procedure whose successful completion could not be guaranteed. So, instead, the Panel turned to the idea of creating a new institution specifically designed to deal with the problems of state failure; and that was what we put forward in our report.

The main features of the Peacebuilding Commission the Panel proposed were as follows:

(i)   The Security Council, acting under the Charter provision that empowered it to establish subsidiary organs, should, after consultation with the Economic and Social Council, establish a Peacebuilding Commission.

(ii)   The core functions of the Commission should be to identify countries which were under stress and risked sliding towards state collapse; to organise in partnership with the national government, proactive assistance in preventing that process from developing further; to assist in the planning for transitions between conflict and post-conflict peacebuilding; and in particular to marshal and sustain the efforts of the international community in post-conflict peacebuilding over whatever period might be necessary.

(iii) Without trying to decide the details the Panel suggested the Commission:

(a) should be reasonably small;

(b) should meet in different configurations, to consider both general policy issues and country-by-country strategies;

(c) should be chaired for at least one year and perhaps longer by a member approved by the Security Council;

(d) should include representation from the Economic and Social Council;

(e) national representatives from the country under consideration should be invited to attend;

(f) the IMF, the World Bank and, when appropriate, regional development banks should be represented by senior officials;

(g) representatives of the principal donor countries and principal troop contributors should be invited to participate;

(h) representatives of regional and subregional organisations should be invited to participate when such organisations were actively involved in the country in question.

In parallel with the establishment of the Peacebuilding Commission, the Panel proposed that a Peacebuilding Support Office should be established in the Secretariat to give the Commission support and to ensure that the Secretary-General was able to integrate system-wide peacebuilding policies and strategies, develop best practices and provide coherent support for field operations.

Regional organisations

The role of regional organisations with some responsibilities in the field of security had been recognised from the outset in the 1945 Charter. Chapter VIII of the Charter (Articles 52 and 53) contained provisions for deconflicting the roles of the world organisation and regional organisations and also envisaged the possibility of regional organisations being used for enforcement action under the authority of the Security Council. Throughout the period of the Cold War, however, these provisions remained a dead letter. It was inconceivable that either of the Cold War alliances, NATO or the Warsaw Pact, would elude a veto from the other side if authority for enforcement action had been sought; and other regional organisations such as the EC, the OAS, the AL or the OAU were not at that stage organised or empowered to undertake missions in the field of peace and security.

With the Cold War at an end and with the UN exhibiting numerous symptoms of peacekeeping overstretch, thought began to be given both at UN headquarters and by the regional organisations themselves to the latter assuming a more proactive role in peace operations. The UN Secretariat organised a series of conferences at which they brought together a wide range of regional and subregional organisations. But nothing much came of all this; it remained talk with little action and, as the first post-Cold War surge in UN peacekeeping activity ebbed in the late 1990s, any feeling of urgency ebbed too. There were other reasons for the lack of progress. At the UN there was a feeling that peacekeeping belonged by right to the organisation and that handing over responsibilities to regional organisations would in some sense diminish the UN itself. More importantly those regional organisations with any real potential in the field of peace operations were either reluctant (OAS) or unable (OAU) to move in this direction or unsuccessful (the EC, now transformed into the EU) in their first ventures. And all concerned were conscious that activating regional organisations did not automatically and arithmetically address the resource problems the UN was facing, since all regional organisations were composed of member states who were also members of the UN. Both the UN and regional organisations were thus lowering their buckets down one single well of human and fiscal resources.

By the time the Panel came to look at these issues in 2004, further shifts had taken place, pushing the debate back towards a renewed effort to mesh the activities of the UN together with those of regional and subregional organisations. The UN's peacekeeping overstretch was once more a daily reality; both the EU, and the OAU's successor organisation, the AU, as well as some of the latter's subregional organisations such as the Economic Community of West African States (ECOWAS), had begun to become seriously and relatively effectively involved in peace operations; and the taboo on the UN working closely with NATO had been broken by cooperation both in various parts of the former Yugoslavia and in Afghanistan. The Panel contained a number of members (Salim Salim, Robert Badinter, Amre Moussa, João Baena Soares, Enrique Iglesias and myself) with working experience of regional organisations and a strong desire to see the cooperation between them and the UN strengthened and systematised. We were given enthusiastic encouragement by the regional organisations themselves, in particular by the EU and the AU; and, when the Panel visited Addis Ababa, it received loud and clear the message that both African governments and civil society organisations wanted to see progress in that direction. The Panel set their recommendations within a general framework of UN support not only for existing regional and subregional organisations, but for such new regional organisations as might be formed in parts of the world where there were either no such organisations or where those that did exist were relatively ineffective. We had indeed been struck in our analytical discussions by how effective some regional organisations, particularly those in Europe (including not only the EU, but also the Council of Europe and the Organisation for Security and Cooperation in Europe), had been in furthering the objectives laid down in the UN Charter; and we were also struck by how often the most bitter and dangerous international disputes (in North East Asia, South Asia and the Gulf region) were to be found where no such effective organisations existed. So, while we did not regard it as part of our remit to tell the countries in these parts of the world to get together on a regional basis, we did give a strong boost to any such developments as might occur: 'We believe the United Nations should encourage the establishment of such groupings, particularly in highly vulnerable parts of the world where no effective security organisations currently exist'.

More concretely the Panel recommended:

(i)   Authorisation from the Security Council should in all cases be sought for regional peace operations. But we added the caveat that in some urgent situations that authorisation might be sought after such operations had commenced.

(ii)   Consultation and cooperation between the UN and regional organisations should be expanded and could be formalised in an agreement, covering such issues as meetings of the heads of organisations, more frequent exchange of information and early warning, co-training of civilian and military personnel and exchange of personnel within peace operations.

(iii) In the case of African regional and subregional capacities, donor countries should commit to a ten-year process of sustained capacity-building support, within the AU strategic framework.

(iv)   Regional organisations that had a capacity for conflict prevention or peacekeeping should place such capacities in the framework of the UN Standby arrangements System.

(v)   Member states should agree to allow the UN to provide equipment support from UN-owned sources to regional operations, as needed.

(vi)   The rules for the UN peacekeeping budget should be amended to give the UN the option on a case-by-case basis to finance regional operations authorised by the Security Council with assessed contributions.

Many of these proposals were simply going with the grain of developments already underway at the UN and in the principal member states. But the last one, (vi), was breaking new ground in a sensitive area. It would mean that all member states would join in financing a regional operation which was in effect being undertaken with their agreement, and in some cases at their behest. Its relevance was soon going to be demonstrated when the AU was pushed, by the reluctance of the government of Sudan to accept a UN peacekeeping mission, into mounting an AU mission in Darfur, and serious financial problems immediately arose. In addition the Panel broke further new ground by stating flatly that it welcomed recent developments in NATO to undertake peacekeeping operations beyond its mandated areas so long as they were authorised by and accountable to the Security Council (as they were in the former Yugoslavia and Afghanistan). It also commended the constructive role NATO could play in assisting in the training and equipping of less well resourced regional organisations and states. Those were views which certainly would not have been expressed by a panel whose membership was drawn from a worldwide pool of expertise during the Cold War period or even during the period immediately following its end.

The Economic and Social Council

ECOSOC had for long been the orphan of the UNs institutional system, neglected and often marginalised in international discussion of the developmental, economic, social, cultural, educational and health issues which it had been established to handle. Twelve articles in the Charter were devoted to it, but those articles were singularly vague about what ECOSOC was supposed to do and lacked any real cutting edge or powers of decision. It was to 'initiate studies and reports', to 'make recommendations', to 'prepare draft conventions' and 'to call international conferences on matters falling within its competence'. From the outset the Cold War paralysed it to an even greater extent than other UN institutions, as its debates came to be dominated by gladiatorial contests between the protagonists of command economies and those of market economies, between the Soviet Union and its satellites and proxies in the Third World, and the West and theirs. Then, in the 1980s a new front in this long and paralysing war was opened up when the developing countries put their faith in what came to be described as a 'new international economic order', which aimed to use international regulatory authority supposedly to bring greater benefits to developing countries. Both command economies and the New International Economic Order were swept away with the end of the Cold War. But by that time much of the terrain which might have been occupied by ECOSOC was firmly in the hands of three major international organisations only very lightly linked to the UN – the IMF, the World Bank and GATT. These three organisations had, during the period of the Cold War, largely escaped from its paralysis by including only countries committed to market economies; they had been boycotted by the Soviet Union and its allies. Following the end of the Cold War all three had rapidly become global organisations with membership moving towards universality.

The Panel's task was to consider what recommendations to make that might increase the relevance and effectiveness of ECOSOC's activities, these having fallen into considerable disrepute in many capitals, which tended to take the IMF, the World Bank and the WTO seriously but to dismiss ECOSOC as a mere talking shop. Broadly the Panel had two options. The first of these was to go for an ambitious and maximalist approach, which would certainly have been interpreted as an attempt to move ECOSOC into the centre of international debate and decision-making on economic, developmental and social issues and as a shift of power away from the other three world bodies. This approach had been the one followed by an earlier panel chaired by the former prime minister of Sweden, Ingvar Carlsson, which had considered the future of the post-Cold War ECOSOC in the 1990s, and had recommended the establishment of an Economic and Social Security Council with a restricted membership (ECOSOC had 54 members) and with decision-making authority. That recommendation had got nowhere, rejected by most of the member states, to whom it was addressed. The second option was to go for a more modest, incremental approach, trying to build up ECOSOC's work, particularly on developmental policy issues. The discussion of ECOSOC in the Panel was not easy. Members from developing countries, who resented the primacy of the three non-UN world organisations and the degree of control over them exercised by the West, hankered after a major boost to the UN's own role in these areas. But Enrique Inglesias, the Panel member with by far the greatest direct experience of economic and social matters, was unconvinced by either the realism or the desirability of attempting such a shift and a majority of other members followed his advice. So we opted for an incremental approach rather than a great leap forward.

At the same time the Panel did spend a good deal of time discussing the pretty unsatisfactory state of world economic governance, divided between different international organisations with purely sectoral responsibilities and heavily influenced as it was by self-selected restricted groupings such as the G8 World Economic Summits and the G77 of developing countries, whose membership was in no way globally representative. It seemed clear to us that many of the major economic and social challenges of the future, ranging from trade liberalisation through counter-proliferation policies and energy security to the policies underpinning the MDGs and climate change and environmental degradation, could not conceivably be properly confronted and managed by groupings drawn exclusively from one or other side of the developed–developing country divide, largely meaningless as these labels were coming to be in any case. What was surely needed was some more inclusive grouping drawn from the largest economies on both sides of that divide which, while not having any legal decision-making power, could provide impetus, momentum and coherence to the main international organisations. The trouble was that both the existing restricted groupings and these international organisations lay outside the UN structure which established the limits of our own mandate and also that the prescription we favoured was not a UN one but an informal one. Therefore we decided it would not be appropriate to make a formal recommendation on this point. But we analysed the problem in some depth and did point towards the idea of converting the G20 group of finance ministers, which brought together states encompassing 80 per cent of the world's population and 90 per cent of its economic activity, into a leaders' group at the summit level, with regular attendance by the IMF, the World Bank, the WTO and the EU, and with the UN Secretary-General and the president of ECOSOC attending as of right. This approach, which had long been favoured by Canada, a G8 member, was still being resisted by most of the others, the US in particular, although some very tentative steps had been taken to bring representatives from some of the main developing countries to G8 summits.

On the reform of ECOSOC itself, our main recommendations were:

(i)   In order to recognise and manage the interconnections between security and development issues, ECOSOC should establish a Committee on the Social and Economic Aspects of Security Threats.

(ii)   ECOSOC should provide an arena for measuring states' commitments to achieve key development objectives in an open and transparent manner and should transform itself into a 'development cooperation forum' by:

    (a) getting away from its current focus on administrative issues and programme coordination and building an agenda built around the major themes in the Millennium Declaration;

    (b) setting up a small executive committee to provide orientation and direction to its work and interaction with the principal UN funds, programmes and agencies;

    (c) focussing the annual meetings with the IMF and the World Bank on encouraging collective action in implementing the MDGs and the Monterrey Consensus [on commitments to official development aid];

    (d) aiming to provide guidance on development issues to the governing boards of UN funds, programmes and agencies.

The Commission on Human Rights

It had been clear from the very beginning of the Panel's work that human rights would need to figure prominently in its report. The links between respect for human rights, or, more often, the abuse of them, and the two main axes of our work, security and development, were clear. Lack of security and instability often led to massive abuses of human rights, as had been the case in Cambodia, the former Yugoslavia, Rwanda and in many other places; systematic abuses of human rights often too led to instability and lack of security. Similarly abuses of human rights impeded and undermined development policies, while lack of development itself represented a deprivation of human rights. So much, in very general terms, was not in dispute. But in the past it had always proved difficult and controversial to strengthen the UN's human rights machinery and performance and there was no reason to believe it would be less so on this occasion. As recently as 1992, after the end of the Cold War, it had proved impossible, due to Chinese opposition, to insert more than the most vestigial reference to human rights into the statement issued at the time of the Security Council Summit. While it had proved possible to establish the office of the High Commissioner for Human Rights in 1994, that post remained under-staffed and under-funded, and was still not exerting much effective influence in the counsels of the UN or on the human rights performance of its member states. There were no illusions therefore, but that this would prove a difficult nettle to grasp; and getting the member states collectively to grasp it would be even more difficult.

And even though human rights were without doubt going to figure prominently in our report, it was not certain at the beginning that the Panel would have much to say about the CHR. While this body was the principal focus of collective human rights activity at the UN, it was well down the UN's pecking order, being subordinate to ECOSOC and the General Assembly and reporting up through a long chain of potentially obfuscatory, repetitious processes. It was thus, in principle, below the Panel's radar screen, which was directed at the main institutions. Nevertheless, as our work gathered pace, it became clear that we could not possibly avoid addressing the inadequacies of the CHR, a body which only met for a relatively short session once a year and which had long since become a forum for diplomatic manoeuvre and finger-pointing rather than the remedying of human rights abuses.

At one of the Panel's European regional seminars, in Warsaw, in May 2004, I had been asked to introduce the discussion on human rights and had spoken in very critical terms of the performance of the CHR and the need to reform it; somewhat to my surprise, the other members of the Panel present, not all of whom were from Western countries, concurred. It seemed to me that, in the Panel at least, getting agreement on proposals to reform the CHR might prove less difficult than had been feared. Encouraged by this I asked Danilo Turk, the UN Secretariat Assistant-Secretary-General responsible for this area of policy (in 2007 elected to be the President of Slovenia), who was present at the seminar, if he would consult his colleagues in the Secretariat and let me have (privately) any thoughts on possible reforms before the Panel's key plenary sessions in July and September. At the July plenary session the negative critique of the CHR was strongly endorsed by the whole Panel, with no signs of determined opposition from those who remained silent. But we were still short of positive proposals for reform and the Panel itself was short on expertise in the field. So, when we met the Secretary-General in September, having received no guidance from his officials in the meantime, we told him of our view that reform of the CHR was necessary and asked him what he would like to see put forward. His rather disappointing response was that he could not think of anything himself but that we should consult the High Commissioner for Human Rights, Louise Arbour. This we proceeded to do, but not in a very satisfactory way, the consultations being between her and several individual members of the Panel. In retrospect it was a mistake not to have had a full session of the Panel with her, as we had done with the Director-General of the IAEA on the issue of nuclear proliferation.

There had been much external pressure in the intervening months, from non-governmental organisations in particular, for us to propose the abolition of the CHR and its replacement by a Human Rights Council (HRC) which would have greater powers and authority, a smaller membership and would be on a par with ECOSOC, reporting directly to the General Assembly. We considered this idea at length but concluded (wrongly as it turned out) that it would prove a bridge too far for the membership. The risk, as we saw it, was that to propose the immediate creation of a Human Rights Council and fail might result in the existing CHR being left intact and unreformed. So, while we indicated in our report our view that, in the longer term, an HCR was the right way to go, we did not formally propose its creation there and then.

Instead we put forward the following main proposals:

(i)   Membership of the CHR should be made universal.
(ii)   Its members should be prominent and experienced human rights figures (and not diplomats as had come in recent years to be the almost invariable pattern).
(iii) The CHR should be supported in its work by an advisory council or panel of roughly 15 members, who would be independent experts appointed for three years, renewable once. They would be appointed on the joint proposal of the Secretary-General and of the High Commissioner for Human Rights and would advise on both country-specific and thematic issues.
(iv)   The High Commissioner for Human Rights should be asked to prepare an annual report on human rights worldwide, which would serve as a basis for a comprehensive discussion in the CHR.
(v)   The Security Council and the Peacebuilding Commission should request the High Commissioner on Human Rights to report to them regularly about the implementation of all human rights-related provisions of Security Council resolutions, thus enabling focussed, effective monitoring of these provisions.
(vi)   The member states should review the inadequate funding of the office of the High Commissioner for Human Rights and of its activities and provide more resources.

The Panel had thus, again, opted for an incremental rather than for a 'big bang' approach to reform; and it was roundly criticised for this, most sharply by the NGO community in the USA. The idea of expanding the membership of the CHR to include all UN members, irrespective of their human rights record, was particularly excoriated. The Panel's view was that over-concentration on strict membership criteria for belonging to the CHR (or to an HRC) risked missing many points and being frustrated. We doubted whether the aim of a CHR (or HRC) restricted to a small number of squeaky-clean countries ruling on those with less good records was likely to be the best way of making progress. So our aim was to professionalise the work of the CHR, particularly through the proposed advisory panel, and thus to inhibit the manoeuvring of those who wished to turn all the CHR's activities into diplomatic jousting. The choice between the two approaches was a matter of judgement; and, since only one (or none) of the two could be adopted, we shall not know for certain which would have produced better results.

The UN Secretariat

No comprehensive attempt at UN reform could or should have ignored the need for extensive reforms in the UN Secretariat itself. The headquarters staff of the UN were widely, and to some extent justifiably, criticised. Their quality was remarkably uneven, with patches and individuals of excellence, interspersed with those of time-serving mediocrity. They shared those weaknesses with other international bureaucracies such as the EU's Commission, for example, as they did the handicap of the ineluctable requirement to ensure a wide geographical spread in their recruitment of staff. From the Cold War period the UN Secretariat inherited a climate of risk-aversion and from the surge of recruitment in the early years of the organisation and almost total job security thereafter, an age profile amongst their staff heavily weighted towards the upper end. Lack of rotation between headquarters staff and field operations, which had grown exponentially during the post-Cold War period, nurtured a feeling of 'them and us'. Add to this a more than average inclination towards interdepartmental turf-fighting, back-stabbing and intrigue, and there was clearly much that needed changing. But many of the weaknesses of the Secretariat were not of their own making, nor capable of being remedied by the Secretary-General and his senior officials acting on their own. New mandates were showered down on the Secretariat by the General Assembly and the Security Council with little consideration of where the resources, human and material, were going to come from to implement them. Member states lobbied for the appointment of their nationals to Secretariat jobs and thereafter protected them with little regard to their quality and fitness for the post in question. When all was said and done the Secretariat was the most micro-managed organisation of its kind in the world, and it had 192 micro-managers. So any attempt at reform needed to do two rather contradictory things, to increase the professionalism, transparency and accountability of Secretariat officials, from the Secretary-General downwards, but at the same time to free them up from the intrusive hand of member state micro-management. And any attempt also had to avoid falling into the trap of accepting the thesis of mainly right wing politicians in the USA that Secretariat reform was the be-all and end-all of UN reform as a whole.

The Panel, all of whose members had direct experience of these problems, had also to steer between two extremes, either being so broad-brush in its proposals as to be meaningless or becoming a micro-manager itself. It was, in this field alone, subjected to a good deal of pushing and shoving, and lobbying from members of the Secretariat with an interest, but proved able to resist these pressures reasonably well. At the top end of the Secretariat it took two clear options, one negative, one positive. The negative option was to say nothing at all about the procedures for appointing the Secretary-General. There was plenty that could have been said; but the general feeling was that, as a group set up to advise the Secretary-General and not the membership, whose job it was to make that appointment, it would in some ways be unfair to land in the outgoing Secretary-General's lap some probably highly contentious ideas about the procedures for appointing his successor. The positive option was to consider carefully the level below the Secretary-General and to propose the creation of a second post of Deputy Secretary-General alongside the existing one established in 1998. We approached that decision by a somewhat circuitous route. Some had suggested that it would make sense to amalgamate two major Secretariat departments, the Department for Peacekeeping Operations (DPKO) and the Department for Political Affairs (DPA), each currently headed by an Under-Secretary-General. There certainly was a need for better coordination and coherence in the work of the two departments, and in some cases there was overlap and time-consuming turf fighting. Moreover the establishment of a Peacebuilding Commission was likely to impose a heavier burden and an even greater need for concerted action. But the more we looked at it, the less the idea of a merger appealed. It would have meant creating a single, massive department whose weight in Secretariat policy-making would have become disproportionate; and its executive, day-to-day control would have been beyond the capacity of one Under-Secretary-General. Also it would have mingled aspects of policy-making, mediation and good offices missions on the one hand and the deployment and management of large peacekeeping operations on the other, which posed quite different challenges and which would be unlikely to benefit from unified treatment.

So we opted instead for the idea of coordinating the work of the two departments and of the newly proposed Peacebuilding Bureau through a second Deputy-Secretary-General who would work exclusively on peace and security issues. This proposal had two additional attractions. It would compel the proper definition of the responsibilities of the existing Deputy-Secretary-General, which had never taken place since the first appointment had been made some years earlier. And it would take some of the weight off the Secretary-General, whose unavoidably heavy travel schedule was difficult to reconcile with the need to take rapid and sensitive decisions on 17 or more peacekeeping operations and a number of efforts at conflict prevention. We were, however, clear that this proposal should only be made if it enjoyed the full support of the Secretary-General. Annan was somewhat hesitant at first and subject to much in-house lobbying, but in the end he let us know that he would like the proposal to be made and would support it.

In addition to this proposal our main recommendations for Secretariat reform were:

(i)   The relationship between the General Assembly and the Secretariat should be reviewed with the aim of substantially increasing the flexibility provided to the Secretary-General in the management of his staff.

(ii)   The Secretary-General's reform proposals of 1997 and 2002 (two earlier Secretariat reform packages aiming at increasing transparency and accountability) should now, without further delay, be fully implemented.

(iii)   There should be a one-time review and replacement of personnel, including through early retirement, to ensure that the Secretariat was staffed with the right people to undertake the tasks at hand, including for mediation and peacebuilding support and for the office of the Deputy-Secretary-General for peace and security.

(iv)   The Secretary-General should immediately be provided with 60 posts for the purpose of establishing all the increased Secretariat capacity proposed in the Panel's report.

Proposal (iv), which was sure to produce a negative reaction from the proponents of zero-growth budgets, amounted to 1 per cent of the total staff of the Secretariat. The 'golden handshake' scheme proposed ((iii) above), was a good deal less draconian than it appeared, given the bunched age profile of Secretariat officials. The Panel never doubted that, as ever, proposals to give the UN more resources and greater flexibility would run into a storm of protest, not least from those member states whose leaders continually called for a more effective world organisation. We were not to be disappointed.

Amending the UN Charter

The procedures for amending the UN Charter are complex and hard to fulfil. This is no bad thing, since the original Charter was a powerful document, which would never have been agreed and ratified if it had not been negotiated in the shadow of two world wars. Changes could as well have been for the worse as for the better. So, over the nearly 60 years of the UN's existence, the only changes agreed and implemented had been a modest expansion of the membership of the Security Council to 15 and a somewhat larger expansion of the ECOSOC to 54. A group of legal advisers from the member states met on a continuing basis to consider various ideas for Charter change but their meetings provided no more than intellectual activity for fine legal minds; nothing was ever agreed.

It was therefore with the greatest caution that the Panel approached the idea of Charter change. There was a consensus that Pandora's Box should only be opened to the minimum degree necessary. Of the proposals the Panel made, only that for the enlargement of the Security Council actually necessitated amendment of the Charter. But, given that that proposal would require the cumbersome procedures of amendment to be engaged, we tacked on to it (but did not propose any action to amend the Charter without agreement on Security Council enlargement) a modest series of what could be called 'tidying up' amendments. These were:

(i)   Removing all references to enemy states [the punitive provisions of the Charter with regard to Germany, Italy, Japan and Hungary, long since out of date].
(ii)   Deletion of Chapter XIII on the Trusteeship Council [dependent on the establishment of a Peacebuilding Commission which did not require Charter change].
(iii)   Deletion of Article 47 establishing a Military Staff Committee (MSC) and all other references to that Committee.

Of these proposals, none was the slightest bit contentious within or outside the Panel, except for the abolition of the MSC. This relic of the post-Second World War settlement had met on a monthly basis for 55 years and never transacted, or even tried to transact, any business. It met and it adjourned. The reasons for its inactivity were clear. Once the Cold War was under way there was no question of agreement being reached on any form of military enforcement action that involved both sides of the Cold War divide. But, more fundamentally than that, an institution which gave absolute control over the UN's military activities to the five victors in the Second World War, to the exclusion not only of the wider UN membership but even of the other members of the Security Council, as the MSC did, was clearly not a body which had any place in the UN of the twenty-first century. At the time of the first Gulf War, in 1990–1, the Soviet Union, which had always had a soft spot for an institution that had been invented by Stalin, tried to breathe life into the Committee; but it was met by flat opposition from the other permanent members, the Chinese being no less adamant than the three Western permanent members. When the Panel sought to list the Committee for deletion, it transpired that the Soviet Union had transferred its attachment to the MSC to the Russian Federation, and a somewhat embarrassed Yevgeny Primakov was persuaded to argue for its retention to a bemused Panel audience that could see no point in it. Faced with a total absence of support, Primakov gracefully conceded the point. But the Panel did address the serious and continuing need for the Security Council to have professional military advice available to it on demand. This need was particularly strongly felt by the rotating members of the Council, who often had no access to military advice from their own capitals. We recommended therefore that the Secretary-General's Military Adviser (at the time a two-star officer) should be double-hatted so that he could provide advice directly to the Security Council whenever a need was felt for that.

*   *   *   *

The Panel's report, which it submitted to the Secretary-General shortly after its last plenary session in November 2004, ran to rather less than 100 pages, relative brevity for such UN offerings. It contained 101 formal proposals for action, covering the whole field of the UN's principal activities and institutions. It was the single most comprehensive reform package put forward in the nearly 60 years since the UN was established. It was now consigned to the bear-pit of negotiations between the member states.

As the account of the Panel's debates and the analysis of its proposals contained in this chapter have shown, in almost every case the Panel opted for practical, incremental improvements rather than for what could be called 'blue sky' thinking. The object was to secure reforms in the immediate future, not to sketch an ideal UN for 20 or 30 years' time. We did in fact consider a fair number of the blue-sky ideas which had been put forward in earlier reports or learned journals, and discussed extensively at seminars over the years since the end of the Cold War: abolition or substantial alteration of the veto power in the Security Council; establishment of an Economic and Social Security Council; recruitment of a UN Rapid Reaction Force permanently at the disposal of the Secretary-General; and revival of the Trusteeship Council to handle the cases of failed states. In every case we concluded not that the ideas were bad ones – in several instances members of the Panel thought they were good ideas which deserved support – but that there was somewhere between a minimal and no chance at all of their being accepted by the member states. To put forward ideas whose rejection was nearly certain was likely to damage the overall credibility of the Panel's report and of the UN as a whole. Even if Kofi Annan had not himself discouraged us from going down that road, there was no appetite among members of the Panel to do so. Nor were the proposals we did put forward lacking in ambition. Taken as a whole they represented a recipe for change which battle-scarred survivors of previous attempts to introduce reforms at the UN readily recognised as unprecedented.

When handing the report over to the Secretary-General, the Panel asked its chairman to send with it a covering letter setting out two important considerations for the future. The first of these related to the specific issues and disputes which we had been asked to avoid:

> . . . no amount of systemic changes to the way the United Nations handles both old and new threats to peace and security will enable it to discharge effectively its role under the Charter if efforts are not redoubled to resolve a number of long-running disputes which continue to fester, and to feed the new threats we now face. Foremost among those are the issues of Palestine, Kashmir and the Korean Peninsula.

The second consideration related to the clearly impending clash over enlargement of the Security Council:

> ... it would be a major error to allow the discussions needed to move towards a decision [on the enlargement of the Security Council] to divert attention from the decisions on the many other necessary proposals for change, the validity and viability of which do not depend on Security Council enlargement.

Not much time was to pass before the justification for both these warnings was to be amply demonstrated.

Chapter XIII

From the launch to the Summit and beyond

With the submission of its report to the Secretary-General in November 2004, the Panel's formal existence came to an end. It was decided not to bring its members to New York for the launch and publication of the report in December, but to leave that to the Secretary-General and the Panel's Chairman. The Secretary-General asked the members to stay engaged and to do all they could to promote the proposals in their report, including by public debate, but he did not wish them to be involved in the follow-up, for which he recruited a group of New York-based UN ambassadors to act as 'friends' of the process and, much later, a senior political figure from each of the main UN regional constituencies to reinforce that effort. At the same time he set September 2005 as the date for a summit meeting in New York to celebrate the organisation's 60th anniversary and to act as the final decision-making event in the UN reform process which he had himself set under way with his speech to the General Assembly in September 2003.

That the Secretary-General was content with the report and felt that it had lived up to his precepts of being both ambitious and practical was not in doubt. Not only did his own letter of transmission of the report to the member states offer unqualified support to its recommendations but, when he came in March 2005 to table his own reform paper 'In Larger Freedom', he tracked almost all the Panel's recommendations, with a very few exceptions, which will be noted later in this chapter. But neither Annan nor the Panel members had any doubts from the outset that it was going to be steep, uphill work to get those recommendations accepted and even more challenging to get the ones accepted to be effectively implemented. Change is, as we have seen, not something that comes easily at the UN. A small, determined group of wreckers, and one usually exists on any proposal, even when a large majority supports it, can very often run an idea into the sand or down one of those procedural by-ways in which the UN excels and from which it never emerges. Moreover, while the UN had been traumatised by the Iraq experience in 2003, it was far from clear that many countries on either side of the argument were yet ready to bind up the wounds then inflicted and move forward together. A slightly different fault-line, the one between developed and developing countries, also yawned wider than at almost any time in the past, with the developing countries deeply suspicious of and resistant to any prescriptions which they regarded as emanating from the developed world. And then Annan's own authority as Secretary-General was being daily challenged over the oil-for-food enquiry, with calls for his resignation and a vicious campaign of personal denigration under way in some sections of the media.

And, if these broad, political obstacles were not enough, there were plenty of substantive difficulties likely to be raised by the subject matter of the proposals themselves. The ideas for systematising guidelines for the Security Council's authorisation of the use of force, while not directly related to the case of Iraq, clearly raised many of the some extremely neuralgic issues. The proposed international norm of 'the responsibility to protect' was highly controversial, as the reaction to various speeches on humanitarian intervention had shown. Issues relating to strengthening the regimes against the proliferation of WMD bristled with both technical and political problems. Anything which looked like upgrading and making more effective the UN's human rights machinery was sensitive to a whole range of countries, including two permanent members. And it was far from clear that many member states really wanted a more influential and effective Secretariat and were willing to lift the dead hand of micro-management, which they had wielded hitherto to such paralysing effect. So, even without the obviously contentious issue of Security Council enlargement, it was never going to be easy to assemble a worthwhile package of reforms.

The period between the launch of the report and the September 2005 summit meeting can roughly be divided into four phases: the launch itself; an approximately three-month period of public and private debate, and much bilateral and multilateral consultation between governments; an increasingly intensive, and towards the end frantic, negotiating process on what came to be called the 'Outcomes Document' for the Summit; and the summit meeting itself from 14 to 16 September 2005. In that same time period came the publication of the companion piece to the Panel's report, Professor Jeffrey Sachs' report on progress made, or rather the lack of it, towards achieving the MDGs, which had been set in 2000 for achievement by 2015, and the Secretary-General's own report 'In Larger Freedom'.

During this ten-month period the world did not, of course, stand still, and many of the main developments at and affecting the UN were ones which did not favour the emergence of a substantial reform package. The UN itself, and above all its Secretary-General, were submerged in the Iraq oil-for-food scandal involving sanctions evasion and bribes paid by the Iraqi regime of Saddam Hussein on oil sales and on the purchase of humanitarian supplies. The UN-based enquiry chaired by Paul Volcker, the former chairman of the US Federal Reserve Bank, and the various attempts by members and committees of the US Congress to get in on the act, attracted far and away more public and political attention and comment than did the programme for UN reform. The involvement of Kofi Annan's own son Kojo in one of the firms involved in the oil-for-food scheme and his lack of frankness in his dealings with his father massively increased the pressure on Annan himself and took a heavy toll on his resilience and capacity to give an effective lead in the campaign for reform. Oil-for-food became the ultimate weapon of mass distraction. Added to that were reports of sexual abuse by UN peacekeepers in the Congo and several highly publicised personal cases in the upper reaches of the UN hierarchy. Apart from those institutional blows, the USA, a key player in any reform effort, remained distracted by the growing insurgency in Iraq and by the, eventually failed, effort to gain confirmation from the Senate for the president's nominee as UN Ambassador, John Bolton, no friend of the UN and destined to wreak havoc with the Summit preparations, when eventually, unconfirmed, he got to New York in August. And the wounds caused by the paralysis in the Security Council and the subsequent invasion of Iraq by US- and UK-led forces in 2003 showed no signs of healing. In the Security Council the members grappled inadequately with the running crisis in Darfur. And much of the attention on the reform package itself was concentrated on the diplomatic gyrations of the G4 countries' efforts to get two-thirds support for their bid to achieve permanent membership of the Security Council and of the equally vigorous efforts of those determined to frustrate that objective. So, even while the need for UN reform was paid almost universal lip service, the conditions for achieving it were lacking and the political will to negotiate flexibly and to cut deals was in short supply.

The launch of the Panel's report

At the best of times the UN struggles to get its message across to the public and to defend itself when it is on the receiving end of criticism in the media. At the end of 2004 it faced both these challenges simultaneously. The UN is handicapped in these respects in ways which do not afflict national governments. Its potential audience is not a relatively homogenous national one but an incredibly heterogeneous global one, which needs to be addressed in a tone of voice which takes account of very different traditions and practices. Its resources for public-information work are miniscule compared with those available to its member governments and have recently been further reduced by budgetary constraints, limiting its outreach; for example, in recent years all but one of the UN's information offices in Western Europe have been closed. Nor can the UN afford to fight a 'gloves-off' media campaign when it comes under attack in one or more member states. Add to this that its headquarters is embedded in a country, the USA, and a city, New York, with a vibrant but carnivorous media industry, catering not for the world but for one member state, and you have a conjunction of factors which go some way towards explaining why the UN has not been more successful in making its voice heard.

A number of members of the Panel, myself included, and the Panel's Director of Research, Stephen Stedman, began to focus from early in 2004 on those weaknesses and the best ways to overcome them, at least in the context of the Panel's report. It was clear from the outset that simply applying the UN Department of Press and Information's routine procedures was not going to suffice for a report which was the single most far-reaching and ambitious package of reforms to be put forward in the organisation's history. The first challenge was to the Panel itself to produce a report which was clearly enough written, sufficiently compelling in its arguments for specific changes and brief enough to appeal to an audience beyond the somewhat incestuous community of UN diplomats, bureaucrats and journalists who worked on First Avenue and their counterparts in national capitals. Whether that objective was successfully achieved is perhaps best judged by others than the present author; the considered reaction of many commentators would seem to indicate that it was. The next challenge was to ensure that the Secretary-General's own response to the report was put on the record promptly and, to the extent possible, to avoid any differences of emphasis or substance between him and the Panel. Achieving this was, in purely bureaucratic terms, made somewhat easier by the fact that a period of about a month was needed between the completion of the report in early November (and its being made available to the Secretary-General) and its actual publication in the UN's official languages after translation from the English language original. In the event Kofi Annan decided to give his wholehearted and comprehensive endorsement to the Panel's report and recommendations, and this was set out in a three-page foreword to the report which was published with it. This firm endorsement was clearly facilitated by the way the Panel and the Secretary-General had worked closely together throughout the process of its preparation.

There remained the launch itself, and here fortune, or rather ill fate, played a predominant role. The storm over the management of the UN's Iraqi oil-for-food programme and allegations of corruption at the UN and elsewhere had been gathering force all through 2004. The enquiry under Paul Volcker, set up by Annan, had begun its work after the summer holidays that year. I had myself had a meeting with Volcker at the time of the September session of the Panel, not to give evidence – since the scheme in question had only come into operation after my own departure from New York as the UK's UN Ambassador in July 1995 – but to go over with him the background and the operation of economic sanctions against Iraq in the years before the oil-for-food scheme came into operation. It was already clear that this enquiry was going to be one of great complexity. But I confess that I did not at the time fully grasp how combustible it would prove to be and how it would risk drowning out all discussion of other UN issues, particularly in the USA. This imbalance was largely an American phenomenon. Elsewhere around the world the media naturally covered the main emerging news items on the oil-for-food scandal but not to the extent of crowding out all other consideration of the UN. In the USA, however, in Washington as well as New York, a lynch mob was in hot pursuit of its quarry, and many of the pursuers were no friends of the UN, people who were not remotely interested in UN reform, indeed probably preferred that the UN should not be successfully reformed. It was in this US climate that the UN and its senior officials lived; and, during the autumn of 2004 and thereafter, it was an intensely destabilising one. In the event the launch of the Panel's report in early December coincided exactly with one of the periodic crescendos in the oil-for-food process and also with some not-unconnected changes in senior appointments in the Secretariat, including the retirement of two of Annan's closest collaborators. The timing could not have been worse.

The launch had in fact been reasonably carefully planned and well-trailed in advance. The BBC, and in particular its World Service, with which I was in close touch, had a whole series of presentations lined up; and other news outlets no doubt did too. *The Economist* had, rather unusually, agreed to let Annan set out the case for reform and the main features of the report in a substantial signed article. As the launch day approached, more and more leaks of the content of the report began to emerge. This was quite normal at the UN. Indeed the Panel's report had up to then been surprisingly leak-proof, apart from the one item over Security Council enlargement in July 2004. These leaks did not in any case seem to me a matter of any great concern since they were largely accurate. But that was not how it looked in New York, where nerves were anyway sorely frayed. Suddenly an off-the-cuff decision was taken, without any consultation, to release the report in New York two days ahead of schedule. The Secretary-General, besieged by a press corps focussed exclusively on oil-for-food, pulled out of the full-scale presentation planned and left it to the Chairman of the Panel, Anand Panyarachun, whose forte was not public diplomacy. Most of the expert presentations, certainly those of the BBC, were simply axed. Copies of the report were not properly pre-positioned and available. All in all it was a fiasco, and, as so often with the UN, a self-inflicted and avoidable one.

The debate on reform gathers pace

Despite the mishandling of the launch of the Panel's report, interest in it picked up vigorously in the early months of 2005, as did informal consultations between the governments which were now being asked to reach decisions on its many policy proposals. Seminars and conferences

proliferated, at which these recommendations were discussed and criticised; but the overwhelming balance of the reactions was strongly
positive. This was particularly true in Europe where, apart from the
divisive issue of Security Council enlargement, there was virtual unanimity right across civil society organisations, the institutions of the EU
and national governments that the reforms proposed made good sense
and should be supported. In America too there was much positive comment, although the proposals for handling human rights, and in particular the idea of expanding membership of the CHR rather than
reducing it, came in for some strong criticism, especially from those
who were in favour of pressing for the immediate establishment of an
HRC with increased powers. But in the USA both the debate and the
support for UN reform was strongest amongst the critics of the Bush
administration's foreign policy. The Administration itself remained for
many months wrapped in silence on the subject, preoccupied by the
deteriorating situation in Iraq, the transition at the State Department
from Colin Powell to Condoleezza Rice as Secretary of State, and the
absence of a US Ambassador to the UN as the battle over the nomination of John Bolton to that post raged on in the Senate.

When I passed through Washington on other business in the spring
of 2005, I was astonished by how far back in policy formulation even
officials in the State Department directly concerned with policy
towards the UN were. The issues raised by many of the Panel's proposals were clearly still sitting in the 'too difficult' tray. Outside the developed world the interest and the debate was less intense, reflecting the
weaknesses of the UN's information system and of civil society institutions and the strong tendency for the issues under discussion to be handled exclusively by governing elites. And even those elites were not very
fully informed. Kofi Annan, who made it his duty to attend all the main
regional, high-level meetings to drum up support for UN reform, told
me he was often astonished and appalled by the level of ignorance at
head-of-government level of the proposals being put forward. There
was also resistance to breaking away from the dichotomy of development and security, with the former seen as the overwhelming priority
of developing countries to the exclusion of all else, a view which was
boosted by increasing mistrust of the policies of the US Administration
and its single-minded focus on the 'war on terror'.

The debate also got under way in New York, but in the early
months of the year not yet in the form of actual negotiation on precise

proposals. For that to start everyone was waiting for the complementary report on progress towards the MDGs and for the Secretary-General's own report setting the scene for the September summit. But even in those early debates battle lines began to be drawn, with a strong group of almost-unconditional supporters of the reforms proposed and a somewhat smaller, and unproclaimed, group of 'spoilers' set on running most of them into the sand. In between, the majority of the membership were still making up their minds. On one matter, however, the proposals for enlarging the Security Council, informal negotiation was already well under way. The G4 countries were meeting together, concerting tactics and lobbying hard for the Panel's Formula A, while the opponents of creating new permanent members were doing likewise for Formula B.

The report on the MDGs from the group chaired by Professor Jeffrey Sachs landed on desks towards the end of January with a heavy thud (with its supporting documents it ran to more than 1,000 pages). But its basic messages were simple and clear. During the five years since they were set by the summit meeting in 2000, progress towards the goals had fallen far short of what was needed if they were to be achieved by the chosen target date of 2015; all the key programmes needed to meet the goals were under-resourced and the frequently reiterated UN target for the developed countries of contributing 0.7 per cent of their gross national income (GNI) to development aid was nowhere near being met; the developing countries themselves were failing to mount the necessary programmes for poverty eradication, health and education; and among the developing countries the plight of sub-Saharan Africa was by a long way the worst. The report therefore recommended a whole range of policy changes to strengthen existing programmes; it pressed for a substantial overall increase in development aid and debt relief; and it proposed that each developing country be asked to table plans that would enable it to reach the MDGs, with a commitment being given by the developed countries to fund such programmes. Sachs compensated for the length of his report by undertaking a high-profile and effective media campaign explaining his group's findings and their recommended responses.

In March 2005 Kofi Annan sent to the member states 'In Larger Freedom' (a phrase drawn from the preamble to the UN Charter). This effectively drew together the threads of the two reports which the member states already had and, with a very few changes, endorsed their recommendations. So far as the Panel's report was concerned, two significant changes were made. While the proposal to establish a new Peacebuilding Commission had on the whole been welcomed right across the developed/developing divide and already looked set fair to be agreed at the September summit, very strong objections had been raised by many developing countries to the new Commission having any responsibility for conflict prevention. They clearly saw this as the thin end of an interventionist wedge and wanted the Commission's mandate to be confined to post-conflict peacebuilding. Faced with determined lobbying, Annan gave in, and in his March document lopped off from the Peacebuilding Commission's mandate any responsibility for helping states under stress before they failed. Whatever the tactical considerations in favour of making this concession (and in my view it was made far too soon, long before the time for the inevitable trade-offs which would be needed if an overall package was to be agreed), it was a serious weakening of one of the Panel's key proposals and unbalanced the whole treatment of conflict prevention. Annan's second significant change was to replace the Panel's proposals on human rights with a bid for the immediate establishment of an HRC.

Thus one of Annan's two changes fell short of what the Panel had proposed, while the other was more ambitious; and for the latter he certainly deserves considerable credit. Annan also made a firm pitch in his document for treating the package of proposals he had endorsed as a single, coherent whole, not to be subjected to the cherry picking and the reductive process of traditional UN negotiation. This was a bold try, doomed at best to partial success, since no one, not even the members of the Panel, believed that all the proposals would go through. But it did demonstrate the Secretary-General's determination to throw his own weight behind the reform campaign. The pity was that that weight had been, and continued to be, diminished by the oil-for-food saga.

The negotiating process

Once it had been decided by the Secretary-General and his senior staff that the climax of the reform campaign was to be the September 2005 summit meeting in New York, to which all Heads of State and Government of the member states were invited, it was unavoidable that the final stages of the preparations for that meeting would have to involve the totality of the countries represented in the General Assembly. This unwieldy format for negotiation, involving over 190 national representatives, bristled with drawbacks. It pointed from the outset towards a lowest-common-denominator outcome, longer on words than action. It gave the fullest possible scope to 'spoilers', of whom there were a determined handful. But the harsh reality was that it was not avoidable. The proposed reforms involved many decisions that had to be endorsed by the whole membership, or at least particular specified majorities among them, and which imposed obligations and responsibilities on all of them. Any attempt to avoid completely that final unwieldy phase of negotiation would have been intensely divisive and doomed to failure.

But there were different options about the way the final stage of global negotiation was to be prepared. One option was to have a multi-track approach under which the different parts of the UN institutional machinery which would be directly affected by the proposals put forward would be asked to prepare the ground. Thus the Security Council would consider the proposals which involved it, as would ECOSOC, the Governing Board of the IAEA and so on, to mention only some of the institutions involved. This multi-track preparatory process could have been conducted in a way which did not remove the final decision-making from the overall membership but which did keep that final stage relatively short and ensured that it did not start from scratch.

The main alternative option to this approach was to have a single, global General Assembly negotiating forum from the outset, operating throughout the negotiating period from April to September. I myself was a strong proponent of the multi-track approach and, through the latter part of 2004, I did my best to convince the main players with whom I was in contact, Kofi Annan himself, his Deputy, Louise Fréchette, other senior Secretariat officials, and various representatives of the British government, of the benefits of this approach and of the drawbacks of the other. But I found I was a voice crying in the wilderness. No one was prepared to face down the pressure from the majority of UN ambassadors to get in on the negotiating act from the very beginning. The atmosphere in New York was febrile, full of mistrust, of the Security Council in particular, and risk-taking was out of fashion. So the negotiating process from April onwards was placed in the hands of the then President of the General Assembly, the Foreign Minister of Gabon, Jean Ping, and his successor in September for the 2005–6 session, Jan Eliasson, who became Swedish foreign minister while he was in office. That as much was achieved at the September summit and thereafter is a tribute to the skill and determination with which these two drove the process forward. But I remain of the view that the multi-track approach and a shorter, final phase of global negotiation could have delivered better results.

One vestige of the multi-track approach did, however, emerge and that was the handling of the two alternative proposals for enlarging the Security Council. The aspirants to permanent membership of the Security Council, known as the G4 (Brazil, Germany, India and Japan), were not prepared to consign the fate of their principal objective in the UN reform negotiations to the triage of a general negotiation. They therefore kept a tight grip on their own campaign and pursued it single-mindedly in parallel with the general negotiations; and in this they were naturally followed by the opponents of the creation of new permanent members. This de-coupling of the Security Council enlargement negotiations from those on the rest of the proposals was encouraged by Kofi Annan, who, like the members of the Panel, was determined to avoid a situation in which a deadlock over Security Council enlargement brought about the demise of the whole package. Annan also persuaded the G4 that the only chance they had of success was to pursue a two-stage decision-making process, with a General Assembly vote ahead of the Summit in favour of the principle of enlarging the Security Council and creating a new category of permanent members without the veto, and a second vote after the Summit naming the new permanent members and endorsing the necessary Charter amendments. Both decisions required a two-thirds majority and, ultimately, the support of all of the existing P5. This decision-making process also favoured eventual de-coupling if it failed to deliver a result, as in the event proved to be the case.

Just how close the G4 came to achieving their objective it is hard to say since in the end the matter was never put to a vote. My own guess is not very close. Much publicity was given to the results of their increasingly frenetic canvassing for support, but the figures quoted tended to ignore one of the iron rules of UN electioneering: that you needed to reduce by about one-third the number of supporting votes you were promised. Moreover there were serious obstacles both amongst the existing P5 and over the issue of African candidates for permanent membership, and neither of these obstacles came close to being overcome. It was very clear that China remained strongly opposed to permanent membership for Japan, with whom its relations were going through a particularly sticky patch. The Chinese found one of those convenient mantras which they so often use to encapsulate a policy. A decision of this importance must, they said, be a matter of consensus, not of a majority vote. Given the views of the group of countries opposed to any new permanent members, this consensus requirement was simply a conversation-stopper. The Americans were less elegantly agile than the Chinese, but no less of an obstacle. They did not much like the idea of any enlargement, seeing it as likely to diminish their own ability to influence the Council. They only ever formally endorsed one country for permanent membership, Japan; and they were happy to hide behind the Chinese case for consensus. The African problem was equally serious and was the rock on which the G4 campaign was finally shipwrecked. Unlike the other regions there was no obvious single African candidate for permanent membership, indeed there were at least three (Egypt, Nigeria and South Africa); but three African permanent members would unbalance the Council and make it too large. To complicate matters even further, the Africans were not ready to surrender the veto, which was an absolute condition for many of those who had promised their support to the G4.

So, early in August, faced with this African position, the G4 campaign was abandoned and with it the hope that the Security Council would on this occasion be enlarged. The Panel's alternative proposal (Formula B), which provided for the creation of a new category of longer-term elective members, was never given serious consideration. The G4 set their faces firmly against it, refusing even to consider the possibility that, together with the proposed review clause, it might be capable of being fashioned into a stepping-stone towards their own objective. This 'all or nothing' approach deterred any support building up for Formula B.

Another casualty was the proposal for the Security Council to endorse a set of guidelines which would govern its decisions on the use of force. This gathered broad support across the board, including at least one permanent member (the UK, which tried to persuade the USA to accept it); but the USA remained firmly opposed and others were no doubt happy to shelter behind that opposition. It too then withered on the vine.

But perhaps the most serious setback of all during the negotiating process was the loss of the whole section of the Panel's proposals dealing with WMD. As luck would have it, one of the quinquennial reviews of the NPT was due to take place in May 2005, right in the middle of the summit preparations. This review conference did not in fact need to take any decisions at all, since the extension in perpetuity of the NPT had been settled in 1995; and it did not take any, not even proving capable of adopting its own agenda. A determined band of 'spoilers', who included Egypt, Iran, Pakistan, Syria and Venezuela, used the occasion, however, to rubbish the Panel's proposals. Also the USA did little to support the proposals and nothing at all to respond to the criticism of its own failure in recent years to move towards nuclear disarmament. After the end of this conference Kofi Annan did his best to revive the pre-summit preparations on WMD. A cross-regional grouping of foreign ministers, chaired by Norway and including the UK in its role as a permanent member of the Security Council, was constituted and went to work to try to bridge differences. But the spoilers remained active and, shortly before the summit, it was agreed that the section of the outcome document on WMD was so thin as to be worse than nothing. The whole section was then dropped. At a time when the Security Council was preparing to deal with two nuclear transgressors, North Korea and Iran, this sent the worst possible signal of infirmity of purpose.

Some parts of the reform package fared better than this; and others lived on dangerously into the final stages of the pre-summit negotiations. The Peacebuilding Commission continued to receive overwhelming support, although a long and tangled debate ensued over the precise nature of its links and subordination to the Security Council and ECOSOC. There was general support for the proposals to strengthen regional peacekeeping. Among the proposals which lived on dangerously were those relating to human rights and the new HRC, the concept of 'the responsibility to protect' and the issue of terrorism, which everyone condemned trenchantly but on which many were still hesitant to agree a legal definition which would outlaw unambiguously any targeting of innocent civilians in any circumstances. In many cases the language which survived the successive iterations of the Outcomes Document was watered down to an extent which deprived it of any immediate, self-executing effect and added up to little more than an invitation to a renewed an open-ended post-summit negotiation. This was unfortunately the case with the proposals for Secretariat reform.

One important area was, however, reasonably successfully out-sourced and that was the financial commitments of the developed countries to strengthening efforts to achieve the MDG. The G8 World Economic Summit was due to take place in Scotland under UK Presidency in July 2005; and Tony Blair set his sights on extracting from that meeting specific commitments on increased aid, particularly to Africa, and a boost to debt relief. This was successfully achieved, including new and important commitments by some at least of the partici-pants to timetables for reaching the 0.7 per cent of GNI UN target for aid. These results from the Gleneagles G8 meeting were built into the summit preparations and managed to settle the somewhat miscon-ceived debate in New York over what had been seen as a 'grand bargain' between the developed countries who were to put up more cash in return for the developing countries agreeing to stronger security meas-ures. This idea, which flew in the face of the Panel's single-agenda approach, now faded, and the summit's Outcomes Document firmly endorsed the latter approach.

The final stage of the pre-summit preparations was more comic opera than serious negotiation. The arrival on the scene at the begin-ning of August of the new US Ambassador to the UN, John Bolton, still not confirmed by the Senate but appointed under a somewhat odd 'recess appointment' procedure, was followed by a tidal wave of several hundred last-minute amendments. Some of these were mere quibbles; others, such as the elimination of every reference to the MDGs, which the Bush Administration had never previously contested, were intensely provocative; and others weakened an already diluted text or reopened contentious issues. This US move was, naturally, grist to the mill of the spoilers, who happily set about deconstructing more of the Outcomes Document. Fortunately, both the Secretary-General and the president of the General Assembly stood firm and, with the strong backing of the EU under UK presidency, saw off most of the proposed amendments, which it transpired did not have solid support in Washington. The net result was more damaging to Bolton's negotiating credibility than to the summit Outcomes Document. But, inevitably, some of the less promi-nent of the Panel's proposals got lost in the melee, including that for providing UN financial support to regional peacekeeping operations, an idea which, had it been agreed, would have facilitated the handling of the Darfur crisis by an AU mission.

The Summit

The UN Summit meeting of 14–16 September was the culmination of a process, in itself not a particularly newsworthy occasion, certainly not one that could easily be explained in a sound bite or a few sentences. A long succession of world leaders followed each other to the podium and tried in the few minutes allocated to them to sum up their country's view of the UN and their expectations of a reformed organisation. Not surprisingly these views were often discordant, and in most cases they were primarily addressed to their home audiences rather than to each other. No decisions were taken at the Summit meeting other than the formal endorsement of the consensus reached a couple of days earlier on the Outcomes Document, when UN ambassadors were finally faced with the awful prospect of a meeting taking place without any agreed conclusions. This anticlimactic event epitomised both some of the strengths and some of the weaknesses of the UN. It was necessary, because reforms needed to be endorsed by the whole membership and they needed to be endorsed at the highest level since they often involved far-reaching changes which would affect all member states. In this they mirrored the indispensability of the organisation. Decisions had to be agreed in advance, because it was simply impractical to try to negotiate them among nearly 200 principals. This emphasised the difficulty the organisation had, at every level and in every one of its institutions, to reach meaningful, operational decisions, especially ones designed to reform institutions and practices that had existed for many years. And both the meeting itself and the decisions that were taken there were difficult to communicate to the media and to the peoples of the member states in whose names they were being taken. So the overall media reaction was negative and dismissive.

But, looking behind this rather superficial picture, a more complex outcome could be discerned. In overall terms the interdependence of all countries, even the most powerful, the need to work for collective responses to the threats and challenges that faced us all, and the critical role that the UN needed to play in all this, was endorsed in unequivocal terms. So was the fact that we all faced a single, multi-faceted agenda if greater security and prosperity were to be achieved, to the handling of which all needed to contribute more than they had done in the past. Neither the narrower security agenda, focussed on terrorism and WMD proliferation, nor the idea of two or more agendas which should be traded off against each other was given any backing.

When it came to specifics, the Summit had gone a long way towards the setting up of the new Peacebuilding Commission along the lines proposed, first by the Panel and then, in somewhat truncated form, by the Secretary-General. Although a further negotiating process was provided for, a firm date for reaching decisions of 31 December 2005 was agreed. The Summit had also decided to replace the Human Rights Commission by a new Council; but, on this, nothing beyond the decision of principle had been settled. All the detail remained for further negotiation, no date for the establishment of the new Council was agreed, and it was already clear that there would be a battle royal over the negotiation of these details. Most surprisingly, and perhaps most importantly of all, the Summit had unanimously endorsed the concept of the responsibility to protect, which gave the international community the responsibility to intervene if a member state was either unable or unwilling to protect its own citizens. And the commitment of the developed countries to increased aid and debt relief was matched by the system proposed by the Secretary-General under which developing countries would table programmes to eradicate poverty and achieve the MDGs and would receive support for them. A commitment to Secretariat reform was given but decisions on all the details were postponed pending further proposals by the Secretary-General and further negotiation.

The list of what was missing from the reforms proposed by the Panel and the Secretary-General and which could not be agreed was a long one too. At the head of the list, of course, came Security Council enlargement, yet again frustrated by interstate rivalries; the hope that this deadlock would be broken in the near future had little credibility. The ditching of all the proposals dealing with the proliferation of WMD was a major and damaging setback. On terrorism, strong words and a summit-level meeting of the Security Council in the margins of the wider Summit could not conceal the fact that there were still divisions over the definition of terrorism and its outlawing with no 'ifs' or 'buts'. What was agreed on conflict prevention, and on the use of force in the name of international community, was weak and unconvincing. Of course not one of these problems ducked by the Summit was going to go away or somehow mysteriously slip down or off the international agenda. So in a way every one of these setbacks merely represented a disagreement adjourned, not a full stop. The overall judgement on the Summit has therefore to be 'two cheers at best'. But, when compared with the almost total absence of reform during the whole Cold War period and the meagre results from earlier, sectoral reform efforts in the period since the end of the Cold War, the scorecard looks more respectable. The proposals put forward were certainly the most ambitious package of reforms put on the table since the establishment of the UN, 60 years before; and even the diminished package which was agreed fitted that description too.

The follow-up to the Summit

The reforms agreed at the September summit for the time being remained just words on paper, subject to two further stages. The first was the completion of the diplomatic process negotiating the details of setting up the two new institutions, the Peacebuilding Commission and the HRC, and of responding to the Secretary-General's proposals for secretariat and administrative reform. The second was the far more demanding and open-ended task of actually making the reforms work by applying them to real-world events and conditions.

The negotiations to set up the Peacebuilding Commission were duly completed by the target date set by the Summit of the end of 2005. They were not easy. The tug of war over the relative roles of the Security Council and of the ECOSOC continued right up until the last moment. But, broadly speaking, the Secretary-General's proposals emerged relatively unscathed. The strong link with the Security Council, which was essential so long as issues of peace and security were predominant in a country on the agenda of the Commission, was retained, and attempts to turn the Peacebuilding Commission into simply being a sub-set of the not very effective ECOSOC were resisted. The Peacebuilding Commission began its work in the summer of 2006.

The negotiations on an HRC were even more protracted and hard fought. The Summit had set no deadline for their completion, but most delegations and, most importantly, the president of the 2005–6 General Assembly, Jan Eliasson, were determined that they should be completed before March 2006, when the discredited and superseded CHR was due to hold its next annual meeting. This target was in fact achieved. On this issue the tug of war was over whether or not the new

Council should, as the Secretary-General proposed, with particularly strong support from the USA and also from other Western countries, be a much smaller body than the Commission (which had more than 50 members), with much tougher election procedures making it difficult for human rights transgressors to win a seat. In the end a compromise was brokered which left the Council barely smaller than its predecessor (with 48 members), but with new election procedures which moved away from the old system whereby candidates agreed on a regional slate could not be opposed by those countries outside the region (and which had permitted serial human rights offenders such as Libya not only to get onto the Commission but to chair it), and now required elections in which all had a say. There were too to be peer group reviews of the human rights record of those elected to the Council and the possibility of suspension if a member was found to have transgressed flagrantly. And the Council was to conduct a systematic review of the human rights practices of all member states. Every bit as important, the Council would be able to meet frequently during the course of the year, not just once for a few weeks as had been the case with the Commission; and additional resources for the High Commissioner for Human Rights were also forthcoming following the Summit's decisions. The compromise package eventually had to be voted through, given the refusal of the USA to join consensus, and was passed by a massive majority, with only the USA, Israel and the Marshall Islands voting against. The first elections to membership were held in May 2005 and the new procedures did seem to be acting both as a deterrent and as an obstacle to human rights transgressors, only few countries with major question marks over their records being elected. The Council too began its work in the summer of 2006.

The Secretary-General's proposals for Secretariat reform fared less well. A detailed package was put forward in the spring of 2006 and immediately fell foul of a split between the developed and the developing countries, with the former giving strong support to the Secretary-General's proposals. All attempts at compromise failed, and in the end a vote was taken, in which the numerical superiority of the developing countries blocked the reform package, even though countries providing more than 80 per cent of the UN's resources were in favour of it. This miserable and perilous outcome for the future of the UN was where matters stood when the new Secretary-General, the former South

Korean Foreign Minister Ban Ki-moon, took over from Kofi Annan at the beginning of 2007.

The more testing second phase of follow-up and implementation has as yet hardly begun in any serious way. Signs from the early meetings of the Peacebuilding Commission and of the HRC have not been particularly encouraging. But the most immediate test has been to the newly endorsed concept of the responsibility to protect those whose governments themselves are either unwilling or unable to protect them. Even while the Panel was still meeting, and to a greater extent in the period when the pre-summit negotiations were under way and after it, the conditions in the Darfur region in the west of Sudan exhibited all the classic symptoms which the new concept was designed to deter or to prevent. Sudanese government-armed and supported militia, known as the Janjaweed, were unleashed on the population of Darfur with disastrous consequences in terms of deaths, rapes and other gross abuses of human rights. A low-level insurgency in Darfur continued, despite international efforts to broker a ceasefire, and threatened to spill over into the neighbouring countries of Chad and the Central African Republic. The Security Council's response was hesitant and ineffective. Attempts to bring pressure to bear on the Sudanese Government to mitigate their obdurate refusal to allow the insertion of a substantial UN force to help protect the people of Darfur were frustrated by Russian, Chinese and Arab hesitations. An AU peacekeeping mission proved too small and under-resourced to perform this task. It had always been clear that the practical application of the responsibility to protect would present the international community with some difficult problems. That indeed was why it was so necessary. If these problems cannot be overcome in the context of Darfur, then the major change introduced at the UN Summit could become a waning and devalued asset.

Chapter XIV

Looking back and looking ahead

Looking back

Looking back over the period since the end of the Cold War, and particularly to the years at the beginning of that period, it is hard to avoid the conclusion that the international community squandered a number of opportunities to strengthen the structure and effectiveness of the UN and to equip it better to face the threats and challenges of a new era which were quite different to those of the one which preceded it. During those early years of the 1990s, which, whether by coincidence or not, were almost identical to the US presidential term of President George H. W. Bush, many things went right for the UN and it became clear that the organisation's potential to play a positive role in achieving collective security in the widest sense of that concept were greater than they had ever been before. But it was also clear that the UN could not hope to shoulder those wider responsibilities without better structures, increased resources and the solid support of its main member states when the going got rough. None of these were forthcoming to anything like the extent required. Instead the early successes were frittered away and were soon overlaid in public perception by a series of appalling humanitarian catastrophes. The mutual solidarity which had characterised the response to Iraq's invasion of Kuwait, to the peacekeeping operations in Namibia, Cambodia, El Salvador and elsewhere, was allowed to degenerate into bickering amongst the P5 of the Security Council and to the outright confrontation over Kosovo, as well as, most dramatically, over the decision to invade Iraq in 2003.

Why and how did these opportunities come to be missed? Largely by misadventure, I would suggest. There was no great plot against the UN, no determination by any country or group of countries to ensure that the UN failed to rise to the new challenges. There were of course those who distrusted or disliked the UN, either because it had failed them in their hour of need or because it represented an obstacle to their ambitions, but those views were not a prime cause of most of the disasters which occurred. What did go badly wrong was the failure to give any systematic overall consideration to the tasks which the member states wanted the UN to take on and of how best to handle these effectively. The sheer fecklessness with which the member states piled new tasks onto the UN, new peace operations, new responsibilities in the fields of the environment, of health, of criminal justice, without pausing to consider how the human and financial resources needed to carry them out were to be provided, was often breathtaking. The 1990s were a period when many member states, particularly the developed ones, were reaping a massive 'peace dividend' from the ending of the Cold War and the consequent reduction of military spending. And yet little, if any, of that dividend was diverted into the adequate funding of multilateral peace operations or into the restructuring of the armed forces of the member states that was needed if they were to participate in and support those operations. Little, too, went towards addressing the wider security issues arising from poverty, pandemic diseases, malnutrition and environmental degradation. Most countries remained far short of the UN target of 0.7 per cent of GNI for official development aid. All this bred an atmosphere of cynicism and mistrust, particularly amongst the developing countries whose dividends from the ending of the Cold War were not obvious.

Of the new, emerging hard security threats, the one that stands out as having received no serious treatment until long after it became evident that it was a worldwide phenomenon, with serous ramifications to other threats, was state failure, the collapse of state institutions and the rule of law, leading often to wider regional mayhem sucking in weak neighbouring countries. During the Cold War this phenomenon had occasionally arisen but it had tended then to be handled, often crudely and brutally, by one of the two superpowers or by the country's neighbours. Now this phenomenon landed in the lap of the UN; and it was on the increase. Within a relatively short period of time, state failure had created the conditions for harbouring terrorism (Afghanistan), for acts of genocide (Bosnia and Rwanda), for massive starvation (Somalia), and for uncontrollable floods of refugees (Haiti); and yet nothing much was done to try to prevent states slipping towards failure. Peace operations in these states, after they had failed and the situation had subsequently been stabilised, were often too short term and were inadequate to the tasks in hand. The solitary example of Macedonia, where a preventive deployment of peacekeepers helped to stabilise a situation before it tipped over into violence, remained just that, solitary.

So much for the weaknesses of the international community's response to the post-Cold War opportunities. What is, however, striking is how resilient the UN proved under the impact of a number of disastrous setbacks. From the trough of the failure of the peace operations in Bosnia, Rwanda and Somalia, the organisation was soon in as much demand as ever, to handle the independence of East Timor and complex peace operations in Sierra Leone and Liberia. From the next trough following the invasion of Iraq and the killing of the leader and many of the members of the UN team in Baghdad, there was a similar snap back. By the end of 2006 the Security Council had authorised the deployment of some 100,000 peacekeepers worldwide.

These cycles say something about the UN's indispensability in the post-Cold War world, surely one of its fundamental strengths and a cause of some optimism for the future. The reason for this indispensability is rather clear: there is no obvious alternative. Such alternatives as have been touted, different variations of the idea of 'coalitions of the willing', were shown to lack international legitimacy and recruiting power. The idea of simply letting states fail, leaving crises to burn out on their own, is not easy to defend in an era of globalised communications and in the light of the complex and damaging knock-on effects of such neglect. Nowhere has this indispensability been more evident than in the steady advance of international justice. In the 45 years of the Cold War no serious attempt was made to follow up the examples of the Nuremberg and Tokyo war crimes tribunals. Since the Cold War ended the international community has moved strongly to reject the culture of impunity with the establishment of the Yugoslav and Rwanda tribunals and, more recently, the setting up of an International Criminal Court. This Court, whose work is only just getting under way, would seem to have successfully ridden out a determined attempt by right-wing opponents in Washington to strangle it at birth. This same trend has now led to a major conceptual breakthrough, with the endorsement of the responsibility to protect; however halting the implementation of that doctrine may prove to be, a fundamental shift has taken place, with the interpretation of the Charter that any country can do pretty well what it likes to its own citizens within its own borders having been set aside.

One further reason for the UN's resilience over this period was perhaps the realisation that, however great the setbacks to a number of peace operations, however shocking the shortcomings in the UN's performance in certain circumstances might have proved to be, it hardly made sense to pile the whole blame onto the UN itself and to draw dramatically negative conclusions for the future. The Rwandan genocide was the work of Hutu extremists, the Srebrenica massacre and the killings in Kosovo were a consequence of Milosevic's ambitions to construct a 'greater Serbia' and the brutality of troops operating with his approval; and the killings in Darfur are mainly being carried out by irregular groups encouraged by the government of Sudan. During the Cold War period no one would have even dreamed that the UN could have played a role in preventing such occurrences; and no one ever asked it to do so. Now expectations have gone up dramatically and have outpaced the capacity to meet them. But the lesson so far learned is surely that the UN needs to become more effective – not that we can dispense with it.

The period covered by this book spans almost exactly the terms in office of two Secretary-Generals: Boutros Boutros-Ghali and Kofi Annan. It touches briefly too on the final part of Javier Perez de Cuellar's ten years in the job, which, however, belonged more to the Cold War era than to its aftermath, and not at all on Ban Ki-moon's term, which began only as this book was completed. My judgement, which would not, no doubt, be shared by all, was that both its post-Cold War leaders served the UN well through an exceptionally demanding and turbulent period in its history. Boutros-Ghali fell foul of the USA for reasons which were by no means all of his own making; and the latter part of Annan's term was clouded by the Iraqi oil-for-food scandal. The record of both demonstrated what an almost impossibly difficult job this has become with the expansion of the UN's role, activities and significance after the end of the Cold War. Comparison with their Cold War-period predecessors makes little sense because so much less was demanded of them. The job now is almost impossible not in the rather sloppy, journalistic 'mission impossible' sort of way, but because it consists of two quite different jobs, both of which amount to an almost full-time responsibility and both of which require quite different qualities and qualifications. The first job is that of the high-wire super-diplomat, able to speak to heads of government and foreign ministers, to facilitate conflict prevention and resolution and to drive forward the whole range of the UN's agenda, often on matters of considerable national sensitivity. This aspect of the job requires constant travel and attendance at most of the main regional summits, which have grown greatly in number in recent years. The other side of the job is that of the chief administrative officer referred to in the Charter, but an administrator of infinitely more complex activities than existed during the Cold War period.

The 17 or so peacekeeping operations which may be running at any one time are in themselves hugely demanding of time, energy and judgement. But the Secretariat's responsibilities go much wider than just peace and security. It was this overstretch in the function of the Secretary-General which led to the first ever appointment in 1998 of a Deputy Secretary-General. But, in a manner all too typical of the UN, that appointment has not yet worked as well as it might have done because of the lack of a clear allocation of responsibilities and some delegation of authority to the Deputy. Far too frequently the Deputy has acted as a kind of shadow Secretary-General, not a complement to him.

It is not altogether surprising that the expansion of the UN's activities following the end of the Cold War showed up the weaknesses in the organisation and operation of the Secretariat, and not only because the member states were reluctant to provide new resources, human or otherwise. During the Cold War parts of the Secretariat were quiet corners indeed, whose inhabitants became used to unexciting, but not particularly useful, functions of a purely routine kind. Given the job security provided to UN officials and the heavy recruitment of officials in the early years of the UN's existence, the age profile in the Secretariat became notably unbalanced towards the upper end. And the massive expansion in field activities, with the increase in the number and size of peacekeeping missions, was not matched by any increased mobility between those staff working at headquarters and those out in the field, thus creating an increasing 'them and us' problem. In some ways the UN came to resemble a pre-First World War diplomatic service in which some officials served all their careers as bureaucrats at headquarters and others were in the field all the time but seldom brought their field expertise to headquarters. That model had been totally discredited and abandoned by national administrations but lived on in the UN Secretariat. If one adds to that recruitment practices which gave excessive weight to the achievement of regional (but not gender) balance over any kind of meritocratic approach, you had a lot of problems.

All these weaknesses were well known to the senior management in the Secretariat and to the member states, but the former did too little to remedy them and many of the latter opposed the most obvious remedies which were discussed. This inertia in the system and resistance to reform was by no means special to the UN. As one who had worked both in and with the EU Commission in Brussels for many years, I recognise many familiar symptoms and practices. But the difficulty of achieving any reforms at all and the insistence by the member states on micro-managing every part of the Secretariat from the Secretary-General downwards was unique to the UN. A cruel light was shone on all this by the Iraqi oil-for-food scandal, which broke into the open soon after the US-led invasion of Iraq revealed the inner workings of Iraq's sanctions-evasion systems; this issue then gradually came to dominate the agenda during much of 2004 and 2005. The Volcker enquiry's report revealed much that was indefensible in the Secretariat's management practices and lack of transparency and accountability. But it also revealed how deeply complicit the member states were in those failings. When the dust had settled, the amount of wrongdoing and even of maladministration could be seen to have been a lot less than the lynch mob of the US media and Congressional staffers were wont to suggest; but the overall impact on the Secretariat's reputation had been seriously damaging.

As to peace operations, the massive expansion of the post-Cold War period had revealed plenty of weaknesses there too. Starting at their origin, the Security Council proved itself all too prone to handing down mandates which were either unclear, unrealistic or contradictory. The 'safe area' mandates in Bosnia, where a short-term expedient became an unsustainable long-term policy, was a case in point. The problems over unclear or inoperable mandates were then compounded by the General Assembly, which had budgetary control, which it exercised with little awareness of the negative impact on the viability of operations. The switch from what might be described as 'classic' peacekeeping operations, where the UN supplied a military force to administer a ceasefire or a peace agreement between two warring governments, to multifaceted operations in failed states, including ones where hostilities were continuing, in which humanitarian relief, disarming warring parties, reconstituting the rule of law and police forces and civil administrations were required functions, posed both practical and conceptual problems which were not at first well understood. The longstanding problem of rapidity of deployment of peacekeepers, essential if forces opposed to a ceasefire or settlement were not to intervene before the peacekeepers even arrived, got worse not better, as overstretch took its toll on troop contributors. And the solution most actively canvassed, of providing the Secretary-General with a dedicated rapid-reaction force, looked no more likely to overcome the legal, political and logistical obstacles that faced it than had been the case when it was first put forward decades before. At least in this peacekeeping area some reforms were introduced. The proposals in the Brahimi Report of 2000 contained much of what was most immediately needed to strengthen the UN's peace operations and some at least of it was implemented. The idea of the UN itself conducting enforcement operations was dropped following the Bosnian experience. But the borderline between the more robust peacekeeping which was needed when attempts were made to destabilise an operation and a fully-fledged enforcement operation was hard to define and even harder to apply. The mounting of 'hybrid' peace operations, where the UN worked in a fully integrated way with a regional organisation such as the AU, remained largely uncharted territory even as it emerged as an approach which fitted the political circumstances better than a fully-fledged UN operation, as is the case in Darfur and Somalia.

One other important weakness revealed as the UN moved closer to the centre of the world's diplomatic stage was the difficulty it had in presenting, explaining and defending its policies. This had always been the case, but during the Cold War it had mattered less. Now, in combination with the emergence of a 24-hours-a-day global media industry, it mattered a great deal. The difficulty the UN had in communicating effectively hampered any effort to reform the organisation and also, on the ground, damaged the conduct of individual peacekeeping operations. It handicapped the UN in handling two aspects of the new media world in which it had to live: the 'push' factor when faced with tragic events and the cry of 'something must be done' went up; and the 'pull' factor when things went wrong with a peacekeeping operation and pressure for withdrawal and abandonment became strong. It also contributed to the roller-coaster presentation of the UN's image either, in success, believed to be capable of anything or, in failure, to be capable of nothing. There were limits as to what could be done to face up to those challenges. It was clear that the UN could not afford itself to get into a sustained media confrontation with one or a group of its member states; to that extent its hands were tied. It was also clear that the responsibility for supporting and explaining the UN to their public opinion rested every bit as much with the member states as with the organisation itself. Blaming the UN when things went awry – as the USA did quite ruthlessly over Somalia, even though the military operation in question was fully under national control – was counterproductive; it simply damaged the reputation of the organisation and undermined support for it when next you turned to it with a request for action. These limits notwithstanding, the UN did not manage to face the media challenge effectively. A more professional approach, which does not mean an approach in which communications are consigned to a small, under-resourced and often demoralised group of experts, but rather one where all senior UN representatives, both at headquarters and in the field, are able to perform on radio and television convincingly and persuasively, is clearly needed.

When I reached New York direct from Brussels in September 1990, the UN and the EU might have been living on different planets. Each knew little about the other, interaction was minimal, and there was a lurking suspicion in the two bureaucracies that they were somehow rivals, in competition with each other. This changed fundamentally in the post-Cold War period, not least because both organisations were being called upon to expand their activities into new areas and found that they needed to work together and could help each other considerably. At the outset the main manifestation of EU activity in New York was directed towards ensuring a unified approach to General Assembly resolutions; a fair degree of success was achieved, exaggerated somewhat by the fact that most General Assembly resolutions were adopted by consensus and that many of them did not anyway signify very much in practical terms. The Security Council remained firmly off-limits, guarded by an Anglo-French Cerberus dedicated to ensuring that the privileges of Europe's two permanent members were not encroached upon by the development of the Common Foreign and Security Policy.

Gradually as cooperation between the UN and EU built up through a number of peacekeeping operations, most particularly in the Balkans, in Bosnia, Macedonia and Kosovo, as the EU impact in a number of policy areas of fundamental importance to the UN, such as the whole range of development issues and the environment, became more significant, it began to dawn on both sides of the Atlantic that far from being rivals they were in fact natural allies. Only a strong UN could help the EU deliver that 'effective multilateralism' which was one of the main planks of the European Security Strategy adopted by the EU Summit in December 2003; and only sustained support from an organisation representing 27 member states and providing more than 40 per cent of the UN's financing was going to enable the UN to function effectively and to reform itself. The taboo on discussing Security Council business at the EU Ambassadors' weekly meetings in New York disappeared shortly after my arrival there.

The EU and its member states in fact became the main protagonists of the Secretary-General's reform proposals. And its influence extended even further, given the tendency of a number of its neighbours to follow the same line. It became also the most obvious broker of compromises between the developing countries and a US administration which many of them distrusted and disliked. The EU also provided substantial relief to the UN's peacekeeping overstretch, taking on, as it gradually did, many of the main conflict-prevention and peacekeeping activities in the European region, with the UN operating as a legitimising authority but not as an executor of policy.

This relatively brief backward look over the post-Cold War period does give some idea of what went wrong and what went right. It also demonstrates what an extraordinary period of change and upheaval it was at the UN. On the basis of that analysis it is time now to look ahead.

Looking ahead

Looking ahead can either be simply a process of speculative prediction or it can be a blend of prediction and advocacy. The final section of this book falls into the second rather than the first of these categories. The track record of prediction has not been particularly impressive. To take only a couple of examples from the period covered by the present study – how many academic experts and practitioners predicted either the end of the Cold War and the disintegration of the Soviet Empire or the relatively bloodless collapse of the apartheid regime in South Africa even a year of two before they actually occurred? Not very many is the honest answer. And yet these events fundamentally transformed the international scene and shaped the world in which we now live. The UN will always be at the mercy of these sorts of unexpected developments, and how it responds to them will determine its future to a much greater extent than any approach planned far in advance. Mankind's successes have lain more in adapting itself to the future when it becomes the present than in predicting it ahead of time. What the UN needs most is a capacity for adaptation, which requires the political will of its members to adapt it to face new challenges as they emerge.

Many of the UN's advocates and supporters fear that the organisation could become marginal and discredited, and many of its critics and detractors hope that will happen. But developments since the end of the Cold War would seem to make that rather unlikely. Despite many setbacks and disasters, despite the humiliations of Bosnia and of Iraq in 2003, the international community keeps turning back to the UN for solutions to problems which none of the individual member states can address successfully on their own. This underlying indispensability is strengthened by the fact that there is no obvious alternative. The idea that 'coalitions of the willing' would supplant the UN has foundered in the Iraqi quagmire. The concept that an alliance of democracies could take its place seems to defy any rigorous analysis. How could a grouping which will lack global legitimacy and which, by definition, will exclude the rising power of China, provide the answers to problems ranging from international security to climate change? Regional and subregional organisations certainly have a major and probably growing role to play, but it is now better understood than it was that, rather than being rivals, these organisations and the UN are natural allies which need each other and which benefit from each other's strengths. The real risk for the UN, and the one which both its critics and its supporters should fear and do their best to avoid, is that the organisation will remain both indispensable and relatively ineffective. That is a bad combination of qualities for all concerned. Avoiding it is the basis of the case for making the UN more effective. Making the UN more effective is not simply a matter of introducing systemic reforms, important though that certainly is, but also of making better use of the instruments already at hand and effectively addressing the burning questions of the hour. This final section of the book will look first at the second of these challenges and then at the future for UN reform.

It should hardly need to be said, but it does, that one of the most immediate challenges is to make those reforms that have been introduced following the September 2005 summit – the HRC, the Peacebuilding Commission, the responsibility to protect – actually work. That certainly cannot be taken for granted. Each of them seems to have got off to a slow and rather shaky start. Performance should not be judged on the basis of a few months or a few meetings. These reforms addressed areas of policy in which the UN's past performance had been feeble and inadequate. The Universal Declaration on Human Rights is about to celebrate its 60th anniversary and yet it is still more honoured in the breach than the observance. The UN's human rights machinery has lacked teeth and it has lacked real political leverage. The new Council and a better-resourced office of the High Commissioner for Human Rights will need to make progress over time to remedy those defects. The UN's performance on peacebuilding has been laudable but it has often been poorly coordinated with the efforts of other international bodies such as the International Financial Institutions, and regional organisations, and it has not been sustained over the lengthy period of time needed to set a failed state on its feet again and to enable it to rebuild viable state institutions. The Peacebuilding Commission will need to be able to plug those gaps if it is to perform a useful function; and it will need gradually to build up a record of success stories if it is to be valued. The doctrine of the responsibility to protect was born from the failures of the immediate post-Cold War period. It is receiving its baptism of fire in Darfur. But people are still suffering and dying in that province of Sudan and it is proving every bit as difficult to move from words to deeds as had to be expected. Outright failure in Darfur or, worse still, in other similar cases as they arise could transform what appeared at the time to be a major breakthrough into a meaningless mantra.

There are, of course, many other immediate challenges facing the UN than just making those three reforms work. The Middle East Peace Process is one of them, and it is one that will certainly be high on the international agenda for a long period ahead, because a comprehensive peace settlement is not just around the corner, to put it diplomatically. The UN's role so far has been at best fitful, at worst negligent. It has been distrusted by Israel, marginalised by the USA and manipulated largely for propaganda purposes by the Arab states. But it is a member of the Quartet (the USA, the EU, Russia and the UN) which is the only piece of international machinery existing capable of driving a peace process forward and it surely needs to strengthen its input into that. As the crisis in the Lebanon in July 2006 showed, the UN's indispensability is as important a factor in the Middle East as it is anywhere else. Instead of being largely reactive it needs to become part of a sustained process designed to assemble the elements of a settlement and to do that it will have to achieve a degree of impartiality; and it will need to work more closely with the EU, the other member of the Quartet which has hitherto failed to pull its full weight.

Another immediate challenge is the threat to the nuclear non-proliferation regime from the nuclear programmes of North Korea and Iran. Both countries have now had rather modest, targeted sanctions imposed on them by unanimous decisions of the Security Council. But neither those sanctions nor any strengthened version of them likely to be negotiable will on their own bring about satisfactory outcomes to these problems. To achieve that, the security concerns of those two countries which are driving their policies, whether legitimate or not, will need to be addressed imaginatively and within a framework which goes wider than the technicalities of the nuclear issue itself. In both cases groupings exist – in the case of North Korea, the six-nation group composed of China, Japan, North Korea, Russia, South Korea and the USA; in the case of Iran, the EU-3 (France, Germany and the UK) backed up by China, Russia and the USA – to handle a process of dialogue and negotiation, but so far the political will to make them work has been lacking on all sides. The UN cannot and should not stand outside this process. It will in any case be a crucial component of any solutions, since strengthened IAEA safeguards procedures will need to be provided for if they are to have any credibility. The hard fact is that without solutions to those cases it will prove far more difficult to shore up the already fragile nuclear non-proliferation regime. The idea that that can somehow be achieved despite North Korea and Iranian possession of nuclear weapons is an illusion. Far more likely in those circumstances would be a wider breakout from the disciplines of the NPT regime in both regions with damaging consequences for the UN and international security.

Peacekeeping is likely to remain a core UN function for the foreseeable future and more of it will probably be of the complex, multifaceted, failed-state variety than of the classic ceasefire line monitoring of earlier days. Although the UN's peacekeeping capacity has been considerably strengthened in the last few years, mainly on the basis of the recommendations of the Brahimi report, there remain many shortcomings to be remedied. The first and most longstanding of these is slowness of deployment. This is in many cases still getting worse, despite ample evidence that delay in deployment gives spoilers time to undermine the peace process and strengthen their grip on the damaged society in question. One trouble is that the most obvious solution, providing the Secretary-General with a rapid-reaction force for deployment at his will, still does not seem likely to become realistic any time soon, if ever. The problems are both technical and political. The former include costs, the logistics of equipping the force and moving it around, the questions of siting its base and of jurisdiction over its personnel; and a small force could easily find itself heavily overutilised, with pressure to despatch it to one peacekeeping operation after another. Political problems are more intangible if just as real, including doubts as to whether the membership would be prepared to give the Secretary-General so much authority, even with the overriding control remaining with the Security Council, particularly when it would be likely to involve life-and-death decisions affecting their own nationals. Better surely than waiting for this ideal solution to come along would be to look for alternatives. The EU's system of battle groups ready for rapid deployment could be one such, particularly if it could be replicated by one or two non-European, developing-country traditional troop contributors such as India, Pakistan and Bangladesh. This would only work if the groups earmarked for rapid deployment were certain to be relieved by longer-term peacekeepers without undue delay. It would require a considerable increase in the sophistication and reliability of the present stand-by arrangements.

A second area requiring attention is to strengthen the civilian dimension of peace operations and its interface with the military. The demand for civilian police personnel far outstrips supply; and yet, in states that have failed or are perilously weak after a prolonged period of hostilities, reconstituting the rule of law is a top priority. The same is true for legal personnel and administrators to help rebuild justice systems and an impartial civil service. The civilian side of peacekeeping missions are often the poor relations of the military, understaffed and underresourced. The same is true of communications policy, not only with the global media but most importantly with the population of the country in which the mission is deployed. If the UN cannot explain and defend its activities in the vernacular language or languages of the local population, there is little chance that it will be able to sustain their support, without which no peace operation will succeed.

Probably the biggest challenge in peacekeeping is to develop ways of integrating UN and regional operations and of strengthening the capacity of certain regional organisations, the AU in particular, to carry out peace operations on their own. The September 2005 UN summit took some of the necessary decisions of principle, so far as capacity building in Africa and logistic support were concerned. But it balked at the key recommendation that, where a regional organisation such as the AU is undertaking a peace operation on behalf of or at the request of the UN, the operation should be financed by the whole UN membership on the basis of assessed contributions. The African countries cannot be expected and will not be able to finance such costly operations on their own. The lack of full financial support and the consequent need for precarious, hand-to-mouth expedients is already handicapping the AU mission in Darfur and the proposed mission in Somalia. That shortsighted refusal needs to be reversed. The integration of regional and UN elements in a single peace operation bristles with difficulties but, when it becomes the only way to obtain the consent of the host government, as seems to be the case in Darfur, it will need to be made to work. In any event African missions are likely to need UN support in providing the civilian elements of peace operations if that aspect of the operation is not to be skimped.

The fourth aspect of peacekeeping which needs to be addressed urgently and in a durable way, and which has so far not been handled at all adequately is that of human rights abuses by peacekeepers against the civilian population. The expectation that somehow, with upwards of 100,000 peacekeeping personnel deployed worldwide, such abuses will never occur would be a triumph of hope over experience. What is essential is to remove the impression of virtual impunity for such offences due to the gaps between national and international jurisdictions. And that impression will need to be removed not just on paper but in reality. If the UN has to blacklist certain countries which prove unwilling or unable to follow-up allegations of misconduct effectively, then that may have to be done, unattractive though such a recourse would be in a world all too short of peacekeeping resources.

The increased commitments to aid and debt relief and by the developing countries to poverty eradication programmes, which were endorsed at the September 2005 summit, should, if they are acted on effectively, improve the hitherto halting progress towards achieving the MDGs set for 2015. But implementation of these commitments will need careful and detailed monitoring and certainly cannot be taken for granted. It would be surprising if there were not some backsliding, which the UN will need to press to reverse. Moreover it is as near certain as it can be that a further high-level stocktaking and remedial action will be needed well before 2015 if the whole MDGs concept is not to lose credibility and leverage. It will also be necessary to consider what, if any, new quantitative targets should be set for development policy after 2015, and how best to take account of what are likely to be some very sharp regional differences in performance by developing countries, with Africa probably continuing to lag some way behind Asia and Latin America. The link between good governance, including respect for human rights, and successful development will remain as real as ever but no easier to handle. All these will be primary tasks for the UN's ECOSOC, for which it will need to equip itself with procedures which enable it to operate more effectively than in the past.

Climate change will inevitably be high on the UN's agenda throughout the decades ahead. No challenge so clearly epitomises the global nature of the main problems facing the international community and the inadequacy, indeed futility, of action taken only at national or regional level to control it. Now that the compelling scientific and economic considerations pointing towards the need for action are out in the open and being hotly debated, it should be possible to make more progress than the minimal and marginal decisions that have so far been achieved. There are at least some signs that two main groups which stood outside the disciplines imposed by the Kyoto Protocol, the developed-country deniers, the USA and Australia, and the big developing countries which were excused any limits on carbon emissions, China, India, Brazil and others, are beginning to reconsider their attitudes. From reconsideration to effective action to limit global carbon emissions will be a long step and no doubt one fraught with many technical and political difficulties. The UN has to be, as it has been from the outset, at the heart of such negotiations and it will have to persevere, however discouraging the outlook may be at any particular time. Above all it will need to overcome the perception gap between developed and developing countries that climate change is somehow a developed country fad and that, insofar as there is a serious problem, it is largely the fault of the developed countries and up to them to resolve. To do all that successfully it will need an institutional framework which not only assists such negotiation but enables the follow-up action to monitor and support commitments entered into to be effective and impartial. That points to the need for a fully-fledged UN Environment Agency to take the place of the present UN Environment Programme which is underpowered both financially and politically.

So much for the UN making better use of the instruments at hand. What is the place in all this for a continuing reform process and what form should it take? That the UN still needs further reform and will continue to do so is not really in doubt. The reform campaign of 2003–6 achieved, at best, only partial success. Most of the proposals which were set aside then or blocked were not misconceived or unnecessary; they were just too difficult and sensitive for the member states to accept at a time when mutual confidence was low and the UN was being rocked by external factors such as the Iraqi oil-for-food scandal. Like every international organisation the UN needs a continuing process of reform if it is to adapt to changing circumstances and challenges and if it is not gradually to become irrelevant and marginal. To abandon the whole concept of the need for reform would be an abdication of responsibility both by the Secretariat and by the stakeholders in the system, the member states. But reform does need to be thought of as a process and not as a once-and-for-all event; and it can come in many forms. I doubt myself whether it would be wise to launch again in the near future an overall reform package such as Kofi Annan initiated in 2003. That he was right to do so at that time I do not doubt. The organisation was at a low ebb and a determined effort to lift it out of that predicament was very necessary. But the 2003–6 campaign revealed the limits of what can realistically be achieved in that way; and it came at a cost: the wide, if erroneous perception that the UN was unreformable. So, even if an overall initiative like that one may be needed again at some time in the future, it is not likely to be desirable or to be successful in the short term. More likely to succeed in the years ahead would be a series of sectoral reforms, a multitrack process which addresses reforms wherever in the UN system they are functionally most needed and where the support is strong enough to give a reasonable chance of success at the outset.

The first candidate for any sectoral approach has surely to be the reform of the Secretariat itself; and the arrival in office of a new Secretary-General at the beginning of 2007 provided both an opportunity and a need. The blocking of Kofi Annan's Secretariat reform package in the summer of 2006 was a sad and humiliating setback for all concerned, the blocked and the blockers. Most of the issues addressed in that package need urgently to be addressed. It should be possible, without losing the essence of what was being proposed, for some repackaging and adjustment, together with the creation of mutual confidence between the new Secretary-General and the membership, to open up the way to agreement. The UN does need to prune its excessive list of mandates, to reduce the minute degree of micromanagement that goes on, to rejuvenate its personnel to make their functions more transparent and accountable, and to break down the gulf between those who operate in the field and those who operate at headquarters. It could make sense too to take up again the Panel's proposal for the creation of a second Deputy Secretary-General job dedicated to pulling together all the threads of policy on peace and security, and thus ensuring a more hands-on senior secretariat input to this crucial area than the Secretary-General, with his heavy travel schedule, can hope to achieve.

Then there needs to be a determined effort made to strengthen the international disciplines against the proliferation of WMD. Just as it is true that efforts to strengthen the nuclear non-proliferation regime are unlikely to succeed without negotiated solutions being found to the problems posed by the North Korean and Iranian nuclear programmes, it is equally true that solutions to those two problems will not be enough in themselves to set the regime on a sustainable future course. To achieve that, a number of multilateral steps need to be taken: the NWS need to resume fulfilling their commitment to move towards nuclear disarmament by bringing about further reductions in warheads and delivery vehicles and eschewing the development of new systems; the CTBT needs to be brought into force following US ratification, thus raising the barrier to any state planning a nuclear test; a Fissile Material Cut-Off Treaty needs to be negotiated; the IAEA's Additional Protocol, strengthening safeguards inspection procedures, should become the gold standard applied by all, if necessary following a decision by the Security Council making it mandatory; the Security Council should ask the Director-General of the IAEA to submit to it regular reports on the worldwide status of safeguards enabling doubtful cases to be taken up at an earlier stage and before the horse has bolted; and the implications for non-proliferation of the near certainty of a major expansion of civil nuclear power generation under the twin pressures of high oil prices and the need to curb carbon emissions should be addressed. If the high proliferation risks endemic in the building of new uranium enrichment and spent nuclear fuel reprocessing facilities are to be avoided, there will surely need to be some international guarantee of the supply of these services, operated impartially by the IAEA. The sooner such a system is up and running the better. Nor should the necessary focus on nuclear non-proliferation distract all attention from the threat from the possible development of biological weapons. While there is a global interdiction on these weapons, to which all pay lip service, there is no inspection system to trigger off warnings of possible transgressions nor, outside a few developed countries, has anything been put in place to handle possible biological incidents following terrorist or other action. These are gaps that should be filled.

There is one area of reform – Security Council enlargement – about which it is difficult to be sanguine in the wake of the second failure to reach agreement in the last ten years. The obstacles to achieving what the G4 remain set on achieving, an enlargement which includes the creation of a number of new permanent seats, remain intact and formidable. China's acceptance of Japan as a permanent member; the US's acceptance of a greater enlargement than they would like; Russia's agreement to a dilution of their present status; a solution to the quandary of which African country or countries should become a permanent member; a reduction in the hostility of those countries which will not become permanent members – Italy, Canada, Pakistan, Indonesia, Mexico, Argentina – to name the most prominent; all those developments may be achievable over time but they do not look like being achieved any time soon. Meanwhile to continue to treat this as the be-all-and-end-all of UN reform, as many commentators do, causes nothing but damage to the overall process of reform and to the organisation's legitimacy and credibility. A further failed attempt at enlargement in the near future would be a setback that needs to be avoided. One possibility would be to look again at the idea of creating a new category of elected, long-term, renewable seats as a stepping stone to a future decision on new permanent members. If the G4 were to soften their opposition to this approach, it could gain a wide measure of support; but, if they remain firmly opposed to it, it will stay just as stuck as the other main option.

The systems of global economic decision-making and governance remain dispersed across a number of different organisations – the WTO, the International Monetary Fund, the World Bank – of which the UN is only one and by no means the senior partner, and this is likely to continue to be the situation in the decades ahead. The case for either creating an overarching global institution in the economic and social field or for giving that role to the UN is not convincing and has convinced none of the main players who would have to agree. In a world committed to increasingly open markets and to removing barriers to trade and capital movements, it hardly makes sense conceptually to be thinking of a global decision-making body of this sort. What is needed, however, is a forum in which a restricted number of the main players can deliberate on the main economic and social challenges facing the world and provide momentum to efforts to reach decisions in the appropriate, but often more unwieldy, sectoral bodies. It was to respond to this need that the annual G8 Summits were instituted. When they began, the G8 membership (Canada, France, Germany, Italy, Japan, Russia, the UK and the USA, with the EU also involved) still represented a dominant proportion of the world economy. With the rapid rise of China and India and the somewhat slower emergence of other developing country economies, that is no longer the case. Moreover none of the main foreseeable challenges such as world trade negotiations or climate change can conceivably be steered any longer by the G8 alone. The obvious answer is for the G8 to metamorphose into a somewhat larger group – the Canadian government has for long advocated a leadership group of about 20 – which would include the largest developing economies. In recent years some of these countries have been invited along to G8 Summits on a purely ad hoc basis, as have the heads of the UN, the International Financial Institutions and the WTO. The time is now coming when the main developing countries should be included as of right in a somewhat larger grouping so that they can share the political responsibility for addressing the burning economic and social issues of the hour which cannot in any case be resolved without their full participation.

This look ahead has mainly so far focussed on policies and institutions. But individual countries remain and will continue to remain the key building blocks and drivers of both. The idea that the UN, or any other organisation, is on the way to establishing a system of world government, subsuming and obliterating national governments, is a pipe dream with no basis in reality. The fear that there is a titanic struggle being waged between those who wish to keep all decision-making on global issues unilateral and national and those who want it all to be regulated by multilateral organisations to the exclusion of national governments is hardly less unreal. Nowhere do these unreal ideas come up against the harsh realities of international politics more bruisingly than at the UN and nowhere at the UN more so than in the role of the P5 of the Security Council. In the halcyon period immediately following the end of the Cold War, those five countries genuinely did work together to deal with a number of challenges; the UN was immeasurably strengthened. Subsequently that cooperation frayed and fell into disuse; and the UN was consequently weakened and became the victim of policy paralysis. The lesson is clear; and there have been some recent signs that it has been, at least partially, learned. Naturally P5 unity does not come without any cost. Compromises have to be struck and much time is consumed. But, as the attractions and effectiveness of unilateral action and 'coalitions of the willing' has waned, what are the alternatives? No alternative can in any case provide the combination of clout and international legitimacy which can only be achieved if those five countries and any others that may be added to their number can learn again to work together in a systematic and sustained manner.

It is always invidious to pick out the policies of individual countries or regional groupings as being likely to determine the future of the UN. No doubt some will criticise the omission of a newly reassertive Russia putting its Security Council veto to opportunistic use or of a still under-stated but rapidly rising India. Nevertheless I would suggest that the future of the UN will greatly depend on the policies of two countries, China and the USA, and two groupings, the AU and the EU. Throughout the post-Cold War period so far China's policy at the UN has been cautious and passive. Few vetoes have been cast and those were on Taiwan-related issues. Where China did play a central role, as over the ending of the Cambodian civil war, the main driving motive was regional not global; the same could be said about the handling of North Korea's nuclear programme. But China's 'peaceful rise', as it likes to call it, is now reaching a point where issues much further away than its immediate region are posing difficult policy choices. This has been seen in China's resistance to putting pressure on Sudan over Darfur despite all the evidence of Sudan's responsibility for abuses of international humanitarian law; but also in its willingness to join the rest of the P5 in putting pressure on Iran over its nuclear programme. These two examples can be used to illustrate a genuine policy dilemma for China. Is it to follow a mercantilist, self-serving foreign policy (Darfur) or is it to play a full and cooperative role in handling threats to international peace and security (Iran)? China will no doubt resist making a definitive choice between these two options for as long as possible, but, in the course of time, its increasing influence and economic weight will mean that a pattern will be created demonstrating which of the options is predominant. And that pattern will greatly influence the future development of the UN, either hamstringing it or strengthening it depending on which of the two options predominates.

The United States is no newcomer to being the determinant influence at the UN. It has been that since the day the organisation was born at San Francisco in 1945. In those early days the USA, whose economic and military weight was then, in the immediate aftermath of the Second World War, even more predominant than it was at the end of the Cold War, quite deliberately opted for working together with others to achieve international peace and security rather than choosing either isolation or unilateral self-assertion. Since that time US policy at and towards the UN has zigzagged in a not always predictable and often profoundly negative manner. At times the USA has been strongly supportive of the UN, for example at the time of the Korean War, of the Anglo-French Suez venture and in the period immediately following the end of the Cold War; at others it has been dismissive and critical, depriving the UN of dues owing to it, and has preferred, for mainly domestic political reasons, to use the UN as a punchbag rather than as a forum for finding collective responses to common problems – for example, during the Reagan presidency and, most recently, following the 2003 invasion of Iraq and during the 2003–6 reform campaign.

These wide swings of US policy conceal an underlying reality, which is that the USA and the UN need each other and cannot achieve their proclaimed political objectives without working together. The important question for the future is whether these swings can be damped down and whether the USA can be persuaded to apply itself purposefully and in a sustained manner to working within the UN system to handle world issues and crises. Certainly the experience of the last few years and a review of the prospective challenges of the next few years would seem to point to the desirability from the US's own national interest to work in this way. The immediate euphoria of the post-Cold War world, when all the talk was of the world's only remaining superpower being the supreme arbiter of international affairs, and the neo-conservative hubris of 2003, have given way to a much more sober realisation of the limitations to US power and of its ability to secure its policy objectives by acting on its own. As for the UN, the harsh realities of the system, the power of the veto, the substantial proportion of the organisation's resources which come from the world's largest economy, underline the futility of any approach which aims at consistently isolating the USA and ignoring its views. Hardly less unrealistic is the attitude which sees the disciplines of the UN as being ropes with which to tie down the American Gulliver against its will. That too will not work. This fraught and crucial relationship between the USA and the UN will remain at the heart of all UN policy-making and decision-taking for as far ahead as one can reasonably look. It is likely to be affected a good deal more by the outcome of the 2008 US presidential elections than it is by the installation of a new UN Secretary-General.

The two regional organisations whose role in the UN's future will be as important, the AU and the EU, answer to quite different considerations than the two countries just examined. In the cases of these organisations their unity of purpose and capacity to take coherent and effective action are likely to be a major asset for the UN as a whole; and, conversely, disunity, divided counsels and weakness are likely to be damaging too to the UN. The AU has already, in the few years of its existence, shown that it is a completely different creature to its predecessor, the OAU. Not only do its charter, and the institutions it has established for dealing with peace and security, and democracy and human rights, set out on paper a range of potential actions far more proactive and interventionist than anything previously contemplated, but it has actually begun to give effect to such good intentions by mounting peace operations, denying legitimacy to the overthrow by force of elected governments and undertaking peer group reviews of the human rights records of its members. Since Africa is the home to many of the failed states which the UN is trying to stabilise and restore to normal functioning, these developments are important. But, as has been seen in the case of Zimbabwe, the Africans can also exert a negative influence on the handling of their own problems. It is hard to see the UN succeeding in the exercise of the responsibility to protect or in the pursuit of higher human rights standards in Africa without the whole-hearted support and cooperation of the AU. But it would be a delusion to suppose that the AU can yet undertake all the tasks it has assumed without some external support and assistance. If that backing is not forthcoming, then the risk is that the promising start which the AU has made will not be maintained; and the UN will become even more overloaded than it already is.

The EU has different problems from those of the AU, but the successful pursuit of its Common Foreign and Security Policy is as important for the future of the UN as is the development of the AU. The EU's resource constraints are different from those of Africa and relate mainly to the provision and deployment of peacekeeping forces, not to the finance needed to keep them in the field. The recent faltering in the EU's policy of enlargement also risks undermining the progress that has been made over the last ten years in stabilising the Balkans in which it has played such a large part. The EU's 27 members contribute between 40 per cent and 50 per cent of the UN's resources and often, in the case of voluntary contributions, more than that. Its policy of 'effective multilateralism' fits more closely with mainstream opinion at the UN than that of any other state or group of states. Its close relationship with the USA makes it a potentially important interlocutor and intermediary with other groups when difficult decisions have to be taken at the UN. So it is not fanciful to see the EU as a kind of engine room for a UN which is being asked to take on many new and demanding tasks. But all that depends on it being able to develop a unity of purpose and policy over a wider range of issues than in the past, and on it being able to complement its undoubted reserves of soft power with a somewhat greater capacity to handle crises when the going gets rough. Once again, as in the case of the AU, should the EU not succeed in developing along the lines it has set for itself, the UN too will be weakened and will be left with a burden which it is not well equipped to carry.

This book has set out to tell the story of the UN's first five tumultuous years following the end of the Cold War and then to analyse and to describe the efforts made to reform the organisation, particularly between 2003 and 2006. It only reflects, of course, the views of one person, albeit one who was involved in these events and who emerged from them, despite all the setbacks and disasters along the way, as convinced as ever that the world needs a UN that is effective and that achieving such a UN is within our grasp. In the end whether it does so will depend on the collective political will of its member states and each one's perception of its own national interest. The UN is a demand-driven organisation, and it cannot afford to be other than that. What it needs is a strong and sustained dose of supply-side reforms, which will enable it to respond more effectively to those demands.

Index